P9-BJA-500

Regional Economic Development

Canada's search for solutions

Billions of dollars are committed every year in Canada to regional development through a variety of programs: federal-provincial shared-cost agreements, freight rate assistance, tax credits, and more. And yet little is known about the success of policy in this field.

Savoie seeks to shed light on Canadian experience of regional development policy. In a comprehensive analysis of past and present programs he considers the various political and economic forces that have shaped the development of policy. He offers a balanced and perceptive assessment of the appropriateness of our objectives for regional development and evaluates the effectiveness of successive governments in meeting those objectives. He concludes with new suggestions for future regional development efforts.

Savoie's comprehensive approach offers an integrated perspective on the implications of regional policy to all who are concerned with Canadian regionalism, federalism, and public policy.

DONALD J. SAVOIE is executive director of the Canadian Institute for Research on Regional Development and professor of public administration, Université de Moncton.

DONALD J. SAVOIE

Regional Economic Development: Canada's search for solutions

UNIVERSITY OF TORONTO PRESS

Toronto Buffalo London

© University of Toronto Press 1986
Toronto Buffalo London
Printed in Canada

ISBN 0-8020-2589-7 (cloth)
ISBN 0-8020-6614-3 (paper)

Canadian Cataloguing in Publication Data

Savoie, Donald J., 1947–
   Regional economic development
   Bibliography: p.
   Includes index.
   ISBN 0-8020-2589-7 (bound). – ISBN 0-8020-6614-3 (pbk.)
   1. Regional planning – Canada. 2. Canada – Economic
   conditions – Regional disparities. 3. Canada –
   Economic policy – 1971–   *I. Title.
   HC115.S28 1985   338.971   C85-099749-6

50,598

To the memory of my parents, Léa and Adelin

CAMROSE LUTHERAN COLLEGE
LIBRARY

Contents

Preface

This study reports on Canada's efforts at promoting regional development. By and large, these efforts are planned and implemented outside the public view, so that one must turn to elected and to permanent government officials to gather the facts and to gain an appreciation of the circumstances under which the efforts were launched. Without the willing co-operation of a number of government officials, this study would clearly not have been possible. They must as always remain anonymous, but no doubt they will be able to recognize their valuable contributions to this book. It remains gratifying to note, however, that only one request for information met with a blank refusal.

I also incurred a great number of other debts in undertaking this study. I am especially grateful to Tom Kent, who read the first draft and who provided valuable insights, and to Professor Ben Higgins, who read the entire study and made a number of important suggestions. Harvey Lithwick provided valuable advice and assistance in revising the work. I also wish to thank Ginette Benoit for having typed all this book with willingness and dispatch. Despite all the help that I have received, I must reserve to myself responsibility for all errors or omissions.

In the preface of my first book, I thank my wife Linda and our children, Julien and Margaux, for their support. I wish to thank them again, but this time even more emphatically. They respected with tolerance and good humour the discipline that I imposed on myself after my decision to write this book. Certainly Linda's unwavering support was crucial to the completion of the study.

Abbreviations

ADA	Area Development Agency
ADB	Atlantic Development Board
ADIA	Area Development Incentives Act
ARDA	Agricultural and Rural Development Act
APEC	Atlantic Provinces Economic Council
CRIB	Canadian Regional Industrial Board
DREE	Department of Regional Economic Expansion
DRIE	Department of Regional Industrial Expansion
ERDA	Economic and Regional Development Agreement
FEDC	Federal Economic Development Co-ordinator
FRED	Fund for Rural Economic Development
GDA	General Development Agreement
ILAP	Industrial and Labour Adjustment Program
IT&C	Industry, Trade and Commerce
MSED	Ministry of State for Economic Development
MSERD	Ministry of State for Economic and Regional Development
OECD	Organization for Economic Co-operation and Development
PCO	Privy Council Office
PMO	Prime Minister's Office
RDIA	Regional Development Incentives Act

PART I BACKGROUND

1

Introduction

Among the countries currently classified by the United Nations as 'industrialized market economies,' Canada is surely one of the most highly regionalized, and its economy is accordingly one of the most badly fragmented. In such a country the 'free market' does not function well for all regions simultaneously, and macroeconomic policies applied uniformly throughout the nation will not suffice to eliminate the faults in market performance. Federal politicians have realized this fact intuitively for some time, and national economic policy has been to some extent regionalized: witness policies regarding freight rates, revenue sharing, unemployment insurance, and the operations of the former federal Department of Regional Economic Expansion (DREE). There is probably no other field of government expenditure in which so much public money is committed but so little is known about the success of the policy. There exist very few objective research studies on regional development efforts in Canada.[1]

Not only are considerable amounts of public funds spent every year on regional development, but many Canadians view striking an appropriate regional balance in the country's economic development as an important tenet of national unity. Former Prime Minister Pierre Elliot Trudeau stressed that the problem of regional development is as threatening to national unity as the language issue.[2] But students of Canadian politics and economics have not given it anywhere near the attention they have given the English-French conflict or the place of Quebec in the federation. The last comprehensive study specifically concerned with the federal government's efforts at promoting regional development was published in 1969. That study unfortunately antedates even the establishment of DREE, which was disbanded in early 1982.[3]

This lack of research has not, however, prevented politicians and observers of Canadian politics and public policy from taking a keen interest in regional development or from engaging in debates on the matter. People from economically disadvantaged areas frequently argue that national economic policies are largely responsible for the economic underdevelopment of their respective regions and that much more should be done in regional development. Meanwhile, those from more developed regions are as likely to argue that far too much public money is committed to inefficient economic activity in slow-growth regions.

As a result, the debate on regional development has tended to lack the information essential to discussion of such an important and potentially divisive issue. In turn, this has given rise to wildly exaggerated claims. A widely read newspaper columnist, for instance, has suggested that Ottawa's program of regional industrial incentives cost taxpayers billions of dollars over several years; in fact, slightly more than $1 billion was spent over the program's entire fourteen-year life span. British Columbia's premier, Bill Bennett, has often claimed that federal policies for regional development are ineffective and should be dropped. The Ontario government, meanwhile, has urged the federal government to stop 'distorting' Canada's industrial structure in the name of regional development.[4]

Other political leaders argue with equal conviction that not enough is being done for regional development. Premier Hatfield of New Brunswick has said that regional development efforts are in reality only compensation for 'the bad policies or the policies that favoured them [i.e., the more developed regions] years ago, and still do.' He maintains that 'there is an attitude here in Ottawa ... that there are certain things that we cannot do down there because we are not so capable of doing them, that there are only certain things that we can do and we should stick with them.'[5]

A number of economists and specialists on public policy have commented on Canada's regional development problems with deep concern. Grant Reuber argues that 'achieving an acceptable and widely accepted reconciliation of national and regional interests poses perhaps the most difficult issue confronting Canadians today.'[6] Others have echoed his sentiment, but no one in recent years has attempted a comprehensive look at Ottawa's regional development goals and at the various programs tried and efforts made, or considered the issues of government organization surrounding the promotion of regional development.

There are understandable reasons why regional development has not received the kind of attention one would expect from the academic community. The subject falls naturally into no single discipline. It is of interest to students of economics, public policy, public administration, political science, sociology, geography, and demography. A number of specialized studies on specific issues in regional development have been carried out, but most have failed to look at regional development from a broad perspective. Perhaps more important, however, efforts at promoting regional development have, by and large, been conducted through federal-provincial programs. Information on intergovernmental programs has not always been readily available to researchers. Further, federal-provincial programs have now become, in their own right, a proper area of specialization.

The advantages of a comprehensive study of Canadian regional development are clear. It can bring together a number of important considerations and shed some light on the total picture. A comprehensive approach can clarify the interdependence of problems in policy-making. No major public policy development, according to G. Bruce Doern, 'is the product of a single linear progression of events and ideas. There are many rivulets of thought.' Heroic assumptions are required if one hopes to study any kind of economic policy-making issues in isolation of political considerations or government organizational issues. Thomas Brewis emphasized the need for a comprehensive approach: 'Those who forget this [need] are likely to find themselves engaged in speculation of little relevance to the world around them.' He explained that 'political ... economic ... administrative considerations' lie at the root of regional development programs.[7]

Conversely, a study that seeks to consider the full range of issues in regional development holds potential drawbacks. The specialists will invariably be more familiar with some issues raised in the study. A number of points and suggestions offered will require additional analysis. But the price is worth paying, if the study encourages further research on regional development. The subject remains large and relatively unexplored. I hope that this book will stimulate more research and look at regional development from a broader perspective than has been attempted in the past.

SOME THEORETICAL CONSIDERATIONS

Regional development economists agree that no single economic theory explains regional disparities. There is no consensus on the appropriate theoretical approach to the question. Richard Lipsey has observed: 'For all the concern about regional area development and regional problems in Canada, we don't really have an underlying theory. We don't know what we would have to do, what are the conditions under which there would be regional equality, however we define equality.'[8]

There have been attempts to develop a theory, or at least an agreed-upon appoach to the study of regional disparities. The Economic Council of Canada sponsored several studies designed specifically to define a theoretical approach to the problem. However, the Council concluded its major effort in this area (*Living Together*) in 1977 without producing a suitable theoretical framework.[9]

Earlier attempts at defining a theoretical approach formed the basis for regional development programs in Canada. For example, the 'growth pole' concept inspired the first policy and program structure of the Department of Regional and Economic Expansion (DREE). French economist François Perroux had argued that economic activity tends to concentrate around certain focal points. Growth, he argued, 'does not appear everywhere and all at once; it reveals itself in certain points or poles, with different degrees of intensity; it spreads through diverse channels.'[10] Efforts to strengthen these focal points in slow-growth regions can start a process of self-sustaining economic growth. These efforts can take the form of incentive grants to businesses to locate there, the provision of land servicing for industrial and housing developments, and so on.

Another French economist, J.R. Boudeville, expanded on the theory and suggested that 'a regional growth pole is a set of expanding industries located in an urban area and inducing further development of economic activity throughout its zone of influence.'[11] Like Perroux, he argued in favour of polarization around certain growth points; any difference between the two authors is essentially one of definition. Boudeville suggested that the growth pole incorporates both the designated urban centre and the growth area; it induces development 'throughout its zone of influence.' However, his development poles are permanent (as growth poles need not be) and seek to adopt methods of production found in the highly developed regions so that they can pass on any success to the rest of the region. Boudeville used the growth pole to explain regional inequalities in geographic areas. He sought to assess the impact of polarized development on regional inequalities.

The concept of the growth pole has evolved considerably since Perroux first wrote on the subject. Boudeville is only one of a number of authors who have developed the concept further. For instance, we now invariably refer to growth centres rather than growth poles. The growth centre implies a much more spatial framework. Analysts are now calling for a more detailed look at potential growth centres concerning the type of industries that should be attracted and the order in which investment decisions should be made. Since new industries and linkages cannot be established overnight, supporters of growth-centre development now urge that new investments be timed so as to establish an efficient growth sequence.[12] Other authors look at growth centres from a broad perspective, embracing all the factors – cultural, economic, and political – that contribute to regional growth, and examine the results of induced urban industrialization.[13]

The 'development' approach also influenced early formulations of Canadian programs for regional development. It holds that regional disparities are caused by the market and that government intervention is essential. It suggests that economic failure breeds other failures and that a region will not be able to attract new economic activities unless it can break away from this vortex.[14] Governments should intervene to break this self-perpetuating cycle of regional disparities. They can prop up demand through transfer payments and can ensure an adequate level of public services through fiscal equalization designed to support provincial governments in the less-developed regions of the country.

The development approach views regional disparities from a broad perspective and calls for a host of measures designed to stimulate growth. These measures include: encouragement of capital accumulation; assistance in creating an adequate industrial infrastructure; an increase in the educational level of the work-force; promotion of the application of new technology; and assistance in modernizing agricultural methods and in constructing new roads, harbours, and sewer systems. This approach requires a multidimensional intervention by government. It deals with problems of regional disparity on a number of fronts, through economic and social initiatives. Just as the symptoms and causes of regional economic disparity vary, so must the instruments to deal with them.[15]

The development approach was inspired by the study of underdeveloped countries and accordingly draws attention to infrastructure, educational facilities, productivity, agriculture, and so on. The approach has fallen out of favour in Canada among both students and practitioners of regional development. They stress that given the progress made in Canada over the past twenty years, the problems of the underdeveloped countries are now so different from those of slow-growth regions that the development approach is no longer applicable.

In more recent years, many regional development planners have looked to the trade theory to gain an appreciation of the regional problem and to come up with new measures. Though developed to deal with the movement of goods and money between nations, the theory has also been adopted to explain the movement between regions within the same nation.[16] It suggests that a region will maximize its economic potential by concentrating its efforts on its economic strengths. If, for example, a region has much capital and little labour, then it promotes economic activity that requires a great deal of capital but little labour. A by-product of this theory is the notion of a region's 'comparative advantage.'

There are numerous examples of regional comparative advantages in Canada. One example is fish processing. The four Atlantic provinces, Quebec, and British Columbia will obviously wish to specialize in this sector because they have the resources. Quebec's hydro power should enhance industrial opportunities in that province; Ontario's comparative advantage lies in its diversified industrial base and its mature urban structure. In short, the trade approach would see Canada's regions specialize in their areas of strength and comparative advantage. With each region building from its strength, market forces would make the necessary adjustments in labour.

A similar approach to that of comparative advantage is 'neo-classical' theory.[17] The latter applies standard methods of economic analysis to regional problems: market forces should be free to set the necessary equilibrium. If unemployment is particularly high in a region, then let the market forces deal with the problem with a minimum of government intervention.

Essentially, unemployment, according to the neo-classical view, is a failure to equate labour supply with demand. The solution, as with other market commodities, is to reduce surplus labour by lowering wages, so that the market can take advantage of lower productivity cost. New economic activity will create employment, albeit perhaps with lower wages than elsewhere in the country. If new economic activity is not created, then worker out-migration becomes the appropriate adjustment mechanism. This will trigger the necessary regional adjustments and bring about regional balance.

The neo-classical approach also questions the appropriateness of federal transfer payments to slow-growth regions: rather than promote self-sustaining economic activity, they may do the opposite. They serve to blunt necessary economic adjustments. Proponents of this view argue that traditionally we have been looking at regional development from the wrong angle. Thomas J. Courchene maintains that Canada is approaching regional policy with 'a concept of gap closing rather than a policy of adjustment accommodation. We see disparity out there ... and we rush to remove it with one set of funds or another rather than letting it adjust itself on its own.'[18]

This view has given rise to a new debate in the field of regional development. Much has been said of late regarding the dependence of slow-growth regions on federal transfer payments. No one doubts that such payments to individuals and provincial governments have produced a more uniform level of public services throughout Canada and have greatly moderated the sting of economic misfortune. However, a region may become dependent on transfer payments to support levels of consumption and services much higher than could be sustained by the economic output of the region. This dependence may blunt the required long-term adjustment that would bring production and consumption back into line. The issue of regional dependence on federal transfer payments illustrates very well the tension between the objectives of regional income and population maintenance on the one hand and self-sustaining economic development and adjustment on the other.

THE CONCEPT OF REGION AND REGIONALISM

The terms *regions*, *regionalism*, and *regional differences* are of vital importance in Canadian policy-making to some analysts, while to others they are unnecessary. Many scholars believe that there should be much more work done in defining such key concepts. Others view regionalism as a gimmick promoted by governments to serve their own self-interests and not those of the Canadian population. Governments, it is suggested, are less concerned with what is being done than with who is doing it and who gets the credit.

Some analysts argue that regions, as opposed to communities or nations, play a predominant role in the economic and social activities of Canadians. In many cases they have 'probably replaced communities as the territorially based unit of group affiliation which arouses in their residents a consciousness of kind and which they regard simply as home.' David Alexander claimed that for Canada to survive as a country it must define goals 'which support and encourage the survival of the region.' Richard Simeon suggests that our political institutions serve to reinforce regionalism and maintains that 'federalism is not only a response to regionalism, but also ensures that it will continue ... It provides an institutional focus for loyalty and identity ... Cleavages which reinforce the territorial divisions [are] highlighted.'[19]

Yet some students of public policy have suggested that in the economic development field the region may not be a valid concept for analysis. They argue that our attention should be directed to 'people prosperity' as opposed to 'place prosperity.' A change of economic activity from one area to another is relevant only in the context of its consequences for individuals. It certainly ought not to be the primary concern. After all, the argument goes, potential opportunities cannot be limited to particular places in which individuals find themselves. Consequently, the appropriate objective is to maximize potential opportunities and economic well-being for individual citizens, not for individual regions.

This view certainly has merit from the perspective of economic efficiency. However, stronger arguments can be made for government concern with 'place prosperity.' In a federation, it is unlikely that all regional or provincial governments will subscribe fully to the view of people prosperity rather than place prosperity. Nova Scotia's government, for example, may well be primarily concerned with people prosperity, or the well-being of all residents within its jurisdiction. Viewed from the perspective of the country as a whole, however, this constitutes an emphasis on place prosperity. Province-building (provincial governments stimulating growth within their jurisdiction) has become a fact of life in Canada.

Canada's population is not perfectly mobile. For many Canadians there are significant cultural costs associated with moving from one region to another in search of economic opportunities. French Canadians, for example, may well have to sacrifice their culture and language (or, at least, that of their children) should they move outside Quebec or a few areas in New Brunswick and Ontario.

Thus, though they may question the wisdom of regionally oriented economic development measures, most opponents accept that such measures will be advanced and implemented. Thomas Courchene has stated: 'I have no illusions that governments will stand idly by and allow the unfettered market to call the adjustment tune. They will intervene.'[20]

CONCLUSION

A brief look at the various theories and approaches to the study of regional development leads one to conclude that regional development policy analysts are in disarray. In an uncharacteristic fashion, the Economic Council of Canada summed up the situation this way: 'Doctors used to try to cure syphilis with mercury and emetics. We now know that mercury works but emetics do not and, moreover, that penicillin is best of all. We suspect that the regional disparity disease is presently being treated with both mercury- and emetic-type remedies, but we do now know which is which. Perhaps one day an economic penicillin will be found.'[21] The Economic Council did not discover such an economic penicillin, nor has one been discovered to date.

Certainly considerable confusion still exists on the most appropriate theoretical approach to regional development. Yet it is in this confusion that Canadian regional development policy has been defined and updated throughout the past three decades. Students and practitioners of regional development have had to work under very difficult circumstances, with very little theoretical framework within which to formulate plans and initiatives.

This study is aimed at defining and analysing regional development programs and policies in Canada over the years. It will then be possible to assess these efforts and make suggestions for the future.

The first part of this study looks at federal-provincial considerations in regional development. Everyone – federal or provincial politicians, public servants, or students of regional development – agrees that federal-provincial co-operation is essential in promoting regional development. Yet it has not always been evident, and I will consider why this is so and in what kind of institutional context federal-provincial co-operation must operate.

The second part of this study explores various government programs in regional development and the forces that have shaped these efforts. It starts with the first explicit regional development initiative, reviews pre-DREE efforts, examines all of DREE's programs, and assesses the organization of the federal government's institutions for economic development. In addition, it considers the extensive non-DREE promotion of regional development, including the role and contribution of provincial governments.

The third and concluding part of the study attempts to assess the effectiveness of these various regional development programs and to propose new ways of studying regional economic disparity. With over twenty years of experience to draw on, we can now ask fundamental questions about the nature of the problem, appropriate objectives, and policy directions and initiatives that might offer more promising prospects. Economic circumstances, both nationally and international- ly, have also changed dramatically in those twenty years. Regional development policy is not immune to changes in political and economic circumstances and must now find its place in a new order of things. This study seeks to assist in this process.

2

Regional economic development and federal-provincial relations

As in most federal systems, Canada's constitution does not assign to either level of government explicit responsibility or powers for economic development or for combatting regional economic disparities. Provincial governments have a major function in economic development because they own natural resources and control most determinants of human resources and land use. The federal government has created for itself a major role, essentially on the basis of its spending power. Equalization payments, income transfers, and shared-cost agreements with the provinces all derive from Ottawa's spending power. In addition, the federal government holds jurisdiction over such matters as foreign and interprovincial trade, and chartered banking, and it shares with the provinces jurisdiction over agriculture and immigration.

Thus, from a constitutional perspective, close federal-provincial co-ordination is required simply because both levels of government have assumed important roles in regional development. Nevertheless, many students of regional development tend to put aside these 'constitutional niceties,' arguing that a classical view of federalism may be appropriate for other policy fields, but not for regional development.[1] As regional development becomes more complex, they point out, so does the interdependence of governments' actions. Measures to promote regional development must be multidimensional and, by their very nature, cut across jurisdictional lines; otherwise, the efforts of one government could well work at cross purposes to those of the other.

The federal government's responsibility for economic development involves the advancement of the country as a whole, just as that of a provincial government is the advancement of the province. The responsibilities of both governments invariably overlap, as do their activities, which flow into one another. It is no longer possible to speak of two levels of government as if everything were neatly divided into hermetically sealed jurisdictions. No one questions the importance of federal-provincial co-operation in regional development. Federal and provincial politicians and officials all stress the benefits of close relations in this area. This was true even in the early 1980s when federal-provincial tension was particularly high over such issues as constitutional reform, the Quebec referendum, and the National Energy Program.[2]

But the discussion of regional economic development, regional disparities, and the regional impact of national policies and programs often becomes an occasion for intergovernmental and interregional debates. Federal-provincial relations have certainly contributed to the notion of an equitable regional distribution of the economic benefits of Canadian federalism and have ensured that our economic debates would not simply be concerned with the functional efficiency of national economic policies. But they have also fuelled resentment between the sparsely populated peripheral regions of the country and the heavily populated and highly industrialized centre. In other words, the centre-periphery dichotomy of the Canadian economy has created among the country's residents different percep-tions of their own economic interests, and federalism has created a framework that has served to promote these differences. Central Canadians favour tariff protec-tion, as do governments in central Canada; western Canadians and their provincial governments favour free trade; Atlantic Canadians see a need for special measures to correct regional economic imbalances, and so do their provincial governments. It is for these reasons that the problem of regional development becomes part of a larger issue of federalism and federal-provincial relations.[3]

FEDERAL-PROVINCIAL CO-OPERATION IN PRACTICE

Reaching agreement on the need for close federal-provincial co-operation in regional development is easy. What is considerably less simple is reaching a consensus on how to achieve such co-operation. Numerous forces shape federal-provincial relations. Regional economic development is often a high-profile activity, more often than not placing governments in a positive light. Richard Simeon writes of 'status, goal and political competition' in federal-provincial relations: 'The federal and provincial governments compete to gain credit, status and importance, and to avoid discredit and blame. They have, in Anthony Downs' metaphor, a territorial sensibility.'[4] Regional development thus provides an attractive target for government competition for status. Not only is it highly visible, but it is also an area where the roles of each level of government are determined more often by politics than by formal jurisdictions.

Regional development has often been a pawn in the continuing struggle between 'nation-building' and 'province-building.' Nation-building held sway for a number of years, particularly between the end of the Second World War and the mid-1960s. Leading, some claim, to a number of 'national' projects – the build-ing of the railways, the construction of the Trans-Canada highway, and the establishment of Air Canada and the Canadian Broadcasting Corporation. By the early 1960s, however, province-building was in the ascendancy, producing expensive educational facilities, modern and competent provincial public services, and extensive involvement in economic development.[5]

A brief look at government revenues illustrates very well the extent of provincial activity. Over a twenty-year period (1959–79) the federal share of total government revenues in Canada declined from over 58 per cent to about 45 per cent, while the provincial share increased from 42 to 55 per cent. The decline of the federal share is even more dramatic when one considers intergovernmental transfers. In 1959, Ottawa had over 52 per cent of the total revenue after such transfers had been accounted for; in 1979, it had less than 34 per cent. In addition, over the same period, Ottawa more than quadrupled the amount of 'tax room' for the provinces in personal income tax.[6]

Shortly after its return to power, the Trudeau government served notice in 1980 that the emphasis on province-building had gone too far and that excessive decentralization was now becoming a threat to the country's survival. It fought successfully in the Quebec referendum and then proceeded to check the general trend toward decentralization with a series of measures designed to strengthen the national government.

Competition between the provinces and Ottawa has been fuelled also by 'competitive political and bureaucratic elites at the two levels of government ... possessed of tenacious instincts for their own preservation and growth.'[7] These élites, it has been suggested, have continually sought to advance either their own interests (invariably bigger budgets, larger programs, more person-years) or their respective views of Canadian society. Those in Ottawa tend to believe that the interests of Canadian society are best served by nation-building, while those who sit in provincial capitals usually espouse province-building.

Another important consideration is the extensive involvement of both levels of government in economic development. Motivated by a firmly held belief that discriminatory federal policies are at the root of their economic woes, the four Atlantic provinces and Quebec are bringing forward initiatives to close the economic gap between them and Ontario. Convinced that any growth in their regions is occurring in spite of, rather than because of, federal policies, the western provinces are also intervening to spur economic development within their borders, so as to reduce their dependence on natural resources and to diversify their economies. Ontario, seeing its industrial base increasingly under pressure from international competition, is also intervening in various economic sectors to promote growth. Ottawa, meanwhile, has not sat idly by. It too has views and initiatives that it considers of vital importance to economic development.[8] The activist approach taken by the various governments makes intergovernmental co-operation considerably more difficult, and it also increases the likelihood of conflict.

VISIBILITY IN FEDERAL-PROVINCIAL PROGRAMS

A further complicating issue in regional economic development is the importance or the visibility of government spending and activities. Federal politicians, in particular, argue that governments must continually compete to win the support of Canadians. Unless a level of government can demonstrate its importance in the political and economic life of the community, people will turn to the other for leadership. An excellent example is Quebec, where it is felt, by federalists at least, that the provincial government is continually seeking ways to discredit Ottawa's efforts to promote Quebec's interests. Federal politicians point also to other provinces, notably Newfoundland and Alberta, for examples of sustained campaigns to discredit the federal government.

To counter these provincial activities, Ottawa is concerned to get due credit for federal money spent. Although its spending power appears to be unconstrained by constitutional limitations, federal money often is allocated to federal-provincial agreements, by which the provinces deliver the programs. This arrangement gives provincial governments an opportunity to claim credit for projects, even when the federal government has paid a major part of the costs. A survey showed that when Ottawa, on its own, delivers a program, 95 per cent of respondents are aware that the federal government is responsible for it, but when the program is delivered through a federal-provincial agreement, only 15 per cent know that the federal government has been involved.[9] Constant jockeying for visibility, therefore, makes federal-provincial co-operation difficult. Projects are assessed in terms of their contribution not simply to the regional economy, but also to the political advancement of a particular government.

Attempts to arrive at an amicable, long-term arrangement to share both the visibility and the public stage have not proved successful, at least from Ottawa's point of view. Between 1975 and 1979, the prime minister signed agreements with the premiers of five provinces to co-operate in informing citizens about participation by both levels of government in federal-provincial programs. The press release accompanying the signing of one of these agreements stated: 'It is often not clear which government is responsible for certain programmes and they [citizens] are therefore not clear as to the amount of contributions made by their provincial or federal tax dollars.'[10]

These agreements have had only limited effect. Even though the basic ground rules have been respected – both governments are mentioned in all standard press releases announcing a new project – many federal politicians believe that this arrangement has not prevented provincial governments from taking credit for any given project on a long-term basis. Canada's then deputy prime minister, Allan MacEachen, in his 1981 presentation to the Breau Task Force on Fiscal Federalism, remarked: 'A number of important public services are jointly financed by the federal government and the provinces ... The federal government has a particular problem of programme visibility ... because [the programs] are delivered by the provinces and because little is done to acknowledge publicly the important federal role.' He added: 'In a federal state, the exercise of political power is always the object of some competition between the two orders of government.'[11] The problem of visibility is not made easier when governments of different political persuasion hold power in Ottawa and in the provinces.

PERSONALITIES IN FEDERAL-PROVINCIAL RELATIONS

Personalities also shape federal-provincial relations. The Standing Senate Committee on National Finance recently produced a special report on government policy and regional disparities that underlined this point: 'Effective intergovernmental cooperation requires interpersonal cooperation at the political and bureaucratic levels.'[12] The effect of particular people on federal-provincial relations can be crucial to regional development, where responsibilities and jurisdictions are not neatly compartmentalized. With the rules of negotiation always changing, individuals can exert considerable influence on both the form of the process and the resulting programs.

DREE's first minister, Jean Marchand, had both a strong personality and the complete confidence of the prime minister. Consequently, he took an aggressive posture toward provincial governments.[13] The provinces approached negotiations with him with some uneasiness: the potential for friction was high, and the atmosphere was not as harmonious as the provinces would have liked. A later DREE minister, Marcel Lessard, a junior cabinet minister with a relaxed personality, emphasized rapport with provincial governments. Several provinces publicly applauded his approach, and conflicts over DREE programs were neither as frequent nor as intense as they were before or after his tenure.[14]

The personalities of permanent officials can also influence relations. Senior federal officials Tom Kent, Robert Montreuil, and Mike Kirby each had a different approach to intergovernmental negotiations, and each affected relations between the provinces and Ottawa.[15] Much depends on whether a senior official has an open or a cautious and bureaucratic approach to federal-provincial negotiations. Other officials will adjust their negotiating strategy to fit his personality. Admittedly, the effect of personality on federal-provincial relations is difficult to determine, and students of regional development do not always have access to the actors. Yet it remains a crucial variable.

ACCOUNTABILITY IN FEDERAL-PROVINCIAL RELATIONS

The structure of Canadian federalism has necessitated frequent interaction among governments. The constitution is ambiguous on important jurisdictional issues, and the financial resources available to governments do not correspond with their responsibilities. Further, national institutions do not adequately accommodate regional interests.

Canadian governments have responded to the need for frequent interaction by setting up a variety of federal-provincial co-ordination mechanisms. At the top stands the annual Federal-Provincial Conference of First Ministers. Under its aegis is an array of ministerial-level conferences and meetings, ministerial committees, and permanent and ad hoc committees of officials, many of which co-ordinate and implement policies and programs. Perhaps no area has seen more of these committees than regional development. Under DREE's General Development Agreements alone, some 1,000 committees of officials were established.[16] Most governments have established special organizations – even ministries – simply to deal with intergovernmental relations.

Frequent consultation can allow interested agencies to participate in strategic planning for regional development. It can also permit flexibility in setting up federal-provincial programs – a highly valued feature. There is, however, a price to pay for this flexibility. A number of politicians and scholars have argued that recent developments in federal-provincial relations have weakened considerably the accountability of governments to their respective legislatures and to the public.[17]

Regional development has not escaped this criticism; in fact, in it the criticism has gone beyond the issue of accountability. Cabinet ministers at both levels of government have complained that they have lost the ability to control new initiatives. One provincial minister said that trying to determine who proposed what under GDA programs 'is like grabbing smoke.' A federal minister added: 'Attempting to stop a proposed subsidiary agreement by the time it comes to me is like attempting to perform an abortion nine months after conception.'[18]

Officials operating federal-provincial regional development programs must provide for more effective accountability of their efforts. This is true not simply because of the criticism on this point, but also because the public sector generally has been asked to become more open and accountable. As a result of this demand a Freedom of Information Act now exists in Canada, and a Royal Commission on Financial Management and Accountability was established in 1976.

This growing concern for accountability may lessen the flexibility of federal-provincial relations and the ability of officials to plan and implement a regional development plan that cuts across jurisdictional lines. Though there are clear advantages to those involved in throwing 'constitutional niceties' out the window, political circumstances no longer permit such a free-wheeling approach. This is yet another dimension that officials must consider in planning regional development.

PROVINCIAL FISCAL CAPACITY

Provincial fiscal capacity has a profound effect on how a government will approach relations with Ottawa. A poor province may not always be able to pull together the necessary expertise to contribute fully to the formulation of policies and programs. In addition, a provincial government unable to 'go it' alone may turn to federal-provincial programs for new initiatives much more readily than will the more self-sufficient.

Poorer provincial governments are at a disadvantage when competing with wealthier provincial governments or, more important, with the federal government, in shaping new federal-provincial initiatives. Some openly admit this. For instance, when commenting on the establishment of Canada's pension plan, a New Brunswick official revealed that 'we just went neutral on [it] ... We just eased out of it. We just didn't have the capacity to tackle it.'[19]

The federal government has recognized this situation and at one point attempted to resolve it. To build up the planning capacity of the less affluent governments, Ottawa in the mid-1970s offered to subsidize the salaries of newly hired public servants in selected provincial governments. In addition, it offered to sign agreements with some provincial governments to give them the ability to plan new initiatives. In both instances, the intended focus of the strengthened capacity was regional development.[20] Provincial governments welcomed this assistance. They feared that if they did not have adequate analytical and planning capacity, the federal government, with its enormous human and financial resources, would simply dictate what initiatives it considered best.

A weak fiscal position can also force a provincial government to discard initiatives it favours for others that have lower priority but are eligible for federal cost-sharing. Some analysts have suggested that the economic weakness of Atlantic governments conditions their response to federal initiatives. Certainly this is so for regional development. A detailed study of the Canada–New Brunswick General Development Agreement revealed the attractiveness of a '20¢ dollar': with Ottawa contributing 80 per cent of the cost of a particular initiative, a twenty-cent investment by the province buys a dollar expenditure within the province. The study revealed also that provincial governments are quick to replace an initiative that does not qualify for the twenty-cent dollar with one that does.[21]

CONCLUSION

In Canada, regional development and federal-provincial co-operation are ineluctably linked. Effective efforts at regional development are simply not possible without effective federal-provincial co-operation. A provincial minister recently put it this way: 'If the feds are going to tell us where they're going to build a bridge, fine. We'll then tell them afterwards where we're going to put the road.'[22]

A study of Ottawa's regional development programs is thus largely an analysis of federal-provincial attempts to co-operate – something that everyone agrees is crucial to success. That said, few observers share the same view as to the most effective means to achieve such co-operation, and there have been a variety of approaches brought forward and tried. There is recognition, however, that the nature of Canadian federalism promotes regional conflicts over economic development and that a wide number of factors influence and shape federal-provincial co-operation in regional development. By and large, these factors make federal-provincial co-operation in regional development more difficult rather than the reverse.

This will be clear in our review of the various policies that have been developed to deal with Canada's regional development problems. Improving federal-provincial co-operation for regional development is in many ways as important as defining new policy instruments and new programs. For this reason, I will be suggesting measures to facilitate such co-operation.

PART II THE EFFORTS

3

Shaping DREE

During the period from Confederation to the mid-1950s, the federal government had no explicit policy of regional development. It directed its economic policy essentially toward the development of the national economy. The prevailing belief was that a strong national economy, based on east-west trade, would benefit all regions. Regional programs, such as the Maritime Freight Rates Act (1927) and the Prairie Farm Rehabilitation Act (1935), were designed to overcome specific problems.

Problems in the fiscal capacities of some provinces started to manifest themselves shortly after Confederation. Ottawa made a number of special and even supposedly final federal subsidies and grants to the provinces. In the 1920s it established a royal commission to look into the financial difficulties of the Maritime provinces. The commission recommended special grants to assist the Maritime provincial governments with their budget deficits and based this proposal on the need for greater equality among the provinces.[1] But, here again, the federal government's concern was not so much with the pace of regional activity as it was with a specific problem – government deficits in the Maritime provinces. In short, the principal motivation behind national economic policy remained growth, not regional balance in the country's economic growth.

THE BEGINNING

Only after the Second World War did the federal government show greater concern for a regional balance in economic activity, perhaps because regional differences became much more apparent in these years. Shortly after the war, the federal Department of Reconstruction called a Dominion-Provincial Conference on Reconstruction. The federal government's submission revealed a total faith in Keynesian public works planning and in the need for federal control over fiscal policy.[2] The federal government offered generous subsidies to provincial governments for planning and implementing public works, provided that the provinces agreed to place fully planned projects into a reserve or 'shelf' to be implemented at a time to be designated by the federal government. Ottawa felt that this plan would enable it to mount a concerted attack on inflation and unemployment by directing projects to selected areas of the country. For a variety of reasons, including continuing prosperity, little came of Ottawa's plan.

What brought the federal government to recognize regional economic imbalances was the fiscal weakness of the poorer provinces. In a very harsh manner, the Depression years had revealed this weakness. The Rowell-Sirois Commission had been established in 1937 to re-examine 'the economic and financial basis of Confederation and ... the distribution of legislative powers in the light of the economic and social developments of the last seventy years.' Essentially pessimistic about the capacity of governments to work together efficiently in joint activities, the commission had favoured a clear delimitation of power. It had concluded that the Canadian fiscal system should enable every province to provide an acceptable standard of services, without having to impose a heavier-than-average tax burden. It had recommended a strengthening of the federal government's economic powers and a series of national grants to the poorer provinces so that they could offer public services broadly equivalent to those in the richer provinces.[3]

Two decades later, in 1957, the federal government set up the fiscal equalization program. It was intended to reduce disparities between regions, to achieve a national standard in public services, and at the same time to equalize provincial government revenues. Ottawa thus undertook to ensure that all provinces would have revenues sufficient to offer an acceptable level of public services. Payments under the equalization schemes were and are unconditional, and eligible provinces need not spend the resources on economic development.[4] The payments help poorer provinces provide services, but do not necessarily assist them in integrating their economies more successfully into the national economy and in supporting regional growth from within.

This limitation does not in any way minimize the importance of the equalization payments. These payments constitute regular commitments on the part of Ottawa to equalizing the fiscal capacities of all provincial governments. In turn, provincial governments in slow-growth regions can provide a level of public service roughly comparable to that available elsewhere. The payments also offer financial stability to provincial governments so that a competent public service can be retained and some degree of forward-looking and long-range planning can be undertaken. In itself, however, the equalization program does not earmark special funding to put in place measures to stimulate self-sustaining economic growth.

Another royal commission was to come forward with suggestions about establishing special development plans. The Royal Commission on Canada's

Economic Prospects (the Gordon Commission) reported in 1957 that 'a bold and comprehensive and coordinated approach' was needed to resolve the underlying problems of the Atlantic region, which required special measures to improve its economic framework. Those measures included a federally sponsored capital project commission to provide needed infrastructure facilities to encourage economic growth. The commission called also for measures to increase the rate of capital investment in the region. In many ways the commission was breaking new ground in advocating special measures to involve the private sector in promoting development in slow-growth regions. Perhaps for this reason the commission remained cautious in its recommendations: 'Special assistance put into effect to assist these areas might well adversely affect the welfare of industries already functioning in most established areas of Canada.'[5]

As with the Rowell-Sirois Commission, the Gordon Commission's recommendations were to play an important role several years after being made public. The Gordon Commission was a creation of Louis St Laurent's Liberal government and reported its findings in 1957. However, 1957 also saw a Progressive Conservative government elected in Ottawa. The new Diefenbaker government did not immediately embrace proposals inspired by a Liberal-appointed commission. The new government, however, was confronted by a recession and was quickly in search of innovative solutions. The recession once again underlined the persistence of regional imbalances. All regions felt the effect of the recession, but nowhere was it as severe as in the four Atlantic provinces. This helped convince the federal government that undirected financial transfers in the form of equalization payments were simply not sufficient to bring about structural changes in the slow-growth regions. Certain ministers in Ottawa were also pointing to what they viewed as unacceptable levels of poverty in numerous rural communities and arguing for special corrective measures.[6]

The 1960 budget speech unveiled the first of many measures Ottawa has developed to combat regional disparities. The budget permitted firms to obtain double the normal rate of capital cost allowances on most of the assets they acquired to produce new products – if they located in designated regions (with high unemployment and slow economic growth).[7]

Shortly after this measure was introduced, Parliament passed the Agriculture Rehabilitation and Development Act (ARDA). It was an attempt to rebuild the depressed rural economy and represented Ottawa's first 'regional' development program. ARDA began as a federal-provincial effort to stimulate agricultural development in order to increase income in rural areas. It aimed to increase small farmers' output and productivity by providing assistance for alternative use of marginal land, creating work opportunities in rural areas, developing water and soil resources, and setting up projects designed to benefit people engaged in natural resource industries other than agriculture, such as fisheries. Later, in 1966, the program was renamed the Agricultural and Rural Development Act, and its objectives were adjusted. ARDA was expanded to include non-agricultural programs in rural areas, designed to absorb surplus labour from farming. Thus reducing rural poverty became ARDA's overriding objective.[8] Notwithstanding these adjustments, however, some Ottawa decision-makers believed that ARDA still had one serious drawback: it lacked an appropriate geographical focus. It was, in the words of one federal official, 'all over the Canadian map.'

The Fund for Rural Economic Development (FRED), introduced in 1966, would deal with this concern.[9] The program could be applied only in designated regions, with widespread low incomes and major problems of economic adjustment. In the end, five regions were identified under FRED: the Interlake region of Manitoba, the Gaspé peninsula in Quebec, the Mactaquac and northeastern regions of New Brunswick, and all of Prince Edward Island. Separate 'comprehensive development plans' were then formulated for those five regions, to develop infrastructure and industry.

The FRED plan for northeastern New Brunswick, for example, consisted of three elements: industrial development services, employment development activities, and industrial infrastructure. The first element was designed to lay the groundwork for industrial initiatives by providing essential research, technicians, and staff. It included the establishment of three regional industrial commissions which were set up to help residents promote the industrial potential of their areas. It also provided support for studies to identify and pursue vigorously specific development prospects and for the provision of management advisory services and training to improve both existing and proposed enterprises.

A more direct stimulus to job creation was provided by the second component of the plan, which was responsible for developing public facilities and providing inducements to private enterprise. Under this heading, assistance was given to projects that were considered capable of creating long-term employment in the natural resources and tourism sectors, but that could not be carried out without some form of public assistance. The program also provided special incentives to selected business enterprises not eligible for assistance under existing programs. An interest-free forgivable loan of 50 per cent of approved capital costs of up to $60,000 for new manufacturing or processing industries and up to 30 per cent for modernizations or expansion was available. It was explicitly designed to encourage new entrepreneurs and further expansion of small existing businesses. A third component provided assistance to residents to relocate to selected centres that offered better employment opportunities.[10]

The federal government introduced in 1962 yet another development initiative – the Atlantic Development Board (ADB).[11] Unlike other regional development programs, this board would be active only in the four Atlantic provinces, as its name implied. Largely inspired by the Gordon Commission, the ADB was initially asked to define measures and initiatives for promoting economic growth and development in the Atlantic region. A planning staff was put together, mainly from within the federal public service. Considerable research was undertaken on the various sectors of the regional economy, and some consultations were held with planners at the provincial level.

Shortly after its creation, the board was given an Atlantic Development Fund to administer. By and large, the fund was employed to assist in the provision or improvement of the region's basic economic infrastructure. Over half of the fund, which totalled $186 million, was spent on highway construction and water and sewerage systems. Some money was spent on electrical generating and transmission facilities and in servicing new industrial parks at various locations throughout the region.

The fund did not provide direct assistance of any kind to private industry to locate new firms in the region. On this point, the ADB was criticized, notably by the Atlantic Provinces Economic Council, in a report on the Atlantic economy published in 1967. It was criticized also on other points. Some argued that ADB spending was unco-ordinated, in that it was never part of a comprehensive plan gearing expenditures toward specific targets. Some said that spending was politically inspired and that in the end it simply became a tool of Jack Pickersgill, a powerful Liberal federal cabinet minister who represented a Newfoundland riding in the House of Commons. The ADB never did deliver a comprehensive regional development plan for the Atlantic provinces, despite its mandate to do so in 1963. There are a variety of reasons offered for this failure. Some observers suggest that the board was never given the political green light to deliver the plan, while others insist that the ADB was disbanded in 1969 too early or precisely when it was on the verge of coming up with a comprehensive plan.[12]

The federal government introduced still other measures to promote regional development in the form of the Area Development Incentives Act (ADIA), and the Area Development Agency (ADA) within the Department of Industry. Legislation establishing ADIA was passed in 1963.[13] The central purpose behind these initiatives was to turn to the private sector to stimulate growth in economically depressed regions. This was to be done by enriching existing tax incentives and by introducing capital grants in designated areas.

Regions of high unemployment and slow growth were the target of these measures. Only regions reporting unemployment rates above a specified threshold level would become eligible. Manufacturing and processing firms were then invited to locate or expand operations in these regions. Three kinds of incentives were applied sequentially: accelerated capital cost allowances, a three-year income-tax exemption, and higher capital cost allowances. In 1965, a program of cash grants was introduced over and above the capital cost allowances.

Assistance was provided automatically on a formula basis. It was applied in a non-discretionary manner to areas chosen solely on the basis of unemployment levels, and Ottawa quickly discovered that it had limited potential as a development tool. Virtually no opportunity existed to relate assistance to development planning. In addition, because of the program's regional formula, the areas eligible for assistance did not include main population or industrial centres within slow-growth regions, where new manufacturing initiatives could be expected to have a better chance of success.

Throughout the 1960s, the federal government also sought to develop human resources.[14] It set up manpower training plans as well as mobility schemes. The Technical and Vocational Training Assistance Act (TVTA) called for agreements to be signed with each province for technical training of youths or for adult retraining. Essentially, the agreements enabled provincial governments to construct training and vocational schools, as well as to develop new manpower training and upgrading courses.

The federal government followed with another manpower development initiative – the Occupational Training Act (OTA). This act included both manpower training and mobility measures designed to deal with the country's structural unemployment. The federal government also sponsored other manpower mobility initiatives through such special development plans as FRED.

This brief outline of regional development initiatives by the federal government during the 1960s suggests that Ottawa was prepared to intervene directly to stimulate growth in lagging regions. Up until 1957, regional economic disparities had only been analyzed by royal commissions and had received little attention in terms of concrete federal initiatives. Within ten years, Ottawa had moved in a very dramatic fashion away from its cautious, conservative, and frugal approach to economic policy to a preoccupation with slow-growth regions.[15] It stacked one development initiative upon another in the belief that these would correct the country's substantial regional disparities.

THE NEED FOR CO-ORDINATION

It became obvious by the mid-1960s that the proliferating regional development programs were largely unrelated. Each new initiative was designed to address a specific problem of economic development, and much of the planning was carried out fairly independently by separate federal departments.[16] Consequently, each program tended to have a different objective and was attached to a different agency, which meant that overall co-ordination of the various programs was impossible. Several departments and agencies were involved in some fashion or other in regional development. These included, to name only a few, the Area Development Agency, the Atlantic Development Board, the Department of Agriculture, and the Department of Forestry and Rural Development. Occasionally, a central agency such as the Department of Finance would attempt to promote some degree of co-ordination, but the efforts were largely unsuccessful. Interdepartmental co-ordination, to the extent that it occurred, resulted from individual deals being struck between the various agencies rather than encouraged co-ordination from the top down.

There was also a problem of co-ordination at the federal-provincial level. Ottawa was increasingly concerned with individual line departments making arrangements on their own with provincial counterparts. With any one province, the federal government could have several unrelated development plans. Thus it could not pursue common goals with individual provinces, and Ottawa and the provinces could not work out strategies for overall economic development.[17]

Thus there was a need for a new institution to bring order and a central purpose to the various agencies and existing regional development programs. Other forces at play also favoured establishment of such a new department.

A PERIOD OF ECONOMIC GROWTH AND REDISTRIBUTIVE POLICIES

The mid- and late 1960s saw strong but uneven growth in the national economy and, relatively speaking, a burgeoning federal treasury. The government moved toward explicit redistributive priorities, as seen in the Canada Pension Plan, the Medical Care Act (Medicare), the Canada Assistance Plan,[18] and programs for economic development, some of which I have just described. Keynesian thinking in Ottawa was clearly dominant, and so was its notion of balance in the national economy.

Strengthening national unity was also a priority with the federal government. The Royal Commission on Bilingualism and Biculturalism tabled a series of reports from 1965 on and called for measures to increase national unity and improve English-French relations. French Canadians, it pointed out, were disadvantaged not just from a cultural perspective, but also from an economic one. The commission's report on official languages, published in 1967, concluded: 'We believe the notion of equal partnership connotes a vast enlargement of the opportunities for francophones in both private and public sectors of the economy.'[19]

The Economic Council of Canada, in its third annual report, in 1966, concluded that 'a favourable national environment may not in itself ensure balanced regional participation.' It called for a stronger commitment on Ottawa's part to developing slow-growth regions. It suggested closer federal-provincial co-operation in regional development matters and recommended that new administrative machinery be set up in Ottawa to take charge. It looked at the advantage of establishing a new line department, but recommended against such a course, opting instead for a strong co-ordinating capacity 'within the central machinery of government.' This, it felt, would enable Ottawa to mount a comprehensive attack on regional disparities, involving numerous government policies and programs. This new capacity, suggested the council, might be best located in the Treasury Board.[20] But even that would not be sufficient, it concluded; special regional development programs were also required. It urged the federal government to 'deconcentrate' federal activities within the regions.

In 1968 Pierre Elliot Trudeau became leader of the ruling Liberal party. He made national unity his central preoccupation and described it as the single motivating force for his involvement in public life. National unity would dominate the agenda of his new government, and it would extend beyond English-French relations. He boldy declared: 'Economic equality ... [is] just as important as equality of language rights ... If the underdevelopment of the Atlantic provinces is not corrected, not by charity or subsidy, but by helping them become areas of economic growth, then the unity of the country is almost as surely destroyed as it would be by the French-English confrontation.'[21]

Shortly after assuming office, Trudeau called a general election and campaigned vigorously on the theme of national unity. The Liberal party was returned to power with a strong majority after five years of minority rule. There was no doubt that the new Trudeau government would give increased priority to regional development, but it was unclear how it would do so. Early in its policy deliberations, the cabinet decided to direct its regional development priorities toward eastern Canada. The minister responsible for defining the policy, Jean Marchand, stated that for some years to come something like 80 per cent of new expenditures earmarked for regional development should be spent east of Trois-Rivières. Only 'modest and controlled' expenditures should be directed to the slow-growth northern and northwestern areas of Ontario, Manitoba, and the northern parts of the three most western provinces. This decision was inspired not simply by the political thinking of the new Trudeau government, but also by economic circumstances. Even cabinet ministers representing constituencies between Windsor and Quebec City saw merit in the argument that national unity was threatened when heavy and persistent unemployment plagued some regions at a time when, in central Canada, the economy was buoyant, to the point of strong inflationary pressure.[22] It was relatively easy to subscribe to the new regional development goal of dispensing economic growth widely enough to bring employment and earning opportunities in the slow-growth regions as close as possible to those in the rest of the country without substantially slowing national growth.

The cabinet decided also that the 'growth-pole' concept would define the new policy.[23] The rationale was simple. The main difference between, say, Ontario and the Maritime provinces, according to Marchand, was that Ontario had major urban centres with vigorous economic growth to which people from northern Ontario could move. The Maritimes had few cities capable of strong growth and of providing employment; consequently, many people remained in economically depressed rural areas. The growth-pole concept, it was believed, could create new opportunities at selected urban centres. Economic growth would take place through movement and change within regions, rather than between regions.

Ottawa would implement the growth-pole concept through two new programs: the special areas program and the Regional Development Incentives Act (RDIA).[24] The two shared the same objective: to encourage manufacturing and processing industry in the slow-growth regions. Industrial centres with the potential for attracting manufacturing and processing firms would be chosen. A special area agreement with the relevant provincial government would then be signed. This would provide for construction or improvement of the infrastructure – roads, water and sewer systems, and schools – within which industrial growth could occur.

With the infrastructure in place, the regional industrial incentives program, through cash grants, would be able to attract new manufacturing industry to the selected centres. The cash grants would lower the cost of setting up production, compensating the investor for locating in economically weak regions. The grant would be sufficiently large that the new production facility would generate the same return on investment that it would have had the firm located in southern Ontario without the grant.

Cash grants constituted a tried and proven approach (under the ADA program) and provided the entrepreneur a basis from which to determine whether the new facility would be economically sound. The new government discarded other possibilities because of important shortcomings. Continuing government assistance – interest subsidies, private-sector loans, or large transportation subsidies for finished goods – were considered both too difficult to administer and politically unacceptable. The government felt also that income tax credits or tax allowances were of limited benefit to new or smaller firms generating only modest profits in early years.[25]

There were a number of decisions about policy still to be taken and new programs to be considered. As well, decisions were required on the host of existing regional development programs, notably ARDA and FRED. Before turning to these issues, the government had to establish an appropriate administrative structure to deliver the new programs, to gain intergovernmental co-operation, and to promote the concept of regional development within the federal government.

DEFINING DREE: CENTRAL AGENCY OR LINE DEPARTMENT?

Prime Minister Trudeau turned to his trusted Quebec lieutenant, Jean Marchand, to spearhead the government's regional development priority. Trudeau, Marchand, and Gérard Pelletier had all come to federal politics largely because of what they saw as unacceptable cultural and linguistic inequalities and regional economic disparities in Canada. Once he became prime minister, Trudeau turned to Pelletier, his secretary of state, to oversee the government's language policies and to Marchand to implement the new regional development policy.

Marchand became minister of forestry and rural development after the 1968 election. Work began immediately on laying the framework for a new department. On Marchand's advice, Trudeau appointed Tom Kent deputy minister–designate of the proposed new department. Kent was a powerful figure in Ottawa. He had played a key policy role in the Liberal party when the party was in opposition and later became principal secretary to Prime Minister Pearson.

Essentially, three options were considered for the new department. The first was a super department of regional development with the necessary clout to get other federal departments to contribute to regional development through their own programs, a program delivery capacity of its own, and an ability to deal with provincial governments. The second option would have brought together all the various regional development agencies and programs into the Department of Manpower and Immigration, renamed Manpower and Regional Development. The third option was a typical line department, able both to deliver programs and to negotiate with the provinces, but with an uncertain ability to influence other federal departments and agencies.

Marchand reports now that the first option was preferred until the very last moment. He states that both he and the prime minister saw merit in the position taken by the Economic Council of Canada outlined above. They were also deeply impressed with the success of la DATAR (Délégation à l'Aménagement du Territoire et à l'Action Régionale) in France. Established in 1963, it had substantial co-ordination ability and influence over line departments in the French government in creating special measures to bring development to slow-growth regions. It could, for example, define regional development plans to which line departments were expected to contribute, and look at the budget from a regional perspective and, correspondingly, influence spending.[26] No doubt, one important reason for its strong co-ordinating ability was the fact that it reported to the prime minister.

With this in mind, Trudeau and Marchand saw two distinct functions for the new department and, initially, two distinct but supportive organizational structures. Research analysis and planning would enable the minister and the cabinet to direct federal departments to tailor their programs for regional development purposes. This function would be located inside the Prime Minister's Office (PMO) but would report to both the prime minister and Marchand. The other function – a program delivery – would be lodged in a typical federal line department reporting only to Marchand.

The proposal, not unexpectedly, met with stiff opposition from the Ottawa bureaucracy, more specifically from officials in the Privy Council Office (PCO).[27] To a purist, the proposal was organizationally untidy, since there would be two administrative structures located in separate organizations, but with one reporting both to the prime minister and to a cabinet minister.[28] This situation was simply unheard of in Canadian public administration, and, given the traditionally incremental bias of PCO officials, it was viewed with a great deal of suspicion. It is the conventional view in Ottawa that a minister cannot be responsible for programs and their fund-seeking, while at the same time having co-ordination authority over the programs of his cabinet colleagues. Such a situation would give the minister an unfair advantage over his colleagues in that he could 'put on his co-ordination hat' to promote his own programs. It is precisely for this reason that the minister of finance, the president of the treasury board, and, more recently, ministers responsible for 'expenditure envelopes' have had no programs to administer.

Marchand now reports that both the prime minister and he were prepared to overlook these administrative 'niceties' in order to ensure that regional development would be given the intended priority. In the end, they rejected the proposal for quite another reason. It was clear to everyone that Marchand would wield considerable power in the new administration without any kind of special co-ordination authority over his cabinet colleagues. Apart from assuming responsibility for regional development, he was named the regional minister responsible for Quebec.

Regional ministers have considerable influence over political decisions and patronage. Cabinet ministers responsible for the two larger regions, Ontario and Quebec, are even more influential, not simply because of the political and economic weight of their regions, but also because of the number of seats they have. Trudeau's principal political advisers feared that adding still more to Marchand's prestige and power by having part of his department located within PMO and PCO and by giving him a special co-ordinating role over the policies and programs of his cabinet colleagues would divide the cabinet. It would, in their view, place the prime minister in a very difficult position with his cabinet and lead to personality conflicts that would be particularly difficult for him to resolve.

In the end, it was agreed that the new department would be a traditional line department. It would still retain its research analysis function and encourage other federal departments and agencies to contribute to federal regional development efforts. It would, however, use persuasion rather than impose co-ordination. Given Marchand's easy access to the prime minister and the priority the new government gave to regional development, Marchand, Trudeau, and others involved in the decision were confident that co-ordination could still take place.

The second option – integrating regional development agencies and programs within Manpower and Immigration – was also rejected. PCO disapproved, and Marchand and Kent, who initially supported the option, chose not to push the concept 'all the way' to the prime minister. Marchand and Kent had spent the previous two years establishing a strong mandate for the Department of Manpower and Immigration. They felt that the department's one weakness was that it could not 'target' or 'direct' its programs to provinces with high unemployment. Incorporating regional agencies and programs would give it such a capacity.

There were other reasons why Marchand and Kent initially favoured this option. A strongly entrenched and weighty line department would be better able to lead an interdepartmental effort than a new central agency or partial central agency. What was envisaged was the kind of industry department that C.D. Howe had turned into the effective power centre in Ottawa and indeed in the Canadian economy. Moreover, an established department would provide a ready-made capacity and strength to plan and deliver programs quickly and avoid reliance on weak and diverse units of the old regional groups.

Officials from PCO and other central agencies 'rang every possible warning bell against a department being so powerful.' Accordingly, Marchand and Kent did not press this option very strongly. They recognized that such a large department would entail a terrible administrative burden. More important, however, they did not want to be drawn into an ongoing bureaucratic fight over such issues as classifications for senior personnel. Choosing an organizational structure that would have been opposed by Ottawa central agencies would have invariably led to frustrating battles over administrative issues. Marchand and Kent believed that they could win these battles, but at a cost. Such battles would have distracted them and other senior officials from getting on with regional programs.

At this stage, there was only one issue left to resolve. Various suggestions had been brought forward for a name for the new department. One popular suggestion was the Department of Regional Development. In fact, before the legislation establishing the proposed department was introduced in the House of Commons, it was widely referred to as such in Ottawa. Marchand resisted this suggestion. He felt that the term *regional development* was already too widely employed in Ontario and in Quebec. The new department's efforts, he insisted, would have to be largely directed outside Ontario and southern Quebec. So that there would be no confusion and no false expectations in these two provinces, Marchand opted for the Department of Regional Economic Expansion (DREE). With the prime minister in full agreement with this suggestion, Marchand could turn to developing his programs and to building his new department.

4

DREE – The early years

Jean Marchand and Tom Kent had a number of important tasks to carry out and decisions to take in setting up DREE in the summer of 1968. New legislation was urgently required, a new organization had to be established, and an adequate budget had to be struck with the Treasury Board. New programs had to be defined and finely tuned and old ones either discarded or revised to fit the new policy. Marchand respected Kent's formidable talents for getting things done, and Kent respected Marchand's political acumen and status in the new government. Both had the confidence of the prime minister. Together they made a powerful team in Ottawa, something the federal bureaucracy quickly understands and respects.[1]

THE DREE LEGISLATION

Marchand expected little difficulty from Parliament in getting new DREE legislation passed, and on this he was correct. If anything, the opposition urged him to go even further than the proposals he presented to Parliament. The new Progressive Conservative leader, Robert Stanfield, was a former premier of Nova Scotia. His home province had long been plagued by slow growth, and he reportedly entered federal politics because of his commitment to regional development. To the extent that one is able to do so in the usually highly partisan House of Commons, Stanfield was generally supportive of Marchand's proposals. He expressed concern, however, that DREE would be left alone to carry the entire load of promoting regional development, while other federal departments simply went on with their own sectoral responsibilities. Said Stanfield: 'There may very well be a tendency on the part of other Ministers to say – Let Jean do it ... This bill does not assure anything like the degree of coordination which there must be among the departments of the government if regional disparity is to be attacked effectively.' The New Democratic Party offered little in the debate. Its leader, Tommy Douglas, lamented the lack of new and specific goals in establishing

DREE. These ill-defined goals, he insisted, did not require a government reorganization. 'There is little advantage in talking about government reorganization,' he said 'unless we know what it is the government is seeking to accomplish.'[2]

Both the prime minister and Marchand dismissed these suggestions. Trudeau argued that the establishment of DREE was necessary 'to achieve real coordination ... of our endeavours and undertakings in such a worthy and vital sphere in respect of our country's future.' Marchand added that his new department 'was the only way to secure the coordination of federal efforts' in regional development.[3]

Political criticism of DREE and its new policy direction came more often and with more conviction from government back-benchers than from the opposition. Members of Parliament representing economically depressed constituencies of rural Quebec and northern New Brunswick, many of whom were Liberals, feared that the emphasis on growth centres would leave their regions with little federal funding for development initiatives. The new approach represented a clear departure from the old regional development policy, in that ARDA and FRED had been expressly designed for their regions or for rural slow-growth regions. Marchand sought to allay MPs' concerns by arguing that his policy would put in place the urban and industrial structures required to give their provinces a new economic depth and strength. Once this was done, attention could then be given to the economically depressed rural areas, or, more specifically, to their constituencies. In short, Marchand assured them that with time their turn would come.[4]

The legislation introduced shortly after the Trudeau government was returned to power and labelled the Government Organization Act was passed in 1969. The DREE Act was short, incomplete, and, from a long-term perspective, hopelessly inadequate. This Marchand knew full well. However, his first priority was to get legislative approval quickly and to provide for the continuation of some existing programs while new ones were being developed. The new legislation repealed both the ADB and FRED. It did not, however, do away with ARDA, ADA, or the Prairie Farm Rehabilitation Act (PFRA). It introduced the Special Areas Program and established the Atlantic Development Council. Within the year Marchand introduced another piece of legislation, the Regional Development Incentives Act.

The Atlantic Development Board (ADB) was replaced by the Atlantic Development Council (ADC), because with DREE capable of delivering infrastructure projects to the Atlantic provinces, the ADB was no longer required. Fearing, however, that Atlantic MPs might feel betrayed by the loss of the ADB, Marchand made provisions for a new body on economic development (the ADC) that would be exclusively concerned with the Atlantic provinces. On paper, the new advisory body resembled the early ADB, except that it could not recommend specifically how money should be spent or have its own staff.

Two points in the new legislation need to be highlighted. Curiously, it said little about the goals of the new department. There was no indication, for example, of whether an increase of income levels in slow-growth regions, greater productivity, or even higher employment levels should be specifically pursued. The wording said merely that special areas could be designated when an area 'in ... [a] province is determined to require, by reason of the exceptional inadequacy of opportunities for productive employment ... special measures to facilitate economic expansion and social adjustment.'[5] The geographical dimension of special areas was not laid out, even in broad terms. There was no mention of the targets to be reached, or when the special-area designation would no longer be necessary.

Defining areas or regions, or, to put it more crudely, deciding who is 'in' and who is 'out' of development schemes, is always politically explosive. There was no doubt a political explanation for Marchand's not defining clearly in the legislation which regions would qualify for the special-areas program. He had already been told in no uncertain terms by many Liberal MPs that they were not pleased with his policy direction. A minister quickly discovers that such debates, particularly when they involve party colleagues, are more suited to the government lobby behind the House than inside, in full view of the opposition and journalists. Why then invite such a possibility by naming designated regions in a bill before the House? This would only serve to force certain government members to defend the interests of their constituencies and thus openly speak against a government bill.

Similarly, ministers and permanent officials are never keen on laying out before Parliament or the general public specific indicators that reveal to what extent goals are being reached.[6] If results fall short of the stated goal, the minister and his department are politically vulnerable. Partisan politics being what they are, it is always preferable to be rather vague about objectives.

The DREE legislation provided flexibility – which was precisely what Marchand was seeking. As we saw earlier, special areas could be designated after simply 'consulting' the relevant provincial government. The format for federal-provincial consultation was not defined, and there were no restrictions placed on the kind of projects that DREE could sponsor in a designated area. Marchand had a free hand to set the tone for these negotiations and for the kind of projects deemed acceptable by DREE.

DEVELOPING THE SPECIAL AREAS PROGRAM

Before they could turn to their new programs, Marchand and Kent had to deal with those that the department had inherited. Some decisions were simple. The new regional incentives would replace the Area Development Incentives program, which in turn would be left to wither away. Initially at least, it was decided to terminate ARDA and FRED programs as quickly as possible. Marchand declared them 'almost dead' one year after the DREE legislation was passed.[7]

On this issue the new department met stiff opposition from a number of provincial governments. Manitoba, Quebec, Prince Edward Island, New Brunswick, Ontario, and British Columbia reacted strongly against DREE's position on both ARDA and FRED. They stressed the valuable contribution those programs had made to certain regions and insisted that suddenly terminating them would play havoc with their economies.[8] In some instances, this opposition bore fruit. Both Ontario and British Columbia, for example, signed new ARDA agreements with DREE in 1970.

Later, and after numerous representations on the part of native associations, Marchand and Kent agreed to expand the ARDA concept. The Special ARDA program had first been introduced in 1971 and consisted of federal-provincial cost-sharing of development projects in rural areas.[9] The program covered incentive grants and related services to assist disadvantaged people, mainly of native ancestry, including status and non-status Indians and metis in rural areas, to undertake commercial ventures from primary-sector producing activities. Advisory committees in each province or territory review and make recommendations on all projects. These committees have equal numbers of members from the federal government, provincial or territorial governments, and native associations.

The program has been particularly well received by native associations and by some provinces, notably Saskatchewan and Manitoba. From its early beginnings under Marchand and Kent, the Special ARDA program has grown, and, more remarkably from a regional development perspective, it has withstood various new policy directions, program changes, and government reorganizations. The program is still operating and has been expanded to provide for training, social adjustment, assistance to primary producers, and infrastructure. Relative to other programs, however, expenditures under Special ARDA are modest. In 1980–81, for example, DREE spent just over $11 million for Special ARDA initiatives.[10]

Despite new Special ARDA initiatives, however, DREE's basic policy direction remained unchanged. The ARDA and FRED programs were slowly winding down. DREE, it became apparent, favoured industrialization and strong urban growth centres and was moving away from schemes to alleviate rural poverty and encourage rural-based development. The cornerstone of this new policy direction was the Special Areas Program, which, together with the new regional incentives program, would encourage industrialists into regions where they would not otherwise go. True to its stated preference, DREE would look primarily to eastern Quebec and the four Atlantic provinces in its attempt to encourage industrial growth.

Before much could be accomplished, it was essential to gain the co-operation of the provinces. They were, according to an observer, told 'Take it or leave it.' DREE had scarcely consulted the provinces at all in developing its new policy direction, in formulating the growth-pole concept, or in determining how it ought to be implemented.[11] In short, DREE's position was clear, and the provinces were well aware of it: if provincial governments wanted federal funding, they had to accept, as given, the new policy.

Accept they did, but not without criticism. Designating areas for special consideration is politically difficult for any government, including provincial governments. Confronted with this situation, they called on Ottawa to designate several communities in their respective provinces rather than the handful that an effective growth-pole approach requires to be successful. In this way, they could at least shift the blame to Ottawa for the non-designation of certain areas. However, Marchand and Kent stood firm. Marchand explained: 'The more you extend it – special areas – the more you weaken it ... We have to stick to our guns.'[12] They were prepared to make some concessions, but not to compromise the effectiveness of their new policy.

Marchand did make one concession that was important to the provincial governments, especially those from the Atlantic region, which are well known for their penchant for highway construction. Provincial politicians stressed time and again to Marchand the importance of highways for regional development: previous regional development schemes, such as FRED, had provided for new routes. DREE finally agreed to provide for highway construction outside the special areas in the case of New Brunswick, Nova Scotia, and Newfoundland.[13]

However, the provinces found co-operation with Ottawa difficult throughout DREE's early years. They were not consulted on general policy or on important decisions about programs. They won what they considered minor concessions on certain projects, but felt these insufficient.

In the end, DREE was able to limit the number of designated special areas to about what it had initially envisaged. Twenty-three such areas were identified, and each became the subject of a federal-provincial agreement. Six of the special areas were expected to realize substantially faster industrial growth than the other designated areas as a result of the incentives programs, and were singled out in order to provide the infrastructure needed to support this growth. These six areas consisted of St John's, Halifax-Dartmouth, Saint John, Moncton, Quebec City, and Trois-Rivières. Because of their locations, Regina and Saskatoon were also designated to assist in financing surrounding community development. In Newfoundland, the Burin Peninsula, Gander, Stephenville, Hawke's Bay, Come-by-Chance, and Goose Bay (Happy Valley) were designated in order to make them more attractive as 'receiving centres' under the Newfoundland Resettlement Program. The Pas and Meadow Lake in Manitoba, and Lesser Slave Lake in Alberta, were designated for industrial incentives to promote the development of resource industries, and to improve community facilities, particularly to the advantage of the Indian and metis populations. The Renfrew-Pembroke area in Ontario and Lac St-Jean in Quebec were designated for industrial incentives, for which they were not eligible under the regular incentives program. Finally, the Ste-Scholastique area, outside Montreal, was designated, as a result of the federal government's decision to construct a new international airport in the area.[14] In this case, assistance was provided to the province to put in place the extensive infrastructure that was required.

These special-area agreements sponsored a great variety of projects: highways, water and sewage systems, industrial parks, tourist attractions, servicing of industrial land, and schools. The federal government covered 50 per cent of the cost of certain projects plus a loan for part or all of the remainder. In the case of highway construction, Ottawa paid up to 100 per cent of the cost. The great majority of projects involved infrastructure. A new industrial park was built in St John's, as were new water and sewer systems, a new arterial highway, and a new high school. Similarly, in other special areas of the province, nearly all the DREE funds were allocated to new water and sewer systems, roads, industrial parks, and schools. The pattern established in Newfoundland was followed elsewhere. The Halifax-Dartmouth area, for example, saw some sixty-five projects exclusively for roads, sewer and water systems, and school construction.

Special-area agreements supported the same kind of initiatives right across the country. New access roads were built to new industrial parks, as in St John's, or to new tourist facilities, as in Trois-Rivières. An engineering building was built for Memorial University in St John's, while a seminary was rebuilt in Quebec City. New water and sewer facilities were constructed in Manitoba's The Pas area, in the Lesser Slave Lake area of Alberta, in Lévis, Quebec, and in Saint John, among others.[15]

All special areas called for the establishment of a federal-provincial liaison committee composed of an equal number of representatives of each government. The role of these committees was to monitor and report on all stages of the planning, design, and implementation of the projects.[16] In other words, these committees had a very limited role in formulating policy or even programs. They were there simply to oversee implementation of projects.

Other federal departments and agencies were consulted or kept informed during development of the agreements. Most showed little interest in participating in formulation or implementation. Consultation was not initiated at the appropriate levels, with both Marchand and Kent preoccupied with setting up the new department and developing strategies and programs. Federal departments saw little merit in contributing to the objectives of another department, perhaps at the risk of compromising their own. In the end, the special-areas program became exclusively DREE's responsibility, with only Central Mortgage and Housing and the Department of Public Works involved in the implementation of certain projects.[17]

THE REGIONAL DEVELOPMENT INCENTIVES PROGRAM

The second major initiative to be developed was the new regional development incentives program. This would be built from the existing ADA program by taking from ADA most of its positive attributes and discarding its less desirable features. Two of the latter were rejected outright. The new program would be discretionary and no longer automatically available to all new production facilities locating in designated areas. Grants would now be available for selected sectors only. The program would also be available over a much wider area, by providing incentives in growth centres and in selected urban areas.

Other features were added. The new program would confine itself to development grants; would set a maximum level, but also provide for offers at less than the maximum if circumstances warranted; and establish a two-part grant structure, one for capital costs and the other according to the number of jobs created. Maximum levels for both were also more generous for the Atlantic provinces.[18]

The part of the grant calculated on the basis of jobs created would not in any way be automatic: large discretionary power was left to the minister. He could require a company 'to demonstrate' that a grant, over and above what was available for capital cost, was necessary to make the project 'viable.' He could also assess the project's contribution to the economic development of the region and then decide whether or not a grant should be offered. These provisions were to guard against windfall profits for companies locating in regions for reasons other than an incentives grant. In addition, they would permit the minister and departmental officials to refuse aid to companies which, in their view, could not stand on their own feet in the long term, regardless of whether a grant was awarded or not.[19]

Perhaps as a result of criticism directed at Ottawa over its lack of consultation with provincial governments, the cabinet requested Marchand and his departmental officials to inform the provinces of the new program before introducing the proposed legislation in Parliament. This they did, and they found the provinces generally supportive. In particular, the three Maritime provinces applauded the proposed program. Newfoundland expressed disappointment that it would not receive some form of additional incentives, beyond that available to the other Atlantic provinces or to the 'mainland.' The province stressed time and again to DREE officials that unless the program were considerably more generous for Newfoundland, new industrial activity would locate on the mainland, notably in Halifax.

Not surprisingly, the most contentious issue confronting the new program was its geographical applicability. Marchand and Kent were adamant on two points: first, that the regions designated be sufficiently limited so as not to dilute the effectiveness of the program to help slow-growth regions, and, second, that unlike the ADA program, the new program should apply in growth centres – Halifax, Moncton, Saint John, and St John's, among others. Their reasoning was tied to the thinking underpinning the growth-pole concept, which suggests that 'nothing succeeds like success.' New enterprises would have strong economic reasons for preferring to locate where other firms already existed, since these would help to finance all kinds of overhead for transportation and community service. A business, particularly if its technology is sophisticated, may run into difficulties by locating in an area with little other industrial activity. These obvious facts, argued Marchand, are the basis of the 'growth centre' or 'industrial centre' approach to development; the chances of starting a growth process that will become self-sustaining depends largely on whether industrial incentives can be concentrated on the stimulation of 'families' of projects at relatively few localities, rather than a series of projects spread over countless little communities.[20]

Regions designated for the program thus included all the Atlantic provinces, eastern and northern Quebec, parts of northern Ontario, and the northernmost regions of the four western provinces. Thus, regions were designated in all ten provinces, and this for a three-year period ending 30 June 1972. The regions designated accounted for about 30 per cent of the Canadian labour force, and the average per capita income within them was approximately 70 per cent of the national average. On the face of it, this coverage may appear excessive in terms of the program's regional applicability, considering the purpose of the growth-pole concept.

However, initially at least, Marchand and Kent got what they wanted. They now report that they were successful in limiting the program's coverage to areas they had first envisaged. Parts of Ontario, Alberta, and British Columbia were designated more as a gesture to ensure that these provinces would not feel completely left out of a federal government program. Marchand and Kent feared that these provinces, given their relatively strong fiscal positions, might establish their own incentives programs, thereby greatly inhibiting the new federal initiative. In any event, the regional incentives program would be complementary to the larger, more expensive special-areas program. With the benefits of these two programs combined, it was felt, industrialists would dismiss smaller communities out of hand and opt for the growth-pole areas to locate new plants. Certainly, viewed with the benefit of hindsight, regional designation of DREE's industrial incentives program in 1969 was highly restrictive.

It was not long before strong political pressure was exerted on Marchand to extend the program's regional designations further. Cabinet ministers and MPs from the Montreal area frequently made the point that Montreal was Quebec's growth pole and that if DREE were serious about regional development, then it ought to designate Montreal under its industrial incentives program. Ministers from other regions did not share this view and did not hesitate to say so to Marchand and to the full cabinet.

Montreal's growth performance rate was not keeping pace with expectations, particularly those of the large number of Liberal MPs from the area. The city's unemployment rate stood at 7.0 per cent in 1972, compared with 4.6 per cent for Toronto. Further, Quebec's economic strength, it was argued time and again, was directly linked to Montreal, and, unless new employment opportunities were created there, little hope was held for the province's peripheral areas. Montreal required special measures, it was argued, to return to a reasonable rate of growth.

In the end, Marchand chose to designate Montreal as a special region, known as 'region C.' In this newly designated region, which consisted of southwestern Quebec, including Hull and Montreal, and three counties of eastern Ontario, the maximum incentive grant was lower than elsewhere. The grant could not exceed 10 per cent of approved capital cost, plus $2,000 for each direct job created. Elsewhere in the designated regions of Quebec and Ontario, the maximum incentive grant was fixed at 25 per cent of approved capital costs and $5,000 for each new job created. A third level of assistance was established for the Atlantic region, which called for a maximum grant of 35 per cent of capital cost and $7,000 per job created. Finally, the changes stipulated that region C's special designation was to be for two years only. This, it was felt, would be sufficient to help Montreal return to a 'reasonable rate of growth.'[21] The changes, however, extended coverage of the designated regions to about 40 per cent of the population and almost 45 per cent of manufacturing employment and established a three-level hierarchy of incentive grants.

The two-year designation for Montreal quickly generated strong interest and a high number of applicants. During the 1971–72 fiscal year, the 360 incentive grants accepted by different firms in the new region C involved capital expenditures of over $225 million and the creation of some 14,000 new jobs. By comparison, 129 DREE incentives grants were accepted by firms in the four Atlantic provinces, involving capital expenditures of over $48 million and the expected creation of slightly less than 5,000 new jobs during the same period.[22]

Marchand also modified his department's industrial incentives program. An amendment to the Regional Development Incentives Act (RDIA) provided for the introduction in 1971 of a loan guarantee program. DREE discovered that its incentives program was 'hampered from time to time by the inability of applicants to raise the long-term financing necessary to establish' new facilities.[23] The new program would enable DREE to deal with this lacuna whenever it was considered appropriate. The program's aim was to encourage lenders to invest loan funds in businesses wishing to locate in economically depressed regions by providing a partial guarantee. Unlike the incentives program, which was limited by legislation to manufacturing and processing businesses, the loan guarantee scheme could also support businesses in the service sector.

The legislation establishing the new program required that the minister of finance concur in any loan guarantee decision. Over time, this provision served to limit the program's effect, in that decision-making became notoriously bureaucratic and slow. It took such inordinate lengths of time to get the ministers of DREE and finance to concur on loan guarantee decisions that DREE officials became reluctant to promote the program. In a ten-year period, less than forty loan guarantee offers were made.[24]

The legislation for the incentives program provided for a termination date; projects had to come into commercial production by 31 December 1976. This was to ensure that a review of the program would take place no later than 1974. As has already been noted, the legislation did not establish the designated regions clearly. Changes could and in fact were introduced through orders-in-council, thus simply requiring cabinet approval. This gave the minister the same kind of flexibility in designating new areas that he had for the Special Areas Program.

In formulating the two new programs, DREE had to meet the requirements of Ottawa's central agencies and its expenditure control process. This DREE did by providing some rather rough calculations of its financial requirements. 'Money was simply no problem in those days,' Marchand and former DREE officials report. Marchand and Kent had secured from the Treasury Board all the funds they required – and then some.

In fact, it soon became obvious that the department would not be able to spend fully its allocated budget. Special projects were approved from time to time to prop up the department's expenditure level. As we have already seen, special short-term highways agreements were signed with the Atlantic provinces. This is not to suggest that such projects were supportive of DREE's growth-pole policy. They simply accommodated some concerns on the part of the Atlantic provinces and enabled DREE to spend its allocated budget. DREE, because of Marchand and Kent, could get projects through the government's expenditure approval process with relative ease and alacrity, because the prime minister had made it clear that regional development held a strong priority in the government's scheme of things. Money was simply no problem for DREE, and everybody in Ottawa was made aware of this. Moreover, DREE's spending gave the federal government a great deal of favourable visibility.

DREE's two major programs were designed in part to attract maximum public awareness to federal spending. In the case of the special-areas program, the federal government had clearly taken the lead, with the provinces adjusting their priorities to reflect the program's requirements. Marchand took an aggressive posture with the provinces, and this did not go unnoticed by the press.

The regional incentives program meanwhile lent itself quite readily to placing the federal government in a favourable light. It allocated grants directly to private investors, thereby bypassing provincial governments. This enabled the federal government to occupy the limelight. The program also offered countless opportunities for government ministers and MPs to go back home on weekends to announce that x number of jobs would be created through a government grant and subsequently to attend ribbon-cutting ceremonies.

However, after three or four years, it became obvious that all was not well. In fact, by late 1971, a fair amount of public criticism was being hurled at DREE. Regions not designated as special areas were arguing more and more that they too could use federal financing for economic development. To many in the non-designated regions, it seemed that the federal government was, in effect, saying that only selected regions should grow and that Ottawa's economic development efforts would be concentrated there.

Criticism was also voiced that far too much federal money was earmarked for infrastructure projects such as water, sewage, and highway construction. One former DREE official reports that there was a widespread saying in Ottawa that 'DREE had too much money chasing too few good projects.' Yet despite such large expenditure budgets, there was no strong evidence to suggest that DREE was making progress in correcting regional economic imbalances. Standard economic indicators were not pointing to any kind of trend toward more balanced growth.

DREE also had no solid evaluation prepared to demonstrate that its programs had contributed to the economic development of eastern Quebec and the Atlantic provinces. 'We knew it in our hearts that progress was made' insists an official, 'but we could not demonstrate it on paper.' A solid evaluation of DREE's efforts was not possible because insufficient time had elapsed to assess their impact. Moreover, analysts argue that too many variables were at play in designated urban centres to say whether any growth was a direct result of DREE spending.[25]

Most, if not all provincial governments were also critical of DREE. The no-nonsense 'take it or leave it' approach adopted by Marchand and Kent did not sit well with the provinces. The call for a closer form of federal-provincial co-operation was made time and again.

The federal government needed a new, more imaginative approach in combating regional disparities. Marchand did not deny that a new approach would probably be desirable, and he informed the cabinet during the summer of 1972 that a review of DREE, its policies, and its programs was necessary. He told the cabinet that no stone should be left unturned and that a 'question mark' should be placed on all DREE activities. Before the review progressed very far, a general election was called.

5

DREE and the General Development Agreements

The Liberal government regrouped in Ottawa after the 1972 election, badly shaken and barely clinging to power. It had won 109 seats to the Conservatives' 107, losing over forty seats in English Canada and suffering some humiliating defeats in traditionally safe Liberal seats.[1] Its clear parliamentary majority had been reduced to an almost untenable minority position.

The government's objective was to win back the support of the electorate and, given its position in Parliament, to win it back in a hurry. Adjustments were required, and Trudeau quickly made them. During the campaign much had been made of the so-called excessive 'French power' in Ottawa. In his new cabinet, Trudeau moved Gérard Pelletier from Secretary of State to Communications and Jean Marchand from Regional Economic Expansion to Transport. As well, the cabinet immediately called for new policy initiatives.

THE 1972–73 DREE POLICY REVIEW

The prime minister appointed another powerful political figure to head DREE, Don Jamieson from Newfoundland. A year earlier, he had named J.D. Love, a career public servant, as deputy minister.[2] Jamieson jumped at the opportunity to continue the policy review initiated by Marchand – and now with a sense of urgency. A group of officials from DREE and other federal departments was brought together under the direction of an assistant deputy minister for planning and co-ordination inside DREE. The scope of the review was all-encompassing. It would ask questions about goals, policies, programs, legislative framework, and government organization. Early on, a decision was taken to inform the provinces that a general policy review had been launched. Consultations with the provinces on the appropriate direction of the review would also be possible, but great care would be taken not to 'lose control of the review' to the provinces or through them to the press.

Fifteen major policy papers were prepared. They were all written inside the federal government, under the guidance of DREE's assistant deputy minister responsible for the review. The policy review reached several major conclusions and came forward with a number of sweeping recommendations. The most important, and one that was stressed time and again, was that in regional development close federal-provincial co-operation was essential. To ensure this, it was recommended that DREE decentralize its operations to provincial capitals. The concept of 'identification and pursuit of development opportunities,' the policy review suggested, should guide DREE's new policy approach: each region was unique and required special measures formulated so as to take full advantage of the opportunities presented. Federal and provincial departments and agencies should participate in a comprehensive fashion in promoting regional development.[3]

Detailed reviews of the economic circumstances and opportunities of the ten provinces were prepared.[4] These reviews later became widely known as DREE's 'yellow books' on provincial economic circumstances. One was also prepared for the Atlantic provinces as a whole, and another for the four western provinces, as well as one for each province. DREE found that the economic structure of the four Atlantic provinces was still quite weak and that it remained the most 'desperate in the country.' A strong federal commitment to stimulate development in the region was still necessary. The review argued that wide-ranging development opportunities nevertheless existed and suggested that the appropriate federal agencies and the provinces jointly try to develop the 'Atlantic Gateway Transportation Concept.'[5] The rationale was that Saint John, Moncton, and Halifax and the ports of Canso and Come-By-Chance would, if properly developed, be able to exploit the Atlantic provinces' strategic location midway between two industrial giants – the United States and western Europe. With fully developed air, sea, rail, and road systems connecting the two markets, the region could become an important transportation, packaging, and distribution centre, serving both North America and Europe.

Individual provincial reviews also revealed that the Atlantic provinces offered a number of sectoral opportunities. Agriculture, fisheries, forestry, mining, and tourism, in particular, held promise for growth. However, they all had problems requiring government initiatives if they were to be resolved. Forestry, for example, had always played a role in New Brunswick's economic development. Now, the sector faced critical resource depletion and inadequate management practices.[6]

Quebec's secondary sector was found to be far too heavily concentrated in slow-growth, low-wage industries.[7] Consequently, Quebec would find it increasingly difficult to create new manufacturing jobs and to keep its wage rate from falling further behind Ontario's. Vitality in the Quebec economy, suggested the review, required renewed vigour from Montreal. Accordingly, efforts should be made to identify developmental opportunities to revitalize that city. It was felt that the new international airport at Ste-Scholastique could provide such opportunities.

Although Ontario's unemployment rate had crept up from 3.1 per cent in 1969 to 4.7 per cent in 1972, no one was suggesting that the province's economy could not respond adequately to market forces or that it would not continue to grow.[8] Nonetheless, the policy review put forward two important recommendations for Ontario: first, that efforts be made to develop a strong liaison on economic development issues between the federal and the Ontario governments; and second, that DREE focus on the socioeconomic problems of northern Ontario. Initiatives ought to be developed for the region and the provincial government encouraged to participate in the process.

In the west, the review pointed out that British Columbia and Alberta and, to a lesser extent, Saskatchewan and Manitoba have renewable and non-renewable natural resources in substantial quantities from which development opportunities could be exploited. All four provinces also had well-developed urban centres or growth poles that could encourage and sustain development.[9] But there were problems, too. Manitoba and Saskatchewan were witnessing out-migration: population growth in Manitoba was virtually static, and Saskatchewan had seen an absolute decline in its population since 1968. British Columbia's population meanwhile was growing annually, but at a cost. Having to absorb a heavy migration of job-seekers from Saskatchewan and Manitoba, British Columbia's unemployment stood at over 8 per cent. In addition, major regions in the western northlands required substantial improvements in their standards of living and in job creation. The native population in particular was subjected to unacceptable socioeconomic conditions and was not participating in and benefiting from economic activities at play in the region.

Opportunities nevertheless were found to exist in all western provinces. Saskatchewan and Manitoba would benefit from initiatives designed to achieve greater value from the processing of agricultural products. Alberta could realize opportunities if efforts were directed to the mineral and agricultural sectors. British Columbia had considerable opportunities for growth in the forestry sector and in its forest industries. The northwest region of the province was identified as one requiring special DREE-led efforts.

All in all, Canada's ten provinces each had peculiar economic circumstances and offered a variety of opportunities for development. All the staff papers on each province and on the western and Atlantic regions were released to the provinces in the form of yellow books. These books, DREE hoped, would pave the way for federal-provincial consultation and ultimately close co-operation.

The message of the policy review was clear. DREE would now be present in all provinces and would be looking for close intergovernmental co-operation.

Certainly, the Atlantic provinces and eastern Quebec would remain DREE's principal client regions, but they could no longer lay claim to 80 per cent of DREE's budget.[10]

From an economic perspective, the growth-pole concept was now out of favour in Ottawa; the new password to DREE funds was 'developmental opportunities.' DREE would pursue 'viable' opportunities whether they were in urban or rural areas, though it would be preferable if they were located in slow-growth regions, and priority status would still be given to these.

Politically, the outcome of the policy review held strong appeal. Badly mauled in the west in the recent election, the Liberal government would be able to increase its presence there in the high-profile field of economic development. In fact, DREE's policy review and the yellow books prepared for the western provinces were deliberately associated with the highly publicized Conference on Western Economic Opportunities, held in 1973. Under the direction of Justice Minister Otto Lang (Saskatchewan's regional minister in the cabinet), the conference was designed to give Ottawa a better understanding of western opportunities and economic problems and the Liberal party increased political visibility in the west.

A delivery mechanism, or a new administrative structure, was now required to implement the new policy. It had to be flexible. Developmental opportunities would not, in some instances, provide long lead-time for planning purposes. They could surface spontaneously, and an ability to respond to them in a flexible manner was essential.

The structure should also facilitate federal-provincial consultation, as well as the active involvement of numerous federal agencies and departments. Exploitation of development opportunities would invariably cut across jurisdictional lines and bureaucratic structures. In his report on the policy review to the House Committee on Regional Development, DREE's new minister pointed out: 'I have become increasingly impressed by the range of opportunities for economic development ... and by the large number of public policies and programmes that bear, or could be brought to bear, upon a concentrated effort to realize some of these opportunities.'[11]

THE GDA AND REGIONAL DEVELOPMENT

The policy review group came up with a new decision-making approach with all the features the new policy required. It was remarkably flexible, capable of supporting any imaginable type of government activity. It provided for the participation of any interested federal department and for close federal-provincial liaison, with either level of government able to propose initiatives.

Negotiated by Ottawa with any province, a General Development Agreement (GDA) provided a broad statement of goals for both levels of government to pursue, outlined the priority areas, and described how joint decisions would be taken.[12] GDAS were enabling documents only and did not in themselves provide for specific action; projects and precise cost-sharing arrangements were instead presented in subsidiary agreements which were attached to the umbrella-type GDAS.

From a strictly administrative point of view, all nine GDAS were basically similar. Each had a ten-year life span; each stipulated that DREE and the provincial government in question would, on a continuing basis, review the socioeconomic circumstances of the province; and each outlined a similar process for joint federal-provincial decision-making. They differed only in cost-sharing for subsidiary agreements. Under the GDA approach, DREE was granted the following authority to share the cost of a subsidiary agreement: up to 90 per cent for Newfoundland, 80 per cent for Nova Scotia and New Brunswick, 60 per cent for Quebec, Manitoba, and Saskatchewan, and 50 per cent for Ontario, Alberta, and British Columbia.

The flexibility recommended by the yellow books was provided by schedule A attached to each GDA and by subsidiary agreements. The schedule presented a brief socioeconomic description of the province, as well as a statement of objectives geared to local economic circumstances. It also outlined a broad development strategy that the two governments agreed to pursue jointly to meet the objectives of the GDA.

Once signed, the GDA provided for three kinds of subsidiary agreements: 'those which co-ordinate existing federal and provincial programmes in support of a particular development opportunity; those which provide specific support not available through other government programmes; and those which establish continuing programmes to fill gaps in the existing range of government development programmes. Since they were not restricted to specific geographical areas or to particular policy areas, subsidiary agreements could thus be developed to fit the needs of any given province or to pursue any type of development opportunity. They were described by DREE as a means of providing maximum flexibility to the policy-makers and as 'action pacts, ... [encompassing] development which the federal government and the signatory province agree will lead to greater economic and social growth in a particular area of the country.'[13]

The GDA required the federal minister and the relevant provincial minister to designate officials who would jointly co-ordinate 'the action to be taken under this agreement.' In many instances, an ongoing Canada-province development committee, consisting of the provincial director-general of DREE, representing the federal government, and a senior official representing the provincial government, oversaw formulation of new agreements. The committee met on a regular basis to accept or reject recommendations submitted by a series of joint subcommittees or work teams, which, in turn, were established to undertake detailed studies and to identify specific projects to which governments could commit funds in developing various subsidiary agreements.

After a subsidiary agreement had been signed, a joint management committee was established to oversee its implementation. These committees consisted of senior federal and provincial officials. As with the development committee, a management committee acted as a formal decision-making body and, in this capacity, reviewed and approved the annual expenditure budget. It also assessed all programs and projects sponsored by the subsidiary agreement and often amended some, discarded others, and came forward with new ones. These management committees had considerable decision-making authority and could identify new projects even after the agreement had been signed.[14]

In introducing the GDA approach, DREE devised measures to encourage other federal departments to tailor their programs and activities to complement those supported by the various subsidiary agreements. For the Atlantic region, DREE planned an annual conference at which federal departments, including central agencies, could discuss Ottawa's efforts at promoting regional economic growth. In short, then, the GDA approach was intended to encourage wide-ranging federal participation in federal-provincial decision-making, rather than having it solely a DREE enterprise.

There were a number of legal and administrative requirements incorporated in all GDAs and in all subsidiary agreements. All GDAs had sections that dealt exclusively with co-ordination: the federal and provincial ministers responsible for the agreement were to meet each year, and 'consult together at such other times as may be mutually agreed, to review the general operation of this Agreement; to consider development opportunities that might be pursued; and to review existing or proposed subsidiary agreement.'[15] Representatives of interested federal and provincial departments were to meet at least once a year to review the development strategy being pursued under the GDA. All subsidiary agreements were to include an evaluation clause providing for periodic assessment of the programs to determine whether they were meeting the stated objectives of the agreements.

Subsidiary agreements were presented in the same format as was the GDA. One section outlined the administrative-legal requirements of the agreement, another required that both levels of government develop and implement a program of public information about projects and activities under the agreement, and yet another stipulated that the two levels of government must fully exchange information on 'any and all aspects of the work undertaken under the agreement.'[16] Moreover, all subsidiary agreements had a schedule (A) that presented the estimated cost as well as the federal-provincial cost-sharing arrangement, and some had a schedule (B) detailing the strategy and the projects of the agreement.

THE DECENTRALIZATION OF DREE

In announcing DREE's new decision-making approach in 1973, Don Jamieson stated that decentralization of DREE's operations and decision-making authority was not only desirable but indeed made necessary by the demands that the GDAS would invariably generate. The GDAS were to involve joint decision-making and required DREE to participate in joint federal-provincial analyses of regional and provincial economic circumstances and opportunities. Such work, it was felt, would be superior and economic circumstances better understood if federal officials lived in the regions.

Thus designed to complement the GDA, DREE's 1973 reorganization substantially reduced the size of the Ottawa head office, established four regional offices, and considerably strengthened the ten existing provincial offices. Leaving only two assistant deputy ministers in Ottawa – one responsible for planning and co-ordination and the other for administrative and financial services – the reorganization relegated the head office to 'coordination and support of field activities.'

With some modifications made for the Quebec and Ontario regional offices, since these two regions consisted of single provinces, a basic organizational structure was developed for the six regional offices. They had little in the way of programs to deliver and were there simply to provide staff support to provincial DREE offices and to conduct general economic analysis and research of their regions.

Action and authority were delegated to the ten provincial offices. In fact, under the reorganization, these received nearly complete authority in program implementation and 'most of the responsibility for programme formulation.'[17] Unlike the early days of DREE, when the Ottawa planning division negotiated agreements directly with provincial governments and afterward delegated some implementing authority to the local offices, the provincial director-general and his office would now represent the focal point of contact on 'all issues' involving DREE and the provincial government. In other words, DREE provincial offices would in future lead all DREE activities affecting their respective provinces. Regional and Ottawa-based DREE officials would have to channel their development relations or policy ideas through the provincial offices and refrain from contacting provincial governments directly. Thus DREE's part in jointly identifying and pursuing development opportunities with provincial governments was, at least in an operational sense, the exclusive responsibility of the provincial DREE offices.

The decentralization of DREE was designed to transform the Ottawa head office into a 'staff' one, and to transfer much of the decision-making authority to the field offices, which were to assume 'line' responsibilities for developing and implementing the department's policies and programs. The intention was to reverse the ratio of head office staff to field office staff from 70:30 to 30:70. Such a massive decentralization of decision-making authority was unparalleled in the history of Canadian public administration. DREE could not draw on past experience in establishing its new organizations. As one former senior DREE official observed, decentralization 'involved a move into uncharted water.'[18]

The potential benefits of decentralization are numerous, and some have already been noted. It can be added that decentralization enables a department to undertake on-site studies and examinations of provincial and local problems and makes program delivery much more sensitive to local conditions and circumstances. Moreover, in DREE's case, decentralization was regarded as an effective way of promoting better relations with provincial governments at the policy level and as indispensable in making the process of joint decision-making under the GDA approach meaningful to them.

Conversely, decentralization also entails potential drawbacks. At the management level, it means establishing new positions and patterns of relations between offices within the organization, as well as obtaining staff commitment to change. At the policy level, decentralization can lead to inconsistencies in program delivery across the country and raise new problems of control and accountability in program formulation and decision-making. Face-to-face contact, for example, is disrupted by the distance separating the various offices. The decentralization of DREE involved a large-scale transfer of decision-making authority to the provincial offices, which had full responsibility for all stages of programs from research analysis to program formulation and implementation, and thence to evaluation and revision. The establishment of formal information and reporting systems became imperative. Otherwise, it was feared, staff in regional offices and in head office would quickly lose touch with current issues and problems facing the department, and DREE provincial offices might operate and formulate programs in isolation from senior departmental management and relevant federal departments.

Some of these potential difficulties were recognized, and a number of systems and procedures were introduced in an attempt to increase interdepartmental consultations, to involve officials from other DREE offices in program formulation, and to ensure that the information requirements of senior DREE officials were met.[19] Provincial DREE officials were encouraged to involve those in regional and head offices in the identification of development opportunities, a computerized information system was established, and precise procedures were outlined for the development of subsidiary agreements and submissions to the Treasury Board.

At the same time that DREE decentralized its operations, interdepartmental consultation gained greater importance. The GDA approach involved other federal departments, but interdepartmental consultation would become more difficult to promote and monitor because of the distance between the actors. Informal contacts, for example, would invariably be less frequent, and it would become more difficult for officials in provincial offices to attend regular interdepartmental committee meetings in Ottawa. However, DREE was never granted any extraordinary authority to ensure the full participation of other federal departments in GDA activities. Don Jamieson made this clear to the House committee when he stated: 'Both the Prime Minister and I ... feel that the main co-ordinating instrument is the cabinet committee system. Rather than try to set up some kind of super ministry or give DREE a dominant role *vis-à-vis* other departments in the operational sense.'[20]

Thus, in developing its comprehensive and co-ordinated approach to regional development, DREE had to rely on traditional methods of promoting interdepartmental relations rather than on a position of authoritative supremacy over other departments. Mainly for this reason, during the early months of decentralization, officials in the provincial offices were often reminded, through staff conferences and departmental position papers, to involve other DREE offices and other federal agencies systematically in formulating new initiatives. To ensure that this would take place, elaborate computerized information systems were developed to alert other DREE offices and relevant federal agencies when a new initiative was being contemplated, so that they too could contribute to its development. Other special co-ordinating measures were put in place. For instance, DREE promised an annual interdepartmental meeting of federal agencies under the various GDAs to ensure the participation of all concerned federal departments.

IMPLEMENTING THE GDA APPROACH

With the GDA concept approved by the cabinet and with the new procedures for federal-provincial co-operation defined, Don Jamieson began a cross-country tour to negotiate individual GDAs. Considerable consultation between DREE officials and provincial government officials had already taken place, and the substance of the proposed GDAs was fairly well defined. Provincial governments by and large reacted favourably to the new approach. They were relieved to see DREE move away from the Special Areas concept and, at least, publicly commit itself to close federal-provincial liaison.

Nevertheless, the provinces foresaw potential problems. Those in the east feared that by moving into all regions of the country, DREE would lessen its commitment and its efforts in Atlantic Canada. Jamieson sought to reassure them by insisting in public and in private meetings with the premiers that 'areas of naturally high growth will not be the concern of DREE.' This of course did not exclude large areas of northern Ontario, Manitoba, and northern Saskatchewan, Alberta, and British Columbia. British Columbia and Alberta did not know quite what to make of DREE's sudden interest in the economic health of their provinces. DREE officials there report that initially they had considerable difficulty in starting a dialogue with provincial officials on the problems of the less-developed regions of their provinces, let alone bringing about intergovernmental co-operation and new program initiatives for these regions. In addition, a number of provincial governments, both east and west, at first were not quite sure what to make of

DREE's intention to establish large offices in provincial capitals. Would it lead, they asked, to joint efforts or was it another attempt by the federal government to dictate the priorities of provincial governments?

Jamieson and his officials were understandably anxious to sign the various GDAS and to get new initiatives introduced. Provincial governments sensed this, and some, particularly in the east, jumped at the opportunity to get federal funding for projects they had long wanted to implement. In the case of New Brunswick, for example, it meant highways agreements.

The minister of DREE signed six GDAS with the provinces in an eight-week period between early February and late March 1974. The other three were signed later that year. No GDA was signed with Prince Edward Island, since that province had already signed a fifteen-year development plan with Ottawa in 1969. The premiers of Newfoundland and New Brunswick signed the GDAS; in all other provinces, a cabinet minister did so.

Virtually every economic sector was covered by the GDAS.[21] In Newfoundland, the GDA sponsored initiatives in tourism, forestry, recreation, fisheries, highways, special projects for Labrador, ocean research, special projects for St John's, mineral development, industrial development, rural development, agriculture, and federal-provincial planning. Nova Scotia's GDA supported mineral development, special projects for the Halifax-Dartmouth area, the Strait of Canso and Cape Breton, agriculture, industrial development, forestry, tourism, energy, dry dock development, and special measures for Sydney Steel Corporation and for Michelin Tires.

The Quebec GDA led to some fifteen subsidiary agreements, which in turn gave rise to numerous projects: establishment of newsprint mills, including one in Amos; industrial studies; mineral research and exploration; construction of a number of industrial parks, including one near Mirabel airport; highway construction; and new tourism facilities.

Ontario signed several subsidiary agreements. One was designed to strengthen the urban system of northern Ontario by providing for new industrial parks and new water and sewer systems in Parry Sound, Timmins, Sudbury, and North Bay. A forestry subsidiary agreement promoted projects to improve forest management, accelerate reforestation, and construct new forest access roads. Community and rural resource development became the subject of another subsidiary agreement: the Upper Ottawa Valley and the Kirkland Lake areas benefited from industrial land development studies, geo-scientific surveys, and hardwood forest renewal schemes. A $180-million subsidiary agreement for strengthening the competitive position of the province's pulp and paper industry was also signed.

The western provinces set up a number of subsidiary agreements with DREE. Manitoba's concerned development of the province's northlands, its industrial sector, agriculture, tourism, water development and drought-proofing, and the development of the Winnipeg core area. Saskatchewan signed agreements for the northland, for development of a major tourist attraction in the Qu'Appelle Valley, for water development and drought-proofing, and for long-term development of its forest industry. Alberta signed six subsidiary agreements with DREE. They involved processing of nutritive products; attempts to improve incomes, living standards, and community facilities in northern Alberta; and further development of the northern transportation system. In British Columbia, the GDA gave rise to numerous initiatives, in highway construction, support of the northeast coal industry, industrial development, agriculture and rural development, tourism, forest management, and development of the Ridley Island port facility.

In 1979, the federal government signed new five-year GDAs with the Northwest Territories and Yukon. DREE's activity began there in 1977–78 with the introduction of special, if modest, ARDA-type programs to assist people of native ancestry to start commercial ventures. DREE's expenditures in the Northwest Territories were $800,000 for the period 1978– 79.[22] The GDAS earmarked relatively modest amounts for community economic development in the Northwest Territories and for renewable resource development projects and tourism in Yukon.

The list of GDA projects goes on and on. Over 130 subsidiary agreements were signed between 1974 and 1982, with a total financial commitment of close to $6 billion. The federal government's share was over $3.3 billion. Appendix A provides a complete list of the GDAs and subsidiary agreements, as well as the amount of public funds involved.

There is little doubt that the strength of the GDA system was in its flexibility. One senior DREE official remarked that the problem of regional economic disparity 'is economic and not constitutional.' 'Jurisdictional lines,' he went on, 'ought to be blurred so that appropriate, viable and coordinated measures to stimulate economic development [could] be brought forward.'[23] The GDAs certainly did this.

Provincial governments grew particularly fond of the GDAs. They applauded their flexibility and the kind of co-operation that they promoted. They had strong reasons to do so. An opportunity presented itself in Halifax with the possible development of a world-class dry dock facility. DREE and the province simply got together and signed an agreement, and the project went ahead. No program limits existed to restrict their activities. Similarly, Quebec felt that a series of recreational parks would help its tourist industry. DREE agreed, and an agreement was signed involving $76 million of public funds. Ontario, wanting to diversify and stabilize the economics of single-industry communities, turned to DREE and signed a $20-million agreement to put in place a series of infrastructure projects.

Shortly after the introduction of the GDAs, it became clear that the relation between Ottawa and the provinces had been reversed. Unlike the situation under Marchand and Kent, when Ottawa had presented projects in a 'take it or leave it' fashion, provincial governments were now proposing initiatives, and the federal government reacted. Admittedly, poorer provinces, contributing only 20 per cent of the cost, were never in a position to adopt a cavalier posture vis-à-vis the federal government. Nevertheless, even they were in an enviable bargaining position, preparing initiatives to which the federal government would respond. If DREE refused to support a particular proposal, the province simply came back with another. Though the GDA system also allowed the federal government to make proposals, this did not occur often.

Another attractive feature of the GDA approach for the less-developed provinces was the cost-sharing formula. With Ottawa contributing 80 to 90 per cent of the cost, virtually any kind of economic initiative became viable. In many ways, Ottawa acted like the Treasury Board – it reviewed proposals from provincial governments, accepting some and rejecting others.

The one recurring criticism levelled at GDAs by less-developed provinces was that DREE had spread its efforts too thinly and had moved away from its firm commitment to the Atlantic provinces. If one compared DREE spending with the pattern established by Marchand and Kent, then this criticism had some validity. By 1977–78, DREE was spending 39 per cent of its resources in the Atlantic provinces, 31 per cent in Quebec, 5 per cent in Ontario, and 21 per cent in the western provinces. In 1970–71, the breakdown had greatly favoured the Atlantic provinces, which received over 50 per cent of DREE funds, with Quebec following at 23 per cent; Ontario received less than 5 per cent, and the western provinces about 16 per cent.[24]

Criticism of the GDAs was heard frequently in Ottawa. Many thought that provincial DREE officials had become too imbued with local attitudes. They were simply echoing provincial governments' priorities and were unable to bring a national, or even interprovincial, perspective to their work.[25] How else could one explain the 'hodge-podge' of projects DREE was supporting? From an Ottawa view, not one of the GDAs pointed to an overall development strategy. They supported rural development if a provincial government favoured it, or tourism projects, or highways construction. Simply put, no one could discern a central and coherent purpose in any of the GDA strategies.

Viewed from Ottawa, provincial DREE and provincial government officials employed the concept of development opportunities to justify whatever project they wanted approved. Building from a region's strength was not evident in the proposals put forward. Over 50 per cent of DREE's expenditures in the Atlantic provinces went for the provision of infrastructure facilities, in particular, highway construction.[26] This was hardly the kind of spending that Finance and Treasury Board officials had expected to see in DREE's pursuit of developmental opportunities or in its mandate to build on the strength of regional economic circumstances.

The Newfoundland GDA combined a sectoral with a spatial approach – with no apparent link between the two. That is, it supported development initiatives for key economic sectors of the province and then went on to support special 'regional' development packages for selected areas of the province. It supported projects in forestry, including forest protection and the construction of access roads. It did the same for industrial development, with substantial funds committed to the construction of an industrial park and new highways linking the park to a community and to another highway. The GDA gave rise also to a rural development agreement which, among other things, provided administrative grants to development and regional councils. A subsidiary agreement for Labrador covered street improvement in certain towns, an auxiliary sewage collector system, a student dormitory for a vocational school, and a new industrial park.

GDA-sponsored initiatives in one province could be in direct conflict or competition with another in a neighbouring province. Eugene Whelan, former minister of agriculture, put it this way: 'When I was ... in New Brunswick, one thing they [farm organizations] were raising Cain about was the fact that DREE was setting up another operation in another [province] of the Maritimes to produce cabbages ... when they already had a surplus of cabbages which they could not get rid of.'[27]

Ottawa-based officials believed that cost-benefit evaluation of proposed GDA initiatives rarely preceded an agreement. Evaluations on shortcomings and accomplishments of projects were also spotty and frequently incomplete. All agreements called for evaluation, but funds were often left unused. Some evaluations simply concluded that it was far too early to attempt assessment. Considerable time was necessary before the full impact of the projects could be felt in the economy, and thus a thorough evaluation would not be possible for several years.

The imprecise nature of the goals and objectives of the GDAs and subsidiary agreements further hindered evaluation. The BC GDA had as one of its objectives 'to promote balanced development among areas of British Columbia.' The New Brunswick GDA called for increasing 'per capita incomes while minimizing net immigration from the province.' A subsidiary agreement with the Ontario government for the Cornwall area aimed 'to create a long-term expansion in employment and income opportunities in the Cornwall area.' Rigorous and clear-cut evaluation of DREE activities was practically impossible.

There was another problem with the GDAs. Not long after they were signed, it became evident that they were not evolving into comprehensive and 'coordinated application ... of federal and provincial ... policies and programmes.' DREE was alone in negotiating subsidiary agreements; other federal departments and agencies were simply not participating. Nor were they supporting the various GDA programs. The elaborate systems that DREE had called for to involve other departments simply broke down. The computerized information system was never fully developed and was never consulted by other departments. In fact, few departments knew that such a system existed. Interdepartmental conferences contributed little to programs: they were not held annually and did not attract enough senior-level officials to make them worthwhile.[28]

The hope that the GDA system would constitute a total federal presence and not simply a DREE one was never fulfilled. Most subsidiary agreements were developed by provincial DREE officials and provincial government officials with little contribution even from other DREE officials. DREE, and the GDA concept in particular, were soon confronted with strong opposition from other federal departments, which charged that DREE was moving into their fields of responsibility with initiatives it was ill-prepared to carry out. They claimed also that interdepartmental consultation was not taking place. One federal minister maintained that DREE went ahead and signed a subsidiary agreement with a provincial government in a sector for which she was responsible, without having the courtesy to inform her or even her departmental officials.[29]

If federal-provincial agreements were required to promote growth in a given sector, line departments in Ottawa argued that the relevant sectoral department should negotiate the agreement. Some argued also that federal-provincial agreements were not always necessary and that they could just as easily deliver the projects. On this point, departments were highly critical of DREE, and some of this criticism was voiced in public. For example, Roméo LeBlanc, federal fisheries minister, said: 'I resisted the DREE agreement in fisheries because I found it difficult … [to accept that] … what I could not do in my defined area of responsibility, I find another department … [doing].'[30]

Smaller provincial governments, however, looked at GDA planning differently. In fact, they criticized what they considered the overly elaborate planning involved in developing GDA initiatives.[31] The GDAs represented more coherent planning than they had been accustomed to, given the size of their governments and the traditionally strong involvement of cabinet ministers in all aspects of government decision-making.

After the 1974 election which returned the Trudeau government with a clear majority of seats, Marcel Lessard replaced Don Jamieson as the minister responsible for DREE. Lessard did not wield the kind of political clout that Marchand or Jamieson had done. He was not a regional minister, as were the first two, and he was new in the cabinet, and thus a 'junior minister.' This fact is important in terms of DREE's credibility in the Ottawa 'system.' It is doubtful, for example, whether cabinet colleagues would have been as critical of DREE in public as LeBlanc and Whelan were if Marchand or Jamieson had been in the portfolio.

Lessard did not alter significantly DREE's policy direction or the kind of programs supported under the various GDAS. He kept busy visiting provincial capitals to attend the annual GDA meetings and to sign new subsidiary agreements. While minister of DREE, Lessard signed more than ten subsidiary agreements each year.

Occasionally, DREE would issue staff papers on the economic circumstances and potential of each province. These papers did not always lead to new initiatives under the various GDAS. Rather they made for good reading, pointed to specific economic difficulties, and commented on the growth rate of each province, as measured by public and private investment, unemployment levels, and gross provincial product. For example, a staff paper in 1976 on the Atlantic provinces, 'Climate for Development,' described how difficult 1974 and 1975 had been for the fishery industry. The paper underlined the problem of weak US markets and the serious question of resource depletion. However, no new initiatives to remedy this situation emerged from DREE.

Particularly toward the end of Lessard's mandate in DREE in 1978, pressure was put on provincial DREE offices and provincial governments to carry out objective evaluations of GDA-sponsored initiatives. These were undertaken but, as always, did not prove very useful. Evaluations were prepared of the highways agreements in the Atlantic provinces. Much of the benefit from the New Brunswick agreement was found to be non-quantifiable and non-economic. New highways had, however, opened up the northern part of the province and had served to establish closer links between the relatively isolated and poor northern regions and the more populated and prosperous southern half of the province.

Evaluations of a number of sectoral agreements were also carried out. Their findings soon became highly predictable: it was much too early to assess fully the impact of a given agreement. They also frequently concluded that a new agreement should replace the expiring one being evaluated: signs were encouraging, progress was being made, efforts should be sustained. A number of evaluations gave rise to 'second-generation' subsidiary agreements. That is, an agricultural subsidiary agreement for New Brunswick, for example, was replaced by a new agricultural agreement. All in all, there were numerous such second-generation agreements signed under the various GDAS.

Rarely were evaluations conducted from an interprovincial perspective; GDA programs were, by nature, provincial in scope and design. One exception was an extensive evaluation carried out in 1979 on the effect of DREE's efforts at developing industrial parks in the Atlantic region. Not unexpectedly, a major theme of the evaluation was that their full impact could not yet be fully assessed. More time was considered necessary, and, with this in mind, a data bank was developed so that another evaluation could be undertaken in 1982. The evaluation revealed also that DREE had invested $31 million in industrial parks in the region; some 5,000 acres were serviced, of which slightly over half were occupied; some 769 firms had located in DREE-assisted parks, creating some 18,000 person-years of employment; and 68 per cent of the firms were new to the communities in which they were now located.[32] Several important questions were left unanswered about the life expectancy of the firms surveyed and about the turnover frequency of those occupying a given building. In addition, no attempt was made to determine where the firms would have located had new parks not been constructed. The proposed evaluation for 1982 was never carried out, and there are no indications that the data bank, which was developed, is serving any useful purpose in program evaluation.

THE REGIONAL DEVELOPMENT INCENTIVES PROGRAM

The regional development incentives program was revised slightly with the advent of the GDA approach in the mid-1970s to make it compatible with the new system. New regions were designated; the program was extended in Manitoba, Saskatchewan, Yukon, the Northwest Territories, Quebec (excluding the Montreal-Hull corridor), and northern Ontario and British Columbia. Provisions were made to offer specialized incentives through the GDA system to support developmental initiatives affecting non-designated areas. The GDA policy review also decentralized the administration of the program down to the provincial-office level. Provincial directors-general were given authority to approve incentive grants of up to $670,000.[33] By and large, however, the incentives program continued to operate much as it had in the past, and it never became an integrated part of the GDA approach.

By 1976, Montreal-area MPs were pressing Marcel Lessard to designate their city under DREE's incentive program. Unemployment in Quebec had risen to 300,000, half of it in the Montreal region. The election of the Parti québécois in November 1976 resulted in a sudden downturn in private investments in the province, and the widespread fear that head offices of major companies would leave Montreal because of proposed language legislation.

Montreal is also Quebec's industrial heartland. The basic economic strength of the province, many believe, is ineluctably linked to Montreal. Many Quebec economists were stressing the importance of the Montreal region to the overall development of the province. A fairly extensive body of literature by Quebec scholars now exists on this issue.[34]

When Lessard first went to the cabinet with the proposal to designate Montreal, he met with opposition. If DREE could justify a presence in Montreal, why could it not also justify one for Vancouver and Toronto? Fundamental questions were asked about DREE's mandate and its role in alleviating regional disparities. Cabinet ministers from the Atlantic provinces remembered well Marchand's comment

CAMROSE LUTHERAN COLLEGE
LIBRARY

about the necessity of spending 80 per cent of DREE's budget east of Trois-Rivières. How would a Montreal designation affect other regions? Would it still be possible, for example, to attract firms into depressed regions if they could obtain a cash grant for starting new production in Montreal?

Lessard now reports that, with considerable help from seven ministers from the Montreal region, he was finally able to convince the cabinet to designate Montreal under the RDIA program. In June 1977, DREE introduced, under the authority of the DREE Act, a discretionary incentives program for selected high-growth manufacturing industries for the Montreal region, with only projects involving a minimum of $100,000 being eligible. Unlike in the Atlantic region, not every new manufacturing or processing facility was to be eligible. Only selected high-growth industries could qualify, including food and beverages, metal products, machinery, transportation equipment, and electrical and chemical products. Projects would be limited by a lower maximum grant than elsewhere: 25 per cent of total capital cost.[35]

In obtaining cabinet approval for Montreal designation, Lessard promised his colleagues to look at the possibility of designating other regions, including northern areas of British Columbia and the Northwest Territories. He also committed DREE to undertake special development efforts in eastern Ontario, notably the Cornwall area.[36]

But the changes introduced by Lessard to Canada's regional development policy were relatively minor and piecemeal. As we shall see, emerging political and economic circumstances would move Lessard and his senior departmental officials to launch a much more ambitious review of DREE's policies and programs.

6

Three aborted policy reviews

By 1978, DREE was being assailed from all sides in Ottawa. The provinces were still generally supportive, although even from them some criticism could be heard. Smaller provincial governments were finding the GDA process highly bureaucratic and cumbersome and probably better-suited to a large bureaucracy like the federal government.[1] In any event, even if provincial governments had been fully supportive, it is not to them, but rather to central agencies in Ottawa, that DREE had to turn for funds and person-years, and in the end to the cabinet, for political support.

Canada was entering a difficult period, both politically and economically. Quebec had elected a separatist government in the fall of 1976. Firmly committed to political sovereignty, the new provincial government had views in direct conflict with those of the prime minister, who was firmly committed to a strong central government. The large Quebec Liberal caucus in Ottawa, with few exceptions, endorsed the views of the prime minister. The election of the Parti québécois signalled an out-and-out 'battle for the hearts and minds' of Québécois.[2] DREE was to be caught in this political cross-fire, as Quebec was an important client and DREE's major program in the province required close federal-provincial co-operation if it were to be effective.

The country's economic picture had also changed dramatically since DREE was first established. Then few had doubted that the economy would continue to prosper. By 1976, however, the economy was stagnant, unemployment was high, and so was the inflation rate. The term *stagflation* had crept into our vocabulary.[3]

Given modest growth, high unemployment, and inflation, many were asking whether Ottawa should continue to prop up slow-growth regions through transfer payments. Were federal cost-sharing agreements inhibiting rather than promoting prosperity in slow-growth regions?[4] There was widespread concern in Ottawa that the GDAS had failed to present the national perspective to provincial governments. The GDAS seemed a one-way street: provinces got what they wanted, but not so the federal government.

DREE was well aware of all these forces at play. In its 1978 annual report, the department noted 'Quebec's vulnerability ... to increasing competition from foreign manufactures' and 'the apparent softness of the Ontario economy.' It also revealed that a policy and legislative review had been launched, 'another stage in the evolution of regional development policy.'[5]

THE LESSARD REVIEW

'Regional economic balance,' DREE argued in its 1978 review, 'has been shifting ... particularly since the middle of this decade.'[6] This shift necessitated a fresh look at the federal government's regional development policy. DREE's last major policy review, in 1973, had foreseen a buoyant Canadian economy that would permit national policies to enhance economic development in slow-growth areas and reduce disparities between regions. Yet by 1978, despite considerable public funds invested in slow-growth regions, regional disparities seemed virtually unchanged. In fact, a marked shift in private investment toward the western provinces was apparent, and closing the disparity gap would now be even more difficult.

DREE officials now looked south of the border for a better understanding of regional imbalance in Canada, on the assumption that similar historical patterns of regional growth and economic fortunes are found on both sides of the border. The New England states, excluding Massachusetts, were found to be remarkably similar to Atlantic Canada in their long-term decline in population and their below-average incomes. The western border states, it was determined, had grown at rates roughly comparable to those of Canada's western provinces. Finally, the Great Lakes states of Michigan and Ohio had exhibited a pattern similar to that of both southern Ontario and Quebec. These findings suggested that regional economic development was influenced more by the continental forces of resource endowment and proximity to markets than by government policy.

The policy review suggested that Ottawa should reorient its regional development policy, changing its basic approach. DREE had directed a relatively high proportion of its funds into various forms of infrastructure. Expenditures of this kind had been useful, and many of the requirements of slow-growth regions had been met. However, the policy review recommended that DREE should be highly selective in such support, tying it to specific investments with strong potential for growth and employment. Marcel Lessard, accompanied by senior DREE officials, explained this new emphasis to the Senate Standing Committee on National Finance: '[DREE is not] a welfare agency ... Our primary objective ... is to help each region of Canada nurture and cultivate those areas and prospects with the best potential for development.' This could be best accomplished by 'intensive analysis ... [to identify] the comparative advantages of each region.'[7] A call for updating DREE's yellow book was made by the minister. This time, the books were prepared in close co-operation with the provinces.

The review proposed taking advantage of the Atlantic provinces' available natural resources and geographic location with an eye to future development. Self-sustaining growth seemed possible in the fishery and fish processing, minerals, and forest-based industries. A new sector with significant growth potential was also identified around the emerging 'ocean industries.'[8]

With the extension of the national fisheries jurisdiction to 200 miles in 1977, the Atlantic region could develop the full potential of this sector. However, it needed a wider range of better-quality products; markets abroad, notably in Europe and Japan; and a rebuilt fishing fleet. The review noted that the fishing industry, together with defence-related activities, environmental research, and, especially, off-shore oil and gas exploration, would offer new development opportunities, providing a comparative advantage to the Atlantic region. It was hoped that a nucleus of medium- and high-technology ocean manufacturing and service industries would subsequently develop.

The Atlantic provinces held other comparative advantages. The mineral sector was expected to grow in relation to the rest of the economy, with additional production of coal in Nova Scotia and potash in New Brunswick and of base metals and iron ore, particularly in Newfoundland and northern New Brunswick. As well, the recent devaluation of the Canadian dollar would help the sector.

A devalued Canadian dollar would also stimulate the region's pulp and paper industry, important in terms of employment. However, to ensure advantage over foreign competitors, firms would have to modernize their plants and counter resource depletion and serious budworm infestation, which were reducing the quality and volume of harvestable timber. An aggressive government plan to protect the forests seemed necessary.

Quebec's economy was facing difficult structural problems: persistently high unemployment, poor productivity, a shortfall in private investment, and the decline of the Montreal urban area. The policy review nevertheless identified a number of comparative advantages in the Quebec economy on which to build real economic growth.[9] The revised DREE yellow book pointed out that Quebec not only had an important domestic market, but was also well positioned geographically to penetrate the American and western European markets. Its major comparative advantage was its relatively inexpensive hydro-electric power. Industry could be attracted simply on this basis, DREE argued. In addition, the province's mineral resources were important and would continue to enhance industrial opportunities. Important deposits of uranium, gold, peat, and asbestos fibre were available. Quebec needed industrial rationalization, however, in the textile, knitwear, clothing, and footwear industries which, for the most part, were no longer internationally competitive. DREE suggested that they rationalize production, consolidate operations, and modernize.

DREE'S new book on Ontario's economic circumstances concluded that 'sustained, strong economic growth can no longer be taken for granted.'[10] The increasing cost of energy and the westward movement of investment capital had weakened Ontario's economic performance. During the 1970s Ontario's economy had not performed as well as the rest of Canada. Though narrowing regional disparities was a noble objective, 'the fact that it is occurring more by means of Ontario's weakening position rather than through other regions' growing strength, with the possible exception of Alberta and British Columbia, should be a matter of national concern.' A weakened Ontario would 'have negative implications for the whole country.'[11]

DREE's review revealed that between 1970 and 1978, Ontario had one of the slowest growth rates of all the provinces: the third lowest in manufacturing investment, and the lowest in residential construction and in per capita disposable income. Ontario's share of the country's newly arriving immigrants declined from 58 per cent in 1974 to 49 per cent in 1978. Ontario's population growth rate exceeded the national average only once in the same period.

Clearly, continuing growth in Ontario could no longer be taken for granted. DREE stressed the difficult problems of industrial adjustment in southern Ontario. The provincial government had stimulated slow-growth areas within the province, but now, DREE insisted, 'Ontario must ... be even more conscious of the overall development of the province itself.'[12]

DREE maintained that significant elements of Ontario's manufacturing industry required adjustment and restructuring in light of changing demands and international competition. The manufacturing sector needed assistance to make the required adjustments on a timely and economically efficient basis and to seize new opportunities in a rapidly changing international market. In the automotive industry, product lines would have to change, and plants be completely re-equipped. Farm machinery was facing an uncertain future due, in part, to its international orientation and its vulnerability to wide cyclical swings. Since it is linked to these two industries, Ontario's steel industry would also need to adjust to changing circumstances. Ontario needed to seize new opportunities for its manufacturing sector, for example, by linking its capacity to major new energy projects in eastern and western Canada.

The prospects for three of the four western provinces looked promising. In line with North America's basic economic trends, the growth of the Canadian western economy had surpassed the national average. Personal income had increased 57 per cent between 1971 and 1978, as compared to 46 per cent nationally; employment had grown by 33 per cent, and the labour force by only 30 per cent.[13]

The main economic challenge for the four western provinces was one of managing growth. The energy sector and associated pipeline projects would offer numerous opportunities. DREE outlined a number of these, including the development of northern oil and gas reserves in the Arctic and the Mackenzie Valley. Four synthetic and heavy oil projects were planned for the mid-1980s, as was the development of Saskatchewan's high-quality uranium reserves. These projects and others, DREE concluded, would bring substantial private investment to the area and create employment. The food and beverage processing industry looked promising, and markets for the region's pulp and paper industry were expected to improve. The shift of financial services westward would continue and further strengthen the region's service sector.

There were, nonetheless, problems in the region that DREE would seek to resolve or have resolved by other government agencies. Manitoba would require stronger economic ties with its three western neighbours to ensure growth. Otherwise, unprecedented growth from resource-related investment in the other western provinces would sharpen the contrast between them and Manitoba. DREE believed that Manitoba could become a regional manufacturing base, and it signed a special industrial development agreement with Manitoba in 1978 to promote industrial activity.[14]

DREE also signalled other western problems that needed attention. An adequate supply of water to meet growing demands for industrial development, agriculture, and expanding municipal services was not as secure as it should be. The policy review predicted that a major shortfall in precipitation over a one- or two-year period would result in a serious water-supply problem – and diversification of the agricultural and industrial base of the western provinces would require a secure water-supply. Problems with soil quality were becoming more and more evident, and additional research and improved soil management were required.[15]

DREE noted regional imbalance in the western economy. Dramatic changes to the economic structure of Canada's north would necessitate adaptation in the west and increased native participation in western development. The western boom seemed unlikely to do away with pockets of regional poverty. In fact, DREE noted with concern that growth was highly concentrated in specific parts of Alberta, British Columbia, and, to a lesser extent, Saskatchewan.

All in all, the policy review revealed that Canada's regional economic circumstances had changed considerably since the review in 1972. DREE would seek to adjust its programs to reflect these changes, and Lessard so informed his cabinet colleagues. DREE concluded that the GDAS still constituted the best possible delivery mechanism. The GDA's most important characteristic, Lessard insisted, was its flexibility. A wide range of approaches and initiatives was possible, and development measures could be tailored to circumstances and to the development priorities of provincial governments. GDAS had proved effective as a tool for federal-provincial co-operation, as witness the broad endorsement that they received at the First Ministers' Conference in February 1978.[16]

DREE acknowledged, however, that the GDAS were not without 'possible drawbacks.' They had not, for instance, been successful in dealing with multi-province issues. All GDA programming was structured on a bilateral basis, and DREE had been incapable of promoting regional or multi-province solutions in such areas as energy, fisheries, and transportation. Also, other federal departments had not become involved in promoting regional development, and the GDAS remained essentially a DREE-only instrument.[17]

The difficulty was that GDA initiatives were developed by provincial governments in consultation with provincial DREE offices. Authority for setting up new programs had effectively been decentralized at that level. However, such authority in other federal departments had remained centralized in Ottawa, inhibiting co-operation.

These problems were not insurmountable, DREE insisted. The low level of support for the GDA process shown by a number of federal departments stemmed from the fact that they were not involved sufficiently early in designing subsidiary agreements. DREE would therefore in future make special efforts to involve federal sectoral departments, invite them whenever appropriate to co-sign and perhaps co-fund agreements, and request that they sit on the various federal-provincial implementation committees. DREE also undertook to adhere more closely to the elaborate interdepartmental consultation procedures laid down when the GDA approach was introduced.

THE REGIONAL INDUSTRIAL INCENTIVES PROGRAM

A review of DREE's regional incentives (RDIA) program found it well established and widely supported by industry. The review proposed minor adjustments: that DREE be allowed to authorize more than one development incentive grant for the modernization of a facility, revision of ceilings so that incentives grants could be adjusted for past inflation, and new payment procedures and schedules for grants.

Marcel Lessard reports that he approved the policy review and the proposed legislative package based on it and submitted them to the cabinet in early 1979.[18] However, before discussion could take place, a general election was called. The cabinet was in no mood, reports Lessard, to approve new policy directions and a new legislative package a few months before facing the electorate.

THE CLARK GOVERNMENT

The Progressive Conservative government of Joe Clark came to power in June 1979. Elmer MacKay, a popular Nova Scotia politician, was named DREE minister. Clark had talked about regional development throughout the election campaign, insisting that 'the fight against regional disparity will be central to our policy as it is central to the Progressive Conservative's concept of national unity.'[19] Curiously, however, MacKay was excluded from Clark's inner cabinet.

Thus, changes to DREE were expected to be structural in nature and likely to involve other departments.

During the campaign, the Conservatives had been critical of DREE programs. 'DREE's difficulties,' in the minds of Conservative politicians, '[were] rooted in the obsessive concern with developing such infrastructure as sewer and water systems that do not offer continuing economic benefits.' The new DREE minister favoured a strong commitment to the four Atlantic provinces and to large projects. He signalled to his colleagues and departmental officials that DREE efforts should be concentrated 'east of the Ottawa river.'[20]

MacKay went outside the department for counsel on regional policy and on DREE's future role. Ian McAllister, an economist at Dalhousie University, offered controversial proposals for restructuring the department: 'DREE, during the latter part of the 1970s, has given the impression of being an expensive, inefficient and secretive bureaucracy'; it 'should essentially be transformed into a small, very senior policy agency.'[21]

The department gave MacKay essentially the same policy and program proposals it had presented to Lessard. Little had changed in terms of economic circumstances at the regional level, and DREE officials saw no need to change significantly their basic policy orientation. The GDAS still represented, in their opinion, the most effective tool for federal-provincial co-ordination and would be particularly well suited to Clark's vision of Canadian federalism. The updated DREE yellow books, initially approved by Lessard, were released during MacKay's tenure – in blue covers, and renamed blue books.

Before MacKay and the Clark government could reorient Ottawa's regional development policy, however, the country was plunged into yet another general election. The only change of any significance the Clark government brought to DREE was a change in deputy ministers. J.D. Love was replaced by Robert Montreuil, another career public servant, who had been DREE's assistant deputy minister for the Quebec region.

THE DE BANE REVIEW

First elected in 1968, Pierre De Bané made regional development his main field of interest in caucus and in Parliament. Though never a resident of the area, De Bané had been parachuted into the Liberal stronghold of Matane in the economically depressed Gaspé region. He was first named to the cabinet as minister of supply and services in late 1978, only a few months before the Trudeau government was defeated. During that brief period, he sought to reorient that department's policies to promote regional development. He initiated a program to identify the eight poorest regions in the country and sent a team of specialists to those regions to find out what local industries produced that the government buys in its day-to-day operations. While in opposition, he had been shadow critic of DREE. In that capacity, he wrote a paper on regional development policy which he circulated widely. It called on DREE to evaluate the regional effect of all federal programs, to take a direct interest in community development, to establish a special regional development fund, and to develop special tax concessions for businesses locating in slow-growth regions.[22]

When the Liberal party returned to power, De Bané specifically asked the prime minister for the DREE portfolio.[23] Immediately after being appointed, he called for a major policy review, feeling strongly that the government's regional development policy needed to be completely overhauled. The guiding principle of the review was that the federal and provincial governments could do more, a great deal more, in promoting regional development.

At the same time, De Bané sought to strengthen DREE's position in Ottawa. He declared that it was unrealistic for the federal government to expect DREE to 'alleviate regional disparities with a budget which in total represented less than 2 per cent of Ottawa's expenditure budget.' He publicly informed the deputy prime minister and the minister of finance that DREE would need a great deal more money if Ottawa was serious about combating regional disparity.[24]

De Bané called a DREE staff conference, to which he invited every departmental official down to relatively junior levels, and he asked them to contribute suggestions for a stronger policy. Those reluctant to voice their views before senior management he invited to write him in complete confidence. At the conference, De Bané echoed the views on regional development that Prime Minister Trudeau had voiced some twelve years earlier: 'Unless the federal government can put in place measures to extend to those people living in slow-growth regions hope and opportunities to turn the economy of their regions and communities around, then the future of the Canadian federation will be bleak indeed.'[25]

De Bané informed the conference that he would not accept the review that the department had submitted to him – essentially the same review that DREE had submitted first to Lessard and then to MacKay. He labelled that review the 'status quo' and rejected it out of hand. He also urged the department to do likewise. He recognized, he said, that a great deal of opposition to DREE existed at both the political and bureaucratic levels. 'To preserve the status quo,' De Bané stated, 'I would have to devote all my efforts and energies over the next twelve months to convince my colleagues of the appropriateness of DREE as we now know it. A very fundamental problem here is that I am not prepared to do that.' He urged his officials to put aside their 'bureaucratic inhibitions' and to come up with new measures 'to alleviate regional disparities.' No effort should be spared to bring about regional balance in economic growth, De Bané insisted. In line with this thinking, he outlined again all the measures he had identified in his paper on regional development. In particular, he stressed community-level development.[26]

Early in his tenure, De Bané embarked on a tour to view at first hand what western European countries were doing in regional development. He called for the establishment of a special study committee inside the Organization for Economic Co-operation and Development (OECD) to look at the issue, a suggestion that the organization later accepted. He also signed a special protocol agreement with the Italian minister responsible for regional development.[27] The accord called on Italy to support De Bané's request for a special OECD meeting on regional development and on both countries to co-operate and exchange views on regional development policy. In these ways, De Bané served notice to his officials that he wanted DREE to adopt an aggressive posture in defining a new regional policy for Canada.

Senior departmental officials, however, remained sceptical that De Bané could deliver a bigger budget and a stronger mandate for the department. Opposition to DREE in Ottawa was still strong, and senior department officials were reluctant to seek a stronger mandate, especially if it gave DREE the authority to assess the regional policies and programs of other departments. They were well aware that De Bané was a junior minister with a reputation in the press for being 'unconventional,' a 'party maverick,' and a 'black sheep.'[28] De Bané certainly raised eyebrows in DREE when he publicly rebuked veteran cabinet minister Allan MacEachen, deputy prime minister and minister of finance, for holding DREE's expenditure budget down to what he felt was an unacceptable level.

Senior DREE officials also saw no evidence for De Bané's claim that regional development held a priority status in Ottawa. The prime minister had made it clear that constitutional renewal and a new energy policy were at the top of the agenda. As he had in 1968, Prime Minister Trudeau turned to two senior Quebec ministers to undertake these tasks. Jean Chrétien, a seasoned politician, was appointed to Justice, and Marc Lalonde, the regional minister for Quebec and a longtime adviser to Trudeau, was named to Energy.

DREE officials remained convinced that had the prime minister and the new government been serious about regional development, he would have appointed a senior cabinet minister to head the department. Nevertheless, they prepared a new policy and legislative package to accommodate at least some of De Bané's views. DREE sponsored a series of public conferences and seminars on local development in an effort to define new development instruments for the department. Senior DREE officials made a number of public speeches stressing comprehensive federal involvement in the promotion of regional development.

Pierre De Bané resisted anything less than a complete overhaul of the federal government's regional policy. He remained convinced that a stronger mandate for DREE was both essential and possible. But there were other forces at play. His cabinet colleagues and government back-benchers, including those from the

Atlantic provinces, were highly critical of the GDAS, which they viewed as instruments substantially financed with federal funds but clearly favouring the political profile of provincial governments. On this issue, the criticism of federal ministers and government MPS became more and more vocal. De Bané explained that he would not renew a subsidiary agreement with Manitoba because Ottawa 'was not getting sufficient political credit for its expenditures.'[29]

The GDA approach was no doubt better suited to times of quiet federal-provincial co-operation, such as prevailed when it was first introduced. However, by the early 1980s, competitive federalism had come to replace co-operative federalism. A bitter referendum campaign over the future of Quebec had just been fought by both Ottawa and the Quebec government. In addition, not one provincial government was of the same political persuasion as was the federal government. It was thus difficult for government MPS to see DREE funds simply transferred to provincial governments which used them to put in place popular economic development initiatives for which they took the credit. MPS went home to their ridings on weekends only to see members of the Parti québécois highly critical of Ottawa, the Prince Edward Island government labelling Trudeau un-Canadian because of his position on the constitution, or Premier Peckford of Newfoundland insisting that the policies of the federal government were working against the best interests of his province. They also saw these same governments claiming credit for a host of GDA-sponsored initiatives for which the federal government had contributed up to 90 per cent of the costs. How then, they asked De Bané, can DREE turn around and agree to finance even more subsidiary agreements?

Well aware of this opposition, and convinced that marginal improvements in DREE's activities would not suffice, De Bané wrote to the prime minister to ask for support for a complete review of federal policy on regional development. He suggested that 'DREE's responsibilities – to ensure that all Canadians have an equal chance to make a living with dignity – can't be handled by one department with one per cent of the federal budget.'[30] Sadly, he reported to the prime minister, the DREE experience had been a failure, because of DREE's inability to muster a concerted federal effort in promoting regional development. The solution, De Bané reasoned, was a much stronger DREE.

Defining departmental mandates is the prerogative of the prime minister. He alone, not the cabinet, must decide which minister will have authority to do what. Frequently mandates overlap and ministers and their departments will jockey to enhance their positions and their spheres of influence. However, only the prime minister can resolve jurisdictional conflicts. Thus, when De Bané wrote to request a stronger mandate for DREE, the prime minister naturally turned to his own officials inside the Privy Council Office for advice.

With the mandate issue in the hands of the prime minister and his advisers, De Bané turned to DREE for new regional development programs. He did not dismiss the GDA approach out of hand, but he asked his department to come up with initiatives that the federal government could finance alone and deliver directly, without the participation of provincial governments. His efforts were strongly endorsed by his cabinet colleagues, a number of whom had publicly called for such an approach.

The Prince Edward Island comprehensive development plan presented an excellent opportunity for De Bané to test this manoeuvre. The plan, signed on 7 March 1969, was divided into three phases, with the last scheduled to come into force on 31 March 1981. Each phase was the subject of new negotiations and new initiatives. Phase I, which ran from 1969 to 1975, dealt with basic infrastructure facilities, such as roads and schools. Phase II, from 1975 to 1981, aimed to strengthen the province's important economic sectors, such as agriculture and fisheries, through incentive grants and marketing studies. Phase III was to continue along the lines established in phase II. De Bané did not attempt to reorient the strategy. Instead, he sought to change the project delivery mechanism. He called for federal departments to deliver a number of projects with DREE funds and to decrease federal funding of provincially delivered projects. He pledged that overall federal support for development projects would not decrease in Prince Edward Island. Under phase III, however, nearly half of the federal funds would be earmarked for direct delivery projects.[31]

De Bané's proposals met with strong opposition from Prince Edward Island's government. Its representatives sought to delay what they referred to as 'unilateral federal initiatives' at least until the end of the comprehensive plan. Changing the rules of the game now, they suggested, would violate the spirit of the fifteen-year accord. It would also mean a substantial loss of jobs in the provincial public service. With the federal government assuming responsibility for delivering initiatives, a number of provincial officials would become redundant.[32]

Notwithstanding these objections, De Bané pressed ahead with his new format for phase III. Confronted with his adamant position, the provincial government finally agreed to De Bané's terms. A group of federal cabinet ministers went to Charlottetown to sign the plan's last phase on behalf of the federal government. DREE and the federal departments of Fisheries, Agriculture, Energy, and Industry, Trade and Commerce would deliver, through federal programs, a number of the plan's initiatives. At a press conference, De Bané explained that the federal government would deliver specific projects because 'regional disparities are the responsibility of both governments.' Joint planning and co-ordination were still possible, he insisted, even if some of the programs were administered through various federal departments.

The plan would not be simply a 'one-shot' federal effort at direct delivery, De Bané vowed. DREE quickly followed with a special five-year $10-million special development plan for southeastern New Brunswick. In this case, however, all the funds were allocated to federal programs. The province could contribute to the plan through its own programs and with its own resources.

A number of direct delivery projects were also earmarked for Quebec. The need for direct delivery was much more urgent there than elsewhere. The provincial government and DREE were not able to agree on a sufficiently large number of new subsidiary agreements to sustain DREE's traditional level of expenditure in Quebec. Confronted with a provincial government that was lukewarm at best on federal-provincial programs and a federal Liberal caucus openly hostile to any transfer of federal funds that would place the Parti québécois in a favourable light, De Bané sought to entice his cabinet colleagues to do more in Quebec, employing, if necessary, DREE funds. One such example was a special agreement between DREE and the Department of Fisheries and Oceans which saw a transfer of DREE funds for the construction and renovation of port facilities in eastern Quebec. In announcing this special agreement, De Bané remarked: 'This transfer of funds is a good example of interdepartmental cooperation [and] ... achieving our goal of reducing regional economic disparities.'[33]

However, DREE had not abandoned cost-sharing with the provinces under the various GDAS. In fact, De Bané did sign a number of traditional subsidiary agreements while in DREE. A new forestry agreement with New Brunswick did not alter the forestry development strategy first introduced under two earlier subsidiary agreements. De Bané also signed a standard subsidiary agreement with New Brunswick to redevelop a portion of the downtown core of Saint John, a forestry subsidiary agreement with Newfoundland, and a water development and drought-proofing subsidiary agreement with Manitoba.

DREE also negotiated a number of pulp and paper subsidiary agreements or major modifications to existing ones with several provinces to modernize and reduce costs in older mills in eastern Canada. The objective here was not to create new jobs, but to protect existing ones. These standard agreements had only one adjustment made to enable the federal government to make payments directly to the companies rather than having to channel funds through provincial governments.

The only major departure from the original GDA approach was the way in which the federal government co-operated with provincial governments. During his stay in DREE, De Bané signed some twenty-one subsidiary agreements that did not constitute a new direction in program substance. De Bané saw little reason for redirecting GDA programs while work was proceeding on a more radical policy and program change. DREE officials also saw that the cabinet was in no mood to support the GDA concept as a federal-provincial tool and saw little hope in being able to reorient Ottawa's regional development policy through the GDA process. In addition, hardly any work had been done in assessing the effectiveness of past DREE efforts. A senior DREE official said: 'It was difficult to get very serious about assessing the impact of our programmes when we were not sure where we were heading or even if we would be around much longer.'

De Bané's new approach to federal-provincial co-operation served to lessen criticism from other federal departments: federal cabinet ministers were no longer hurling charges at DREE. It did little, however, to improve regional development. Though standard GDA programming was less and less popular with De Bané and his cabinet colleagues, De Bané sought a larger budget for DREE. He campaigned for more funds in public as well as in the cabinet and cabinet committees, and DREE gained a substantial increase in its budget. De Bané informed the House Standing Committee on Regional Development in March 1981 that DREE's budget for 1981–82 was much higher than the previous year's, with a net increase of $143 million – a 25 per cent increase – to 'be focused on needy areas.'[34] He noted that this increase compared remarkably well with the budgets of other departments. Perhaps his colleagues were confident that funds would no longer simply be transferred to provincial governments; indeed, more DREE funds could well mean more funding for their own programs.

THE REGIONAL DEVELOPMENT INCENTIVES PROGRAM

Bringing about fundamental changes to the GDA approach and its programs extended, however, beyond De Bané's mandate. It raised questions about government organization, which is the responsibility of the Privy Council Office, and about economic policy, which is the responsibility of the cabinet and, more specifically, the minister of finance. The one program that De Bané and his officials could alter and suggest new measures for without going outside the department was regional incentives.

De Bané wanted at least two important changes in the program. First, he was concerned about its regional designation. By the time he was appointed minister, the program covered fully 93 per cent of Canada's land mass and over 50 per cent of the population. He wanted designations better focused so as not to diffuse Ottawa's efforts. Accordingly, he unveiled a plan to collect and analyse data down to the community level. He reported to the House Standing Committee: 'When I became Minister of DREE I instructed the department to upgrade its data base for small areas.'[35] DREE needed more detailed information so that it could more accurately measure disparities and develop special 'regionally-targetted' measures. De Bané planned to use this new data base to develop a regional disparity index for Canada, which would help DREE designate regions under the industrial incentives program, which would in turn become more generous to the least well-off regions, as defined by the index.

De Bané was successful also in convincing the minister of finance that a new tax credit program was necessary to attract investment to slow-growth regions. The minister of finance reported in his 1980 budget speech that he had agreed to introduce a new special investment tax credit after repeated representations from the minister of DREE. The program was aimed at the 5 per cent of the Canadian population living in regions suffering the most from high family unemployment and low per capita income.

Most manufacturing and processing activities that would qualify under DREE's regional incentives program would qualify also under the new program. Expansions, modernizations, and new facilities were eligible, and no project size limits were to be imposed. The program would be in force for a five-year period, commencing 29 October 1980. The investment tax credit of 50 per cent would be applied to the eligible capital costs of assets acquired for manufacturing and processing.[36]

Second, De Bané wanted to make the incentives program more proactive or *dirigiste* in relation to the private sector. The Bureau of Business and Economic Development was set up to identify, through such techniques as import substitution, export analysis, industry profiles, and corporate and economic intelligence, attractive investment opportunities for the private sector in slow-growth regions.[37] Attempts would be made to select only high–growth potential manufacturing sectors and dynamic industries, so that new activities would sustain themselves. Once it identified opportunities, DREE would go to firms to outline opportunities and offer federal assistance in the form of grants or tax credits. Such representations would always be done at the highest level.

The first sector looked at was high technology. And the first development opportunity the bureau identified was for a small, rural, economically depressed community in Kent County in eastern New Brunswick. With much fanfare, DREE announced that Mitel, a Canadian high-tech company that had enjoyed tremendous growth during the 1970s, would locate two new manufacturing plants in Bouctouche, New Brunswick. The plants were expected to create some 1,000 new jobs. DREE would contribute a $15.7-million incentive grant to the Mitel project, which involved a total capital investment of $48 million.[38] The project was strictly a federal initiative; the provincial government first learned of the project through the news media, as did the residents of the province.

Meanwhile, De Bané and Herb Gray, the minister of industry, trade, and commerce, were exchanging strong words in public over Volkswagen's decision to locate a new parts plant in Barrie, Ontario, in order to take advantage of Ottawa's duty remission program, under which the duty on automobile imports was waived if a company established a plant in Canada.[39] At De Bané's urging, a delegation of federal officials was sent to Germany to meet with Volkswagen. DREE selected two sites, Montreal and Halifax, and offered a cash grant to Volkswagen to locate in either one. The company rejected the one-time grant, arguing that it would need a yearly operating grant to compensate for the fact that parts suppliers were located mainly in southern Ontario.

De Bané suggested that the federal government should refuse the duty remission for Volkswagen if the company pressed ahead with its Barrie location rather than a DREE-designated region. If regional development were to be effective, De Bané had said many times, it requires many instruments. One of them clearly was the duty remission program. Herb Gray rejected De Bané's argument, suggesting that it was better to have Volkswagen locate in Canada, even in southern Ontario, than have the company pick a site in the United States.

When the De Bané–Gray exchange became public, the Quebec government jumped into the debate and urged Ottawa to insist on a Quebec site. Quebec cabinet ministers argued that the province never received its 'fair share' of the Canadian automobile production industry. Quebec's minister of industry, Rodrigue Biron, said that if Ottawa was truly serious about regional development and the promotion of 'real' economic growth in the province, it ought to insist on a Quebec site.[40]

Volkswagen was unmoved by this public debate and remained committed to Barrie. The president of Volkswagen Canada issued a statement that it would not locate anywhere else in Canada, notwithstanding a generous DREE grant.[41] As for duty remission, Volkswagen simply assumed that it would be available, regardless of where it chose to locate in Canada. In the end, the federal cabinet sided with Gray and did not choose to employ duty remission as a means of directing Volkswagen away from southern Ontario. With the economy in a deep recession, a number of ministers were in no mood to call Volkswagen's bluff.

For De Bané, the Volkswagen episode simply confirmed his view that regional development should be the responsibility of all federal departments, not simply DREE, and that a great variety of regional development tools was necessary. Duty remission was but one of them. But before De Bané and DREE could amend their regional development incentives program and define new regional development tools, the prime minister unveiled a major government reorganization. DREE would be disbanded. Its policy role and the GDAS would be transferred to a strengthened Ministry of State for Economic and Regional Development. Its regional incentives program would be incorporated into the programs of a new Department of Regional Industrial Expansion (DRIE). Herb Gray was named minister responsible for DRIE, and De Bané was moved to a newly created portfolio in External Affairs. De Bané's attempt to give DREE a stronger mandate had failed. Only time would tell if a more effective regional development policy would emerge from this new organization.

7

New policies, structures, and programs

On 12 January 1982, Prime Minister Trudeau unveiled a major government reorganization for economic development. The reason for doing so, he pointed out, was that 'it is no longer enough that one department alone is primarily responsible for regional economic development.' The new organization also reflected the new policy direction for promoting Canada's economic development described in detail by the minister of finance in his 1981 budget speech. At that time, Allan MacEachen had spoken about a new economic reality in Canada and consequent changing prospects at the regional level. Substantial opportunities now existed in every major region in the country, suggesting that the federal government should adopt a new policy orientation. [1]

MEGA PROJECTS – THE ROAD TO PROSPERITY

During his 1981 budget speech, Allan MacEachen tabled a document titled 'Economic Development for Canada in the 1980's' which maintained that regional balance was changing as a result of buoyancy in the west, optimism in the east, and unprecedented softness in key economic sectors in central Canada. Underpinning this view were the economic prospects associated with resource-based mega projects.

The Atlantic region, in contrast to historical economic trends, was expected to enjoy a decade of solid growth, largely as a result of off-shore resources. The west, meanwhile, would capture over half of the investment in major projects. Ontario and Quebec would face problems of industrial adjustment, brought about by increased international competition. Yet, opportunities were thought to exist there as well. If properly managed, the economic spin-off from major projects could create numerous employment opportunities in central Canada. Some 60,000 person-years of employment would be created in Ontario from major pipeline projects in western Canada. Thus, the regional challenge in the 1980s would take a new direction. Regions that had previously enjoyed strong growth were now confronted with special problems of adjustment, while those that had traditionally lagged behind were now enjoying prospects for expansion. All in all, both problems and opportunities existed in all regions. Accordingly, the minister of finance stated, 'regional economic development will be central to public policy planning at the federal level.'[2]

The policy direction would take advantage of major economic forces working on the Canadian economy. The policy document pointed to some $440 billion of potential projects, predominantly in energy and resources, that would be launched before the end of the century. By and large, these major projects would be located in the west, in the north, and on the east coast and were expected to bring about a new set of comparative advantages and economic growth not seen in these regions in this century. They would provide an important source of income, improve provincial revenues, and generate new economic activity. Cabinet ministers began to voice a similar message of economic optimism, notably for the future of the Atlantic provinces. The minister of energy, Marc Lalonde, commented: 'What offshore oil and gas provides [in Atlantic Canada] is the opportunity for an accelerated, more dramatic economic turnaround than would otherwise have been thought possible. The basic strength is here. And now we must build on that strength.'[3]

Added to this was anticipated growth in income from grains and other food products, including fisheries. The Department of Finance's policy document noted that 'rapid population growth in the world is placing new demands on food, and in response to rising world prices further expansion and modernization of the agricultural and food sectors throughout Canada is in prospect.' This development, it was felt, would also favour the western and Atlantic provinces. In central Canada, the competitive pressure on manufacturing would require adaptation and regeneration. The policy document thus stressed reorienting and restructuring this sector. The restructuring 'must both reduce the pressure for costly support to less competitive industries and at the same time provide alternative employment opportunities in higher productivity and higher wage sectors.' Much like the argument in the policy document, ministers also suggested that mega projects could help restructure Ontario manufacturing. Senator Bud Olson, minister of economic and regional development, maintained: 'There is a significant underlying base of major project investment that must be looked at, and the cumulative impacts of those projects will and are having significant beneficial impacts in many parts of the country, not only in the provinces where the mega projects are situated.'[4]

In summary, anticipated major projects would enhance the economies of the west, the north, and the Atlantic region. In economic terms, these regions would be able to 'take care of themselves.' The new regional problem was weakening manufacturing in central Canada. It was there that new employment opportunities ought to be created. Many manufacturers producing standard products, such as automobiles and appliances, as well as clothing and footwear, were losing their comparative advantages to foreign competitors. Even if they substantially improved productivity, however, competition would remain strong.

The process of economic growth in central Canada and the peripheral regions would thus be quite different. In the latter, growth would result from the infusion of new capital and labour. Atlantic Canada had a large reservoir of untapped labour to draw from. All that was required for growth in the west and east, then, was a good investment climate, market access, and an adequate supply of labour. In central Canada, however, growth would come about only by drawing resources from declining industries and moving them into growth sectors – in other words, by managing both industrial decline and industrial growth.

In 1969, much had been said about alleviating regional disparities and focusing federal efforts east of Trois-Rivières, and about the importance of regional development for national unity. In 1982, the prime minister's lengthy statement and the finance minister's policy document said nothing about regional disparities. Although regional development would be central to policy-making, it involved something significantly different from what it had been fourteen years earlier. Now regional development referred less to alleviating regional disparities than to development at the regional level.

The prime minister did comment on the DREE experience, but simply to say that the federal government would build from the groundwork laid by the department.[5] DREE, it was felt, had helped ensure adequate infrastructure in all regions: every region had not only roads, water, and sewerage, but also schools, medical facilities, and housing. Some regions with inadequate infrastructure now had prosperous and fast-growing urban centres, such as Calgary, and were no longer slow-growth regions.

NEW GOVERNMENT STRUCTURE

With a new policy in hand, the cabinet had to decide how to structure the government. Could DREE deliver the policy, or was a new organizational structure required? Regional development would now be central to policy-making in Ottawa. Could an ordinary line department such as DREE ensure that this would occur? Conventional wisdom suggested not. A line department can hardly rise above the day-to-day competition among departments for new funds, new person-years, and greater influence. It cannot pretend that it is above this competition while seeking funding for its own programs.

The cabinet decided that a central agency with no program of its own would be better able to influence other departments. It could assess changing economic circumstances and follow up on crucial policy and program decisions. And it could ensure that regional development became part of the whole fabric of government policies and programs.

The cabinet established a new central agency, the Ministry of State for Economic and Regional Development (MSERD), by adding regional policy and co-ordination to the functions of the existing Ministry of State for Economic Development. The ministry was established in late 1978 to co-ordinate and direct economic development policy and to manage the economic policy 'expenditure envelope.' The envelope system integrated into a single process the separate functions of setting priorities, establishing spending limits, and making specific expenditure decisions. Within the envelope system the ministry was to advise deputy ministers and ministers on Ottawa's economic development budget and recommend allocation of funds between programs.[6]

In addition, MSERD was to see that 'regional concerns are elevated to a priority position in all economic decision-making by Cabinet.' Because of this added responsibility, the new ministry had to decentralize part of its operations. Offices comprising eight to twelve person-years were established in every province. These offices were directed by a senior executive, called the federal economic development co-ordinator (FEDC), who 'advises Cabinet, co-ordinates the activities of the federal government in the region, promotes co-operation with the provincial government, labour, business and other economic development groups, ensures that information about government policy is available in the field, and works with other federal departments.' The ministry would, whenever appropriate, also appoint special project directors in the region 'to cut red tape on mega projects and avoid undue delay in project planning, approval and completion.'[7]

The FEDC, however, would direct activities in his region, keeping federal officials in the field informed of the activities and decisions of the Cabinet Committee on Economic and Regional Development. He would also co-ordinate the federal presence in the regions, and 'serve as the chairman of a committee of economic development departments in the region.'

Through this committee and from his own staff work, the FEDC would propose an economic development plan for his province. In turn, this plan would be the basis for federal-provincial negotiations for economic development and also assist in making federal departments and agencies more sensitive to regional circumstances.

The importance of having all federal departments play a more active role in regional development was stressed by the prime minister and MSERD's minister, Senator Olson. While announcing the appointment of the FEDC for Prince Edward Island, for example, Senator Olson declared that the Cabinet Committee on Economic and Regional Development had 'launched a process of review of all existing economic development programmes to determine if they can be further directed toward regional objectives.'[8]

Largely because of the expected role of the FEDC, the new ministry was described by Ottawa as a 'decentralized central agency.' It would provide the full cabinet with regional information developed by federal sectoral departments in the regions or by on-site research and analysis with MSERD. Thus, the information would not, as with DREE, be based almost solely on federal-provincial discussions under the various GDAS.

The agency would, however, remain largely Ottawa-based. The head office would increase its allocation of person-years (originally established in 1978 at more than 100) by almost 200, and the new regional offices received 100 – producing a head office to regional staff ratio of 2 to 1, considerably higher than DREE's ratio of 3 to 7. The rationale for a substantial increase in person-years was built around the need for ensuring that the 'regional dimension' was incorporated in the federal government's decision-making process. To do this, MSERD required an enhanced information system on regional issues. A new position, that of associate secretary or associate deputy minister, was set up. Around it the regional information network would be built, including the regional offices. Moreover, approval was given for the Ottawa office to establish a major projects branch to facilitate a government-wide approach to the development and management of the various major projects.[9]

Nearly two years later, the MSERD legislation was finally amended to incorporate the regional responsibility that was added to MSERD's responsibilities. The legislation was no more explicit on objectives than was the old DREE legislation; it said nothing about goals. It was not clear whether regional balance in economic growth or reducing regional disparities was to be paramount. MSERD's concern, the new legislation stated, was 'expansion of the economy through the development of productive enterprise in every region of Canada.'[10]

ECONOMIC AND REGIONAL DEVELOPMENT AGREEMENTS (ERDAS)

The prime minister declared at the time that he announced the new organization for economic development that 'existing General Development Agreements with the provinces will continue until their expiry date,' to be replaced then by a 'new and simpler set of agreements with the provinces, involving a wider range of federal departments.' The new Economic and Regional Development Agreements (ERDAS) would be formulated under the direction of the relevant FEDC. The reorganization reflected Ottawa's new approach to federal-provincial relations. The policy paper tabled by the minister of finance during his 1981 budget speech made it clear that 'joint implementation of economic development programming may not always be desirable.' ERDA agreements would reflect this new approach. The most positive characteristics of the GDAS would be retained, and less desirable features discarded.[11]

The cabinet thought that the federal government was not obtaining its share of visibility under the GDAS. Accordingly, the new ERDAS, following the plan adopted for Prince Edward Island and subsequently for other DREE initiatives, would stress direct delivery by the federal government.

The cabinet believed that the GDA process had given rise to a process that lacked political control and direction. GDA initiatives were prepared and agreed to through a host of federal-provincial committees staffed exclusively with permanent officials. By the time they surfaced at the political level, planning was so far advanced that little change was possible. Under the new ERDAS, Ottawa would deliver directly certain projects under the aegis of the various subsidiary agreements. The respective responsibilities of the federal and provincial governments were to be much clearer. In future, Ottawa would much sooner employ subsidiary agreements than cost-sharing initiatives delivered by provincial governments as a mechanism for program co-ordination between governments.

ERDAS were designed also to encompass all federal departments and agencies, which were invited to contribute to the various ERDAS, either by signing new subsidiary agreements with the provinces or by delivering specific initiatives. ERDAS were to respect interprovincial considerations and the needs of the national economy. Federal line departments would thus be better able than DREE had been to counter over-reliance on a provincial perspective of economic development.

The cabinet hoped that the ERDAS would give rise to joint planning, with parallel delivery of projects. Future subsidiary agreements might be planned jointly, but with each government delivering its own programs. These types of arrangements were already being signed under GDAS when ERDA was unveiled: under the Canada–Nova Scotia Ocean Industries Agreement and the Northeast British Columbia Coal Agreement, Ottawa and the provinces were to deliver their own programs directly.

ERDAS would also be developed under close political scrutiny. The legislation (Bill C-152) establishing MSERD spelled out the joint planning process: 'Detailed negotiations ... of any subsidiary agreement shall not be undertaken ... unless a plan for economic development to which the draft agreement relates has first been approved by the Minister in concert with other Ministers.' Federal ministers would not be asked to approve proposed agreements when it was too late to affect their contents.

Apart from these changes, the ERDAS were remarkably similar to the GDAS they replaced. Like the GDAS, they were ten-year umbrella-type agreements that did not provide for specific projects.[12] They simply offered a broad statement of goals, outlined priorities, and described how joint decisions would be taken. They were, in short, enabling documents, with projects to be presented in subsidiary agreements.

The similarity between ERDAS and GDAS extended even to wording. Several 'whereas' clauses were followed by a section on definitions, a statement of objectives, a section on subsidiary agreements, and so on. A schedule A was attached to the ERDAS outlining the economic circumstances of the relevant province. As with the GDAS, federal and provincial ministers were asked to meet annually 'to review the economic and regional development environment of the province.'

With a new negotiation process defined, MSERD's new minister, Donald Johnston, embarked on a cross-country tour to meet his provincial counterparts. Johnston found some governments less than enthusiastic over the new approach. They viewed it as a move away from federal-provincial co-operation. In addition, the Atlantic governments argued that ERDAS signified an end to Ottawa's commitment to regional development. Premier Peckford said that his province was being shortchanged on federal monies for regional development under Ottawa's new approach.[13]

Nevertheless, the provinces had little choice but to enter into new negotiations with the federal government. MSERD and the FEDCS had replaced DREE and DREE's provincial directors-general. The GDAS were being replaced by the ERDAS, and no provincial opposition or criticism could change that.

Shortly after their appointments, the FEDCS initiated discussion with the heads of federal departments and agencies in their respective provinces to identify initiatives that they could deliver as part of the new ERDAS. At the same time, the FEDCS approached their provincial counterparts about the ten-year development agreements.

And, one by one, the provinces signed new ERDAS with the federal government. Manitoba was the first, on 25 November 1983.[14] Both the federal and the Manitoba governments publicly applauded the agreement. Donald Johnston remarked: 'This ERDA represents a new kind of federal-provincial co-operation, based on a shared understanding of Manitoba's economy.' His provincial counterpart added that it 'encourages a much wider coordination of federal-provincial activities in the economic development field than ever before.' The two ministers announced that they had also agreed to sign two subsidiary agreements. The first, the Canada-Manitoba Economic Planning Agreement, provided funding for cost-shared studies on the provincial economy. It was patterned on the subsidiary agreements that DREE had signed. The second subsidiary agreement was designed to strengthen Manitoba's mineral industry. It provided funding for a series of geo-scientific studies to identify promising new sites for exploration. It called for measures to improve productivity and safety in the industry, as well as marketing studies and development schemes. Both governments were to invest close to $25 million over a five-year period in a series of complementary programs. The scheme resembled DREE's agreements, except that both governments, rather than just the province, were to deliver the programs.

Attached to the Manitoba ERDA was a memorandum, prepared jointly by the provincial MSERD office and the provincial government, identifying future priority areas for both governments. It called for, among other things, improved transportation, development of human resources, and strengthening of small business.

Saskatchewan was the second province to sign an ERDA.[15] Premier Grant Devine pointed out that the new agreement was the result of 'a cooperative process.' Donald Johnston stated that the agreement was designed to build upon 'the existing strength of Saskatchewan's economy.' Both governments also signed a five-year subsidiary agreement similar to Manitoba's. In addition, they signed a memorandum of understanding concerning a new technology strategy, whereby both governments would examine the need for industrially oriented research centres, identify innovative sectors with major growth potential, and help industry effectively manage technological change.

The Saskatchewan ERDA also identified three other priority areas for the provincial economy. Both governments would attempt to improve the international competitive situation of the province's minerals, heavy oil, forestry, and agriculture; to diversify the provincial economy; and to bring people of native ancestry into the various development opportunities.

At the time Newfoundland signed its ERDA agreement, Premier Peckford was publicly less positive about the new approach than the western premiers had been. He declared: 'We must ensure that regional development funding is properly directed to priority areas. It is also crucial that the federal government ... understand the full dimension of our economic disparities and the appropriate way to solve them.'[16] Two subsidiary agreements covered planning and minerals development and were inspired by previous agreements for these same sectors.

In signing New Brunswick's ERDA, Premier Hatfield agreed to sign a planning subsidiary agreement and spoke of 'the successful joint effort under the General Development Agreement (GDA) to develop the New Brunswick economy.'[17] He hoped that the new agreement would continue the GDA efforts. He later informed the legislative assembly that the province could bid farewell to an 'outstanding decade of federal-provincial co-operation in regional development [the ten-year GDA] but that it was highly unlikely that the new approach would be as successful'; 'the federal government may in the new agreements be less generous.' Further, he declared, 'under the new ERDA, the province will be in constant negotiation with a number of different federal departments, each with its own policies, philosophies and priorities.'[18]

Shortly afterward, the province signed subsidiary agreements on agriculture, on mineral development, and on forestry, similar to past GDA subsidiary agreements on these sectors except with direct federal delivery in some.

Nova Scotia agreed to proceed with the ERDA signing, modelled on the GDA, after receiving some assurance that the federal government would maintain 'funding at DREE levels under the GDA.' Its subsidiary agreements echoed those under the GDA. One on the Strait of Canso was designed to 'provide for a second phase of activity necessary to fully capitalize the infrastructure completed under the first agreement.' The new agreement also called for a number of infrastructure-type projects of the kind sponsored by the first agreement. Funds were earmarked for 'wharf construction, an all-weather highway ... and various small scale infrastructure projects.' Another subsidiary agreement, on minerals, continued along the lines of two earlier GDA subsidiary agreements, of 1974 and 1982. Specifically, a number of programs in the new agreement, notably the geo-scientific and the mineral development studies programs, were identical to those of the earlier 1982 agreement. A planning agreement, modelled on GDA arrangements, made funds available for research and studies into economic conditions and prospects for Nova Scotia.[19]

Prince Edward Island signed an ERDA and six subsidiary agreements, on alternative energy, agri-food development, fisheries, transportation, and planning. These agreements involved a total commitment of both governments in excess of $121 million. Premier Jim Lee and federal cabinet minister Bennett Campbell indicated that subsidiary agreements for industrial development, marketing, and tourism would soon follow.[20]

The sectors affected by Prince Edward Island's ERDA were precisely those in the earlier comprehensive plan. Further, programs under the various subsidiary agreements were also identical to those sponsored by the comprehensive plan. In the new transportation program highway improvements and port development reappeared, as did technology development, market development, and livestock and crop health in the agricultural program. The energy subsidiary agreement made provision for 'completion of the Prince Edward Island energy alternatives study,' started by the comprehensive plan.

Alberta signed an ERDA, a one-year extension to the existing subsidiary agreement on nutritive processing, and memoranda of undertaking for tourism and agriculture. These memoranda outlined principles and a process that would guide both governments in defining future subsidiary agreements for these two sectors. The ERDA identified other sectors holding promise for economic development – forestry, transportation, and science and technology – on which Ottawa and Alberta would concentrate efforts. Finally, it suggested that DRIE and the provincial government jointly consider possible development initiatives for northern Alberta.

A change of government in Ottawa in 1984 did not dampen the federal government's desire for signing ERDAS with all provincial governments. Shortly after the Mulroney government came to office, the new DRIE minister, Sinclair Stevens, signed an ERDA with Ontario. The format established for earlier ERDAS was not disturbed. Ontario welcomed the opportunity to sign an ERDA. Larry Grossman, the provincial treasurer, spoke about co-ordinated efforts for 'economic growth and permanent job creation in Ontario.' Both governments agreed also to a $2-million planning project, designed 'to support cooperative decision-making and improved coordination.' Both governments revealed also that they would shortly sign agreements in forestry and tourism and identified priority areas for future efforts: industrial revitalization, resource management and product development, service-sector stimulation, human resource development, and community development.[21]

Soon afterward, Sinclair Stevens signed an ERDA with Don Phillips, British Columbia's minister of industry and small business development. Stevens echoed the sentiment of his Liberal predecessor, Donald Johnston, when he said: 'ERDA, unlike the former GDA, covers all the departments and ministries which influence economic development and is intended to make sure that a wider range of federal policies and programs will be tailored to the priorities of each province.' He added that '[we] intend to identify the initiatives and opportunities which will strengthen British Columbia's economy and help it reach its full economic potential.' Both ministers also outlined a 'course of action [that] was agreed upon for implementation.' It would include agreements in forestry, minerals development, agriculture, and food development. Other priority areas were to be tourism, transportation development, aquaculture, and human resource development.[22]

Quebec was the last province to sign an ERDA, on 15 December 1984, and the provincial justice minister, Pierre-Marc Johnson, explained the delay: 'Negotiations had bogged down with the previous Liberal government, but things changed radically when the Progressive Conservatives came to power this fall.' The new government, he added, had 'a different way of looking at things and [respects] Quebec's jurisdiction.' Johnson and Sinclair Stevens announced that the two governments would commit $1.6 billion over five years in tourism, culture, forestry, and industrial development. New projects and possibly new sectors would be identified at a later date for the last five years of the ERDA.[23]

The terms of the Quebec ERDA are similar to those in the nine earlier ERDAS. Moreover, the sectors identified for joint government action are essentially the ones in Quebec's GDA. The one difference between Quebec's ERDA and the others is that no provision is made for any joint planning agreement.[24] The Quebec government refused to enter into such a subsidiary agreement, arguing that it preferred to arrive at joint action through consensus rather than through joint planning.

Thus, one by one, the federal and provincial governments signed ERDAS. The ERDAS and GDAS were identical in format, and similar in objectives pursued and types of programs and initiatives sponsored. The ERDAS provided for the federal government to deliver directly initiatives that had been previously delivered by provincial governments under the GDAS.

Before the election of Brian Mulroney's Conservative government, Ottawa grew impatient over Quebec's refusal to sign an ERDA. Donald Johnston explained: 'They [Quebec] seem to want to continue with the old system.' Marc Lalonde added that Ottawa would 'continue to have enough flexibility to conclude a future agreement with the province.' In the mean time, both ministers unveiled a series of new federal projects worth $109 million to be delivered directly. The projects were earmarked for tourism, agriculture, mineral development, communications, transportation, and research and development – sectors similar to those in the Quebec GDA.[25]

THE REGIONAL FUND

At the same time that he announced the new policy and the new government organization, Prime Minister Trudeau declared that a regional fund would be established, such as had been called for by former DREE minister Pierre De Bané. The prime minister stated: 'Money freed up as the existing GDAS expire will be used ... to create a regional fund.' This fund would 'support regional economic development efforts and should reach $200 million by 1984–85.'[26] Shortly after the new government organization was unveiled, several federal ministers referred to the new regional fund and spoke about its importance to regional economic development.

Initially, at least, some confusion existed over the size of the fund and how it would be financed. Responsibility for the various subsidiary agreements was transferred to a number of federal line departments and agencies, which added to the confusion. Further, the new line department DRIE, now responsible for the old DREE programs, was understandably reluctant to transfer part of its unallocated resources to a new regional fund over which it had little control.

The problems with the regional fund, however, were and are more fundamental. The term *region* has still not been properly defined. Consequently, it was unclear whether the fund was to apply to sub-provincial regions, to provinces, or to multi-province areas. More important, it was not clear whether the fund was to apply exclusively to disadvantaged regions.

Could the fund be employed exclusively to support projects that would not otherwise be developed in a disadvantaged region? Those who have called for a regional fund have consistently warned that it should not support projects that a line department should initiate through its ongoing programs. Line departments would then simply turn to the regional fund for total funding whenever an initiative came forward from a disadvantaged region. The department's ongoing program and budget would finance projects from more developed regions, while the regional fund would finance those in other regions. More simply put, the question was whether or not expenditures from the regional fund should be above and beyond the normal program responsibilities of departments in all regions. Unless they were, the purpose of a regional fund would be negated. This issue remains unresolved.

Equally important, the regional distribution of the fund was not made clear. Given that the fund was being financed from 'money freed-up as existing GDAS expire,' one could assume that its regional distribution would have been based on DREE's historical spending pattern under the various GDAS.[27]

THE DEPARTMENT OF REGIONAL INDUSTRIAL EXPANSION (DRIE)

The government reorganization also established a new line department – the Department of Regional Industrial Expansion (DRIE) – through the amalgamation of the regional programs of DREE with the industry, small business, and tourism components of the Department of Industry, Trade and Commerce (IT&C). The trade component of IT&C moved to the Department of External Affairs.[28]

The integration of DREE and IT&C, it was hoped, would capture the most positive characteristics of both DREE's decentralized and regionally sensitive organization and IT&C's centralization and ability to gather industrial intelligence and conduct relations with industry and government. In short, DRIE would not be as decentralized as DREE or as centralized as IT&C.

DRIE was to set up provincial and sub-provincial offices to deliver its programs. These offices have become the new department's principal contact point for DRIE clients applying for assistance under the department's programs. Unlike in DREE, however, they have little say in formulating policy or programs. These functions, along with gathering of industrial intelligence, have become the responsibility of new sectoral branches in DRIE's Ottawa office. DRIE's Ottawa-region staff ratio has been set at 6:4, compared with DREE's 3:7.

Nevertheless, compared to other federal departments and agencies, DRIE is highly decentralized and 'regionally sensitive.' It represents the 'leading edge' in Ottawa's new economic development orientation and the model on which other departments are encouraged to pattern themselves.[29] The new department is expected to integrate regional and sectoral interests, be highly visible in the regions, and emphasize efficient program delivery.

In the new DRIE organization, provincial offices are directed by a senior official who holds the same rank or job classification established under the DREE organization. The offices, however, report directly to Ottawa and do not go through regional offices as was the case under DREE. Typically, a provincial DRIE office can implement programs and has units for economic analysis, development (to identify new opportunities at the local level), public information, and administrative services.

THE INDUSTRIAL AND REGIONAL DEVELOPMENT PROGRAM

The first DRIE minister was Ed Lumley, who rose in the House of Commons on 27 June 1983 to explain Ottawa's new industrial and regional development program. Lumley cautioned that 'combatting regional disparities is difficult even in good economic times ... It is much more difficult in a period when, because of a worldwide downturn, [Canada's] traditional industries are suffering from soft markets, stiff international competition, rapid technological change and rising protectionism from the countries that make up our market.' A new program to meet these circumstances would have to be one that he could 'clearly recommend to the business community, to the Canadian public and to Members of Parliament.' DRIE, Lumley reported, had come up with such a program. It was a 'regionally sensitized, multifacet programme of industrial assistance in all parts of Canada ... This is not a programme available only in certain designated regions. Whatever riding any Member of this House represents, his or her constituents will be eligible for assistance'. The program could accommodate a variety of needs, including investment in infrastructure, for industrial diversification, for the establishment of new plants, and the launching of new product lines.[30]

An important distinguishing characteristics of the new Industrial and Regional Development Program (IRDP) was the 'development index.' Patterned on De Bané's earlier collection of data on small areas, it was to establish the needs of individual regions, as far down as a single census district. All are arranged in four tiers of need (see Appendices B and C). The first, for the most developed 50 per cent of the population covers districts with a need for industrial restructuring. In this tier, financial assistance is available for up to 25 per cent of the cost of modernization and expansion. At the other end of the spectrum is the fourth tier, which includes the 5 per cent of the population living in areas of greatest need (based on level of employment, personal income, and provincial fiscal capacity). In this tier, financial assistance is available for up to 60 per cent of the cost of establishing new plants.

The program can provide financial assistance to both business and non-profit organizations through cash grants, contributions, repayable contributions, participation loans, and loan guarantees. This assistance is available for the various elements of 'product or company cycle': economic analysis studies; innovation (including product development); plant establishment; plant modernization and expansion; marketing (including exact development measures); and restructuring. Appendix B of this book provides a detailed breakdown of the program elements, as well as the possible levels of assistance. Tier 4 regions are eligible under all program elements; tier 1 regions are not. Financial assistance under tier 4 can amount to 70 per cent of costs, while tier 1 varies from 20 to 50 per cent. Appendix C outlines how the development index of the four tiers was arrived at.

Reactions to the program have been mixed. Provincial governments in the Atlantic region have suggested that they were losing their preferential access to DREE funds. The Atlantic Provincial Economic Council has expressed the fear that instead of narrowing the application of regional development schemes, DRIE was extending it. The Senate Committee on Regional Development has argued that the poorest regions of the country could well wind up worse off with DRIE. However, provincial governments elsewhere and some MPS from Ontario and the western provinces have applauded the new DRIE program. Private-sector representatives have so far said very little and remain largely non-committal.[31]

WINDING UP MSERD

In naming his cabinet in June 1984, Prime Minister John Turner announced that one of his most important objectives was to ensure a more 'streamlined and leaner' federal government. The federal government, he insisted, had become 'too elaborate, too complex, too slow, and too expensive.' He unveiled several measures to 'streamline' cabinet decision-making. The number of cabinet committees was reduced from 13 to 10, and the number of cabinet ministers, from 36 to 29. Two central agencies, the Ministry of State for Social Development and the Ministry of State for Economic and Regional Development, were 'wound up.' In announcing his new cabinet structure, Turner mentioned regional development only to say that 'steps [would be taken] to strengthen the regional development role of the Department of Regional Industrial Expansion.'[32]

Specifically, Turner transferred the Federal Economic Development co-ordinators (FEDCS) from MSERD to DRIE. Accompanying the FEDCS to DRIE were the various ERDAS. The Office for Regional Development was established within DRIE. A junior minister, for all practical purposes reporting to the minister of DRIE and operating under the aegis of the DRIE portfolio, was appointed minister of state for regional development. Remi Bujold, representing a Gaspé riding, was promoted from the back benches to fill the post. The industrial and regional development program was left untouched by the Turner reorganization.[33]

There is no doubt that Turner's winding up of MSERD was prompted by a strong commitment to streamline government, not by any desire to strengthen Ottawa's regional development policy. Little was said, for example, by either Turner or any of his senior ministers about the federal government reorienting its regional development policy.

A NEW PROGRESSIVE CONSERVATIVE GOVERNMENT

Canadians returned a record number (211) of Progressive Conservative MPs to Ottawa in the September 1984 election and thereby gave the party a huge majority government. The party's theme throughout the election campaign had been change and the need for a new government to bring about change on a number of fronts. Regional development was no exception.

The Progressive Conservative party had taken dead aim at 'the actions of successive Liberal governments' in regional development. 'When the Liberals dismantled DREE in 1981, the party's policy paper on regional development said, 'they left Canada's least developed regions without their traditional voice.' The paper suggested that the winding up of MSERD 'further reduces the importance attached by the federal government to the task of combatting regional disparity'. DRIE, it added, 'is likely to neglect Canada's poorest regions.'[34]

A Conservative government, Brian Mulroney made clear, would give regional development priority. Two principles would guide his government: consultation, and fair and equitable distribution of regional development funds. The policy paper was less forthcoming on policy goals or directions. It spoke of offering 'rewarding careers' to young people in Atlantic Canada in their home provinces – 'place prosperity' as opposed to 'people prosperity.' The paper referred specifically to 'regional disparities' more than the Trudeau government had, particularly toward the end of its mandate.

Brian Mulroney outlined a number of specific measures during the 1984 election campaign. DRIE would receive a 'specific legislative mandate to promote the least developed regions,' and 'every department will be required to submit to the Standing Committee of Parliament on Economic and Regional Development annual assessments of the effect of departmental policies on specific regions.' DRIE would get a wide range of policy instruments, including tax incentives. In the four Atlantic provinces, efforts would be made to improve the economic infrastructure, including facilities for transportation and communications as well as training programs and improved market research. Commitments were also made to assist communities with chronic unemployment and little economic activity.

Though the Conservative party was highly critical of the Liberals for having 'dismantled' DREE, it did not reestablish DREE when it came to power. In naming his cabinet, Prime Minister Mulroney made no one responsible for regional development. He dropped the minister of state that Turner had introduced a few months earlier, despite having a record 40 ministers in his Cabinet and having several ministers of state responsible for specific fields. Mulroney retained the ministers of state first introduced by the 1982 government reorganization that did away with DREE, such as those for Trade and for External Relations. He also introduced new ministers of state, for Tourism and for Forestry, among others.

Thus the Canadian government has come full circle in fifteen years in organizing itself for the promotion of regional development. DREE was first established to co-ordinate Ottawa's regional development plans. In turn, a reconstituted central agency, MSERD, was set up to ensure government-wide concern for regional development. Later this approach was dropped, and a minister of state responsible for regional development was appointed. With the new Mulroney cabinet, we are now back to the pre-DREE days.

Existing regional development instruments such as the ERDAS will not wither away unattended. The ERDAS will continue, though with changes. Direct delivery will be less frequent. DRIE will continue operations and retain a special role in regional development. The Conservative party pledged to give DRIE a 'specific legislative mandate to promote least developed regions' and to introduce new program instruments to promote regional development.

In the case of IRDP, the Mulroney government quickly limited the program's scope, in line with his election pledge to direct DRIE toward the least developed regions. DRIE minister Sinclair Stevens announced, within two months of his appointment, important restrictions to tier 1 regions, or the most developed regions of the country: 'modernization' and 'expansion' projects would no longer be eligible for assistance. Stevens served notice of transfer to the provinces of responsibility for much of IRDP. Ottawa would administer large grants to national or multinational firms and let provincial governments deal with small and medium-sized businesses.[35]

8

Other regional development efforts

Attempts to achieve regional development in Canada have gone considerably beyond the activities of DREE, MSERD, and DRIE. Certainly, in budgetary terms, these latter have constituted only a small part of Ottawa's effort. Virtually all government activities, except public debt charges and government operations abroad, affect regional development. Provincial governments, similarly, have introduced regional measures supported by neither DREE nor MSERD.

NON-DREE MEASURES

Ottawa has over the years introduced a number of measures to stimulate regional development. The Cape Breton Development Corporation (DEVCO) is but one example. Established in 1967, DEVCO was designed to fill the economic vacuum created by the decline of the coal and steel industries in the late 1950s and the 1960s on Cape Breton Island. Early on DEVCO had concluded that Cape Breton should phase out coal mining by 1981, and its objective was to create jobs to replace those lost by mine closures.

DEVCO's operations have evolved considerably since the corporation was first established. Initially, it sought to attract outside firms with generous incentive schemes to bring new jobs to the island. This phase was followed by new policy directions. In 1972, for example, DEVCO decided to drop the original plan to phase out coal mining by 1981 and instead to modernize. It decided to build a modern coal preparation plant with associated modernization of coal handling. Moreover, negotiations with the Nova Scotia Power Commission led to a large coal-fired generating plant at Lingan. This in turn paved the way for opening up new coal mines such as Prince and Donkin. These developments were supported with federal funds.[1] The Donkin-Morin mine was launched in 1980 at a cost to the federal treasury of $55 million.

DEVCO also launched a series of non-coal development projects, to encourage local entrepreneurship.[2] It planned direct action as well as assistance to local entrepreneurs in the form of high-risk equity and secured loans. DEVCO acted as entrepreneur or direct operator of projects in tourism, farming, and agriculture. Its intention was to broaden Cape Breton's appeal to tourists and also to investors generally by putting together projects that, though not in themselves commercially attractive, would draw enough people to give other private operations a chance to develop. DEVCO would become less involved over time. Nonetheless, its development side continues to draw on federal funds, and the corporation continues to experience annual operating deficits. In 1981, for example, it lost $18 million.[3]

Not all of Ottawa's regional development initiatives, however, have been designed for have-not regions. In the late 1970s and early 1980s Ottawa became concerned with industrial adjustment in southern Ontario and Quebec and introduced two new regional programs to deal with the problem. They offered assistance to the private sector and to industrial communities in much the same fashion that DREE had done in its designated regions.

The Industrial and Labour Adjustment Program (ILAP) was launched in 1981. The minister of finance unveiled it in his 1980 budget speech and earmarked $350 million to it over four years. ILAP was formulated for urban areas particularly hard hit by industrial adjustment 'to promote industrial restructuring and manpower retraining and mobility in areas of particular need.'[4] Communities were designated on the basis of need, as measured by the number of layoffs from an industry, whether the adjustment was recent or chronic, and whether the layoffs were structural or cyclical. Communities with recent adjustment problems were favoured on the grounds that other programs existed to help those with more long-term problems.

In the initial phase, Windsor, Ontario; Sydney, Nova Scotia; and Port-Cartier, Sept-Iles, and Tracy Sorel, Quebec, were designated for a minimum one-year period. Later, L'islet-Montmagny and McAdam, in New Brunswick, and Brantford and Chatham, in Ontario, were also designated. Still later, 'industry specific' restructuring initiatives were introduced.[5] Under ILAP, the federal government provided assistance to firms wishing to locate or restructure in designated communities. The form of assistance varied. A non-repayable contribution of up to 75 per cent of consulting costs associated with development of a new project could be provided, or repayable interest-free contributions of up to 50 per cent of the capital cost of a new project.

The program had mixed success, largely depending on the community. In a one-year period, close to thirty firms obtained ILAP assistance in the Windsor area, ranging from a $77,000 non-repayable grant to a $6-million repayable loan. The program proved much less successful in Sydney, where, during a one-year period, only one firm was able to qualify for assistance.[6] The labour adjustment component was considerably more successful in all designated communities; in some industries laid-off employees could take advantage of several schemes. Special incentives grants for relocation were put in place, as were higher training and upgrading allowances. A portable wage subsidy, which provided $2 per hour to a new employer, was to facilitate re-employment of older workers. In addition, early retirement benefits for displaced workers were offered.

The industry-specific restructuring initiative of ILAP assisted firms in designated sectors, wherever they were located. Assistance resembled that described above and applied to such sectors as the major appliance and components and the auto parts industries. This part of the ILAP program was thus not regional in scope, as were the others. Some observers suggest, however, that this assistance was in fact regional: over 80 per cent of the funds went to communities in southern Ontario, most of the balance to Quebec, and only negligible amounts to New Brunswick and Nova Scotia.[7]

Yet another regionally oriented initiative was the Adjustment Assistance Benefit Program, which granted some $250 million over a five-year period. Funding was secured from ongoing DREE programs such as the RDIA and the GDAS, and from Industry, Trade and Commerce programs. Ottawa sought thereby to update its textile and clothing policy, last revised in 1978. At that time, it had negotiated nine bilateral restraint arrangements and had later concluded eight more. The seventeen arrangements were to expire on 31 December 1981, and Ottawa had stated its preference for freer trade and for the removal of special protection measures over the long term. The new program was 'to revitalize the economies of those communities most vulnerable to foreign competition' in the textile and clothing industries. A newly established Canadian Regional Industrial Board (CRIB), made up of senior business leaders as well as labour and government representatives, is responsible for implementing the program.[8]

The textile and clothing industries are largely concentrated in Quebec and Ontario.[9] Forty-nine per cent of Canada's total employment in the textile industry is in Quebec and 45 per cent in Ontario. Sixty-nine per cent of the total establishments are in Quebec, and 22 per cent in Ontario. Manitoba is a distant third in both industries. The problem was as much regional as it was one of industry or of sectors. In fact, the need for adjustment was concentrated in some thirty cities and towns in Quebec and eastern Ontario, and so creation of new industrial opportunities focused on them.

The new CRIB program was largely inspired by ILAP. Contributions of up to 75 per cent of the costs of consultants for new development projects were available to firms, as were loans of up to $1.5 million, at preferential rates. Firms wishing to establish a new manufacturing and processing activity in a designated region could receive repayable interest-free contributions of up to 50 per cent of the capital costs and up to 50 per cent of pre-production expenses.

The federal government sought to attract firms 'which will have a comparative advantage in the economy of the 1980's – high productivity, high-technology industries.' It intended to go beyond the problem of an increasingly non-competitive industry and turn to the community level to deal with 'the economic and social roots of the regions in which these industries are concentrated.' Thus, the CRIB program provided for contributions of up to 100 per cent of consultants' fees to analyse designated communities and produce plans to develop their full industrial potential. Like ILAP, CRIB facilitated early retirement for long-time textile and clothing workers who had been laid off. Manpower training and portable wage subsidies were also enacted.

Both ILAP and CRIB represent recent ad hoc measures to respond to regional problems; other long-standing measures deal with regional structural problems. One is Ottawa's special freight assistance program for the Atlantic provinces. The Duncan Commission concluded that Confederation had placed an unfair burden on the trade and commerce of the Maritime provinces and recommended a reduction in Canadian National Railway rates there, with the carrier compensated by federal subsidy.[10]

A special assistance program introduced in 1937 established Maritime rates at 20 per cent lower than rates elsewhere. It was revised in 1957 to 30 per cent and in 1969 extended to highway carriers. A further revision in 1974 provided an additional 20 per cent reduction for selected commodities moving to markets outside the Atlantic region. A federal-provincial committee determines which products are eligible for the rate subsidy. New products manufactured in the region may be added to the list. For example, wheel weights for automobiles were recently declared eligible when a firm in Nova Scotia began manufacturing them. Total payments under the freight assistance programs amounted to $60 million in 1980 and $63,400,000 in 1981.[11]

FEDERAL TRANSFER PAYMENTS

The federal government concentrates many of its transfer payment programs on the slow-growing regions. The most important and best known is the equalization program which adjusts for regional variation in the revenue base for provincial taxes. It contributes about 25 per cent of provincial revenue in the Atlantic region and about 10 per cent in Quebec and Manitoba.

Federal transfers to individuals are considerably higher in slow-growth regions than in more developed areas. In the Unemployment Insurance (UI) program, for example, close to 55 per cent of benefits in 1976 went to residents of Quebec and the Atlantic provinces. The program itself is regionally differentiated in favour of areas of high unemployment in that there is a variable entrance requirement, which is lower, in terms of weeks employed, for areas of high unemployment. Over 7 per cent of the population in the Atlantic provinces received UI payments in 1976, compared with less than 2 per cent in Alberta and less than 4 per cent in Ontario.[12]

Other federal transfer payments to individuals are of particular importance to slow-growth regions. Because of population composition, slow-growth regions have benefited more from Ottawa's Family Allowance and Old Age Security programs than the more developed regions. The four Atlantic provinces had over 35 per cent of their population qualify for Family Allowances and over 9 per cent for Old Age Security in 1976, compared with 30 per cent and 8.8 per cent, respectively, for Ontario.[13]

OTTAWA'S GOVERNMENT RELOCATION PROGRAM

In May 1975, Treasury Board president Jean Chrétien obtained cabinet approval to initiate a program for relocating units of the federal public service away from the National Capital Region and other major metropolitan centres. A key objective was to strengthen the federal government's commitment to regional development. Chrétien explained: 'It is ... logical that serious thought be given to the possibility of using the relocation of federal jobs and salaries as another instrument for the promotion of economic activity in the less advantaged regions of this country.'[14]

Chrétien established a task force to assist departments and agencies in identifying units that might be moved and to report on a detailed relocation program. The task force broke down its planning into two phases: the first for units that could be moved easily, and the second for major units with significant economic impact, but requiring close examination and ministerial direction.

The first phase proposed relocation of 24 federal units: 4,600 full-time and 5,500 part-time jobs were to be moved from the National Capital Region to 24 communities in all 10 provinces between 1977 and 1982. A substantial number of these jobs would be filled through local hiring in the receiving communities rather than through a transfer of personnel from Ottawa. Total capital spending was projected at $190 million. The jobs were to be distributed in this manner: 2,235 permanent and 630 temporary for the Atlantic, 1,091 permanent and 1,900 temporary for Quebec, 626 permanent and 1,680 temporary for areas of Ontario outside the National Capital Region, and 551 permanent and 1,870 temporary for the western provinces.[15]

The task force sought also to direct units to areas of slow growth within provinces. For instance, in New Brunswick Bathurst in the northeast and Shediac in the east were allocated federal units involving some 880 jobs. In Quebec, Matane in the Gaspé area was given a unit with 260 jobs. In Nova Scotia, Yarmouth, Sydney, and Antigonish were all designated as receiving communities. In Ontario, a large number of jobs were earmarked for Thunder Bay, North Bay, and Sudbury, in the north. DREE officials who were consulted strongly favoured communities in economically depressed regions. The relocation was planned over a long period so that employees occupying positions being moved outside Ottawa would have sufficient time to find other work in the event they chose not to move. Staggered moves would also minimize the economic impact on the city of Ottawa.

A number of unforeseen issues surfaced that required resolution to ensure the program's long-term success. For instance, employees were resisting the moves. It had been hoped that enough workers would move to ensure continuity of service. Some employees were reluctant to move to communities that did not provide schooling for their children in both official languages. In addition, new management information and control systems had to be set up to provide access by ministers and senior officials in Ottawa to the newly located units.[16]

While these issues and others were being resolved, decentralization was proceeding as planned. Units for Matane and Bathurst, for example, were operational on schedule. Others, like that for Shediac, were set up in temporary accommodation while construction for permanent quarters was undertaken.

The program became the subject of heated political debate. Opposition MPs charged that far too many units were being relocated in Liberal ridings and that the selection process was politically inspired. The government pointed out that some units went to cities with opposition MPs, including Charlottetown and St John's; the great majority of units went to Liberal-held ridings because economically disadvantaged regions tended to vote Liberal. A principal objective of the program, the government insisted, was to strengthen Ottawa's commitment to regional development.

When the Progressive Conservative party was elected to power in 1979, the new government immediately announced a review of the decentralization program. The review, insisted Treasury Board president Sinclair Stevens, was prompted by government restraint: 'It was necessary to review the decentralization programme in the context of the government's expressed priority to restrain government spending and to eliminate all but the most urgent discretionary expenditures.'[17] He announced the cancellation or deferral of thirteen projects that Jean Chrétien had already unveiled, and a resulting $76-million saving. Uncancelled projects were in advanced stages of development, with substantial monies already spent.

When the Liberal party returned to power after only nine months in opposition, the cabinet asked the new Treasury Board president, Donald Johnston, to make recommendations on the decentralization program. A few cancelled or deferred projects were reactivated, notably the Revenue Canada Taxation Data Centre to Jonquière, Quebec. Johnston declared that the federal government was committed to the principle of organizational decentralization, which would continue, but subject to new guidelines.[18] Johnston, like Stevens, considered the program expensive in times of government restraint. Actual costs had proved considerably higher than projected expenditures in most of the relocations. The program also continued to meet stiff opposition from affected public servants and from unions and local associations.

In light of these considerations, Johnston announced that future relocations would be negotiated between individual line departments and the Treasury Board secretariat. The task force on decentralization was disbanded on 31 March 1981. There is little evidence that work has continued on identifying new units for potential allocation or that the second phase of the original program, which had called for long-term planning, has progressed since then.

FEDERAL PROCUREMENT POLICY

The federal government purchases over $20 billion worth of goods and services annually. Although 'each province has now come to view a fair share ... as nothing less than a divine right,' western and Atlantic governments maintain that the bulk of federal purchasing goes to firms in Ontario and Quebec – and they are correct. About 80 per cent of all federal contracts are placed with firms in central Canada. The Department of Supply and Services, argues Allan Tupper, 'seems rather resigned to the continuing pre-eminence of centrally-located firms.' He suggests that 'Ottawa does not appear to have consistently employed purchasing policy as a regional development tool.'[19]

In instances where the federal government is, for all practical purposes, a firm's only client, Ottawa can exert some influence on where such firms would locate new industrial activities. An excellent case in point is Canada's munitions industry. The federal government is its principal client, and federal grants and special shared-cost agreements with selected firms have helped modernize and upgrade a number of production facilities. Despite this dependence on Ottawa, however, over 90 per cent of the 3,000 jobs in the industry are located in Ontario and Quebec.[20]

Defence-generated spending in the aircraft and parts industry primarily benefits Ontario and Quebec.[21] In the 1982–83 fiscal year it gave Ontario over 1,600 person-years of employment, and Quebec over 1,400 person-years. Nation-wide, it produced 3,952 person-years. Offset contracts associated with two major aircraft purchases, the CP-140 and CF-18, are to go by and large to Ontario and Quebec. Ontario will receive about two-thirds of the contracts, and Quebec about one-quarter. New Brunswick and Nova Scotia fare much better in defence spending in the ship-building and repair sector. Though the impact of defence spending is considerably less important in this sector than it is for the aircraft and parts industry, Nova Scotia and New Brunswick together account for nearly 30 per cent of the 1,000 or so person-years generated.

Direct defence-related activities are also attractive to the regions, often offering long-term employment. Though it is more difficult to obtain information on defence spending than on other government activities, available data permits us to draw some conclusions on the importance of defence expenditures and their regional effects.

As a proportion of total government spending, defence expenditures have declined steadily from 42 per cent in 1953 to about 8 per cent in recent years, and a major part (more than 20 per cent) of defence spending occurs outside Canada. Canada's total defence budget in 1982–83 amounted to $6.9 billion; $5.4 billion was spent in Canada, half of it in Ontario. Ontario received about 47 per cent of the 1982–83 defence budget, and accounted for close to 32 per cent of total national economic activity. Nova Scotia received 10.4 per cent of the defence budget while accounting for only 2.2 per cent of national economic activity. New Brunswick got 4.3 per cent of the defence budget, and 1.8 per cent of national economic activity. Provinces that did not fare well included Quebec, with only 18 per cent of the defence budget and 22.5 per cent of national economic activity; Alberta, with 6.4 per cent and 14.4 per cent; British Columbia, with 7.6 per cent and 14.1 per cent; Saskatchewan, with 1.3 per cent and 4.2 per cent; and Newfoundland, with 0.7 per cent and 1.3 per cent.

In direct defence-generated employment Ontario leads again, with over 30 per cent. Nova Scotia has about 15 per cent. Provinces that have less direct defence employment than their share of the national population include Saskatchewan, with less than 2 per cent, and Newfoundland, with about 1 per cent.

No information is available to break down the defence budget on a sub-provincial basis. However, the bulk of defence spending in Nova Scotia is concentrated in the Halifax region, and a large part of defence spending in New Brunswick centres on Fredericton. Defence officials report that the bulk of their spending in Ontario is in the south and east.

THE ROLE OF THE PROVINCES

Depending on how one defines 'region,' all of Canada's provinces may be said to be either highly involved in regional development or practically not at all. If one views an entire province as a region, provinces make substantial efforts to develop provincial or regional economies. In fact, such efforts have prompted students of Canadian federalism to write about province-building.

No provincial government is willing to let market forces and federal policy alone determine the economic health of its province. Particularly since the early 1960s, provincial governments have established agencies to stimulate economic development and to introduce a multitude of 'buy provincial' schemes and industrial assistance measures, in the form of grants and loan guarantees, feasibility studies, and the development of new industrial parks. DREE-supported subsidiary agreements have also contributed to provincial schemes to promote growth, supporting such initiatives as industrial commissions, provincially oriented tourism promotion, agricultural service centres, and pilot projects in forestry.

Competition among provincial governments for development is intense and at times bitter, as when Manitoba, Quebec, Ontario, and New Brunswick competed over a new helicopter manufacturing facility in 1983. (Competition among provincial DREE offices was at times as intense as that among the provincial governments themselves.) The efforts of provincial governments to promote development and the resulting interprovincial competition for new economic activities have taken numerous forms other than those we have already seen under the various GDAS and the subsidiary agreements. Often operating in secrecy, provincial departments of development, frequently supported by a provincial crown corporation, travel the country trying to snare investors. Frequently they arrive only a few days after a firm has been visited by a similar department or crown corporation representing another provincial government. Nova Scotia, with federal help, attracted Michelin and Clairtone. New Brunswick, in turn, enticed Malcolm Bricklin to set up an automobile manufacturing plant, and Newfoundland persuaded John Shehan to build an oil refinery at Come-by-Chance. Alex Campbell, former premier of Prince Edward Island, summed up the situation succinctly: 'We are four separate, jealous, and parochial provinces. We fight each other for subsidies.' Alan Tupper has shown that such intense competition is not found exclusively in the Atlantic provinces.[22]

Such provincial efforts have been only partly successful and have proved costly to provincial treasuries. The cost of maintaining a growing number of public servants to attract footloose economic projects to their provinces is considerable, not to mention subsidies and grants.

Provincial governments are more reluctant to promote growth at the sub-provincial level or in regions within provinces. By and large, they have attempted to remain geographically neutral in economic development, seeking to attract new economic activities to their provinces regardless of location.

There have been some exceptions. Ontario for a time attempted to spur development outside its highly developed southwestern region. The Ontario Development Corporation was given such a mandate in 1963. In 1967, an Equalization of Industrial Loans (EIOL) program was set up to provide forgivable loans to firms wishing to locate or expand in northern or eastern Ontario. This program was dropped in 1973 and replaced by a province-wide program of interest-free loans and deferred payment schemes. The program was somewhat more generous for northern and eastern Ontario than elsewhere in the province. The direction of Ontario's economic development was updated in 1979 and again in 1980. The latest revison saw the establishment of the Board of Industrial Leadership, which was asked to develop a broad economic framework for industrial expansion. The Ontario government had become concerned primarily with attracting new growth to the province and less with directing such growth east or west of Toronto or to the more peripheral northern region.[23]

Saskatchewan has also implemented measures to attract new economic activity to areas of slow growth. The government of Allan Blakeney established the Department of Northern Saskatchewan to oversee all programs in the north and to develop economic initiatives for the region.

On the whole, however, provincial governments have not defined their economic development efforts within a regional context. Their bias in this respect is perhaps more sectoral than is Ottawa's, and certainly they are as concerned, if not more so, with the overall health of their provincial economies as Ottawa is with the national economy.

Provincial governments by and large have made comprehensive efforts at regional development at the sub-provincial level only after DREE had promoted the idea and had agreed to fund much of the cost. In fact, it is widely believed in Ottawa that the only area where DREE took the lead in directing GDA spending was in funds for special 'regional' agreements which were a package of projects designed to spur development in a given region. There are a number of such examples. The government of New Brunswick agreed to a $90-million economic development plan for the northeast only after DREE had agreed to pay 80 per cent of the cost.[24] The same can be said in the case of Newfoundland about a development package for coastal Labrador. The federal government, through DREE, has always led development on Cape Breton Island, in Nova Scotia. DREE was instrumental, through GDA funding, in getting Ontario's government to come up with plans for the northern communities of Sudbury and North Bay, among others. In western Canada, DREE negotiated a series of subsidiary agreements to direct development to the northlands. DREE also signed a nutritive processing agreement with Alberta that provided funding to firms wishing to establish outside the major urban areas.

In some instances, DREE signed agreements only after agreeing to consider funding sectoral-type subsidiary agreements with the provincial governments. Most governments favoured a sectoral approach, rather than a spatial or regional one, to economic development under the various GDAS.

When DREE was not involved, provincial governments tended to ignore location. A good case in point is the nuclear power plant in New Brunswick. Recognizing that a decision on the plant's location was a provincial responsibility, DREE nonetheless urged that a northern site be selected. DREE saw it as an opportunity to bring jobs to this underdeveloped area – and said so. The provincial government, however, decided that a southern site made good business sense and that it would be in 'the general provincial interest.'[25] Many see sub-provincial regional development as a drag on provincial economies, much as many argue that regional development constitutes a drag on the national economy.

THE ROLE OF THE PRIVATE SECTOR

Government intervention in the economy, all the more pervasive in Canada because of two levels of government, has spawned a new dimension regarding decisions as to plant location. Market forces no longer dictate a firm's response to emerging opportunities and its decision on where to locate new or expanded production facilities. With their shareholders' best interests in mind, firms will search out government programs to see if public funds are available to assist in promoting their development strategy. *Canadian Business* magazine reports 'some firms are in the happy position of being able to employ staff or consultants whose sole function is to sniff out all the juicy morsels the politicians and policymakers throw into the public trough.'[26]

This is not to suggest that the private sector applauds all government programs. There is strong evidence that it would like much less government intervention in the economy, on the one hand, and much more consultation between government and industry, on the other. These two themes emerged constantly, for example, in the public hearings sponsored by Canada's Royal Commission on the Economic Union and Development Prospects for Canada.[27]

The private sector's concern over government involvement in the economy may explain in part why most of Ottawa's economic development programs are passive. 'While clearly striving to influence the location of industry, federal incentives are firmly based on the view that corporate decision must ultimately prevail and that the state must limit itself to offering lures to businessmen.'[28] The state has never opted for a 'hands on' approach that 'directs' firms to a given location – 'or else.' Ottawa could, for example, 'black list' a firm and not permit any federal departments or agencies to award contracts to it, or refuse to grant a preferential duty, if the firm refuses to locate in a given community.

Thus, by and large, firms will take advantage of government grants and subsidies to locate in a given region. Occasionally, a major Canadian bank, such as the Bank of Montreal, will publish articles in its monthly review, as it did in 1981, on trends in regional development.[29] Most such articles, however, are descriptive analyses of how well various regions are doing, and few offer solutions.

The lure of government grants and the consequent 'shopping around' by the private sector can lead to 'bidding' wars between governments. This bidding for industry with public funds can in turn result in 'windfalls' for corporations. Governments have no assurance that a firm will not request assistance for a particular location, even after a corporate decision has already been taken to locate there. How is a government to know, for example, if McCain's located a number of production facilities in northwestern New Brunswick because of DREE grants or because the McCain family is from the area? More important, how is a government to know whether McCain's would not have located its plants in the area without DREE grants?

Grants to industry are highly visible and at times give rise to heated public debate over their value. Less visible, but often more lucrative for firms, are tax credits, which do not involve a direct transfer of money. They do represent, however, government revenue forgone. Canada's tax system is complex, and it is difficult to undertake a detailed review from the perspective of regional economic development.

Nonetheless, it is possible to make some observations. A 1979 report from the Department of Finance reveals tax expenditures totalled over $21.5 billion in 1976 and $30 billion in 1979. This compares with a total federal expenditure budget of $50.0 billion for 1979.[30] If one breaks down the total tax expenditure account by functional categories, one discovers that Health and Welfare is the biggest spender. In 1976, tax expenditures for this category amounted to close to $10 billion. This was made up of items involving income maintenance and housing, such as the tax advantage on savings in registered pension plans and retirement savings plans and the non-taxation of capital gains on principal residence.

The next most valuable category was economic development and support. The largest expenditure item there is lower income tax on small businesses. Other important items included the two-year write-off on manufacturing and processing assets and a compository item consisting of the fast write-off for Canadian exploration expense and for development expenses and the 33 1/3 per cent earned depletion allowance. Total tax expenditure in this category for 1976 amounts to close to $4 billion.

It is too early to assess properly the investment tax credit program, designed to attract firms to slow-growth areas. DREE officials monitoring the program reported only that the private sector showed interest in it, especially when the program was first announced. However, tax expenditures under the program have been marginal, when compared to other corporate tax expenditures.

Sufficient information is also available to break down tax expenditures on a province-by-province basis. Ontario, Quebec, Alberta, and British Columbia earn the lion's share of tax expenditures – in 1976, close to 90 per cent of all corporate tax expenditures. On a per capita basis, Alberta leads all provinces in corporate tax expenditures, while the four Atlantic provinces trail badly. In fact, corporations declaring taxable income in Yukon and the Northwest Territories received more tax expenditures than did any one of the four Atlantic provinces. Lack of information prevents assessment of federal tax expenditures at the sub-provincial level.

All in all, though tax expenditures constitute over 50 per cent of the total federal expenditure budget, they play only a negligible role in Ottawa's fostering of regional development. One federal finance official speculated that tax expenditures with a specific regional development purpose never amount to more than 2 per cent of the total federal tax expenditure budget.

PART III AN ASSESSMENT

9

An assessment

A substantial amount of public money has been spent in Canada over the last twenty-five years in the name of regional economic development. DREE expenditures alone amounted to over $7 billion during this period; under the equalization program, over $30 billion was spent. Every province except Ontario has at one time or another received equalization payments. And even Ontario has benefited of late from regional development programs, notably under the ILAP initiatives.

Federal crown corporations, such as DEVCO, have been set up solely to promote economic adjustment and development in a specific community or region. Special industrial and labour adjustment programs (with funding of about $150 million) have been established with a similar mandate. Even national programs, such as Unemployment Insurance, have been adjusted so that they can be more generous to slow-growth regions. Special tax credits have been introduced exclusively for slow-growth regions, about the total costs of which we know virtually nothing. Ottawa also embarked on a major program to relocate public service units from the National Capital Region to slow-growth areas.

A number of questions come immediately to mind. What effect have these expenditures had on slow-growth regions? What have we learned from the various initiatives? And what are the implications of the recent reorientation of federal regional development policy and programs? Before turning to these questions, it is important to look again at the question of regional disparities.

REGIONAL DISPARITIES REVISITED

There does not exist a widely accepted single indicator of regional disparity. The Economic Council of Canada has acknowledged this limitation, while intimating that 'a wide variety of facts suggest that individual well-being does differ from one region to another.'[1] Two indicators, income per capita and unemployment rates, have been widely employed to measure regional disparity in Canada. Data under these two headings have been collected for some time on a regional basis, and they do provide a useful starting point.

There was some progress in reducing regional disparities in income per capita between 1961 and 1981, although the gap started to widen again in the late 1970s. The effects from personal income, transfers from governments (personal income), income received by family earners (average family income), and taxation of personal income (average family disposable income) serve progressively to reduce regional income inequalities. The largest reduction in income disparity occurred in average family disposable income – where income disparities appear smallest – while the least reduction was with respect to earned income per capita – where they are widest. The lowest-income provinces have somewhat caught up with the rest of the nation, in spite of real gains in national income per capita.

In 1961, the four Atlantic provinces, Quebec, Manitoba, and Saskatchewan received less than the national average income, while Ontario, British Columbia, and Alberta were above average. In 1981, Alberta and British Columbia were leading, followed by Ontario. Saskatchewan has been moving very close to the national average, followed by Quebec and Manitoba. The Atlantic provinces still rank last. Newfoundland and Prince Edward Island remain the lowest-income provinces, despite showing the best performance in all income measures in the Atlantic region. New Brunswick is moving closer to Nova Scotia, which has the highest incomes in the Atlantic region, while the latter has generally maintained its income position relative to the national average.

Some have suggested that earned income per capita provides a better measure of a region's economic performance than per capita income. Earned income per capita excludes relative gains from interregional transfer payments. According to this measurement, regional disparities are more pronounced, and disparity has narrowed only slightly from 1961 to 1981, though Prince Edward Island and Saskatchewan made some gains (see Table 1).

Greater progress was made in personal income per capita, as the Atlantic provinces, except Nova Scotia, moved rapidly toward the national average. The fastest advances were made by Saskatchewan, followed by Prince Edward Island and Newfoundland; Ontario showed least growth. The disparity in personal income per capita lessened from a ratio (highest to lowest) of 2.03 in 1961 to 1.69 in 1981 (see Table 2).

The reduction of differences in income per capita has been more pronounced in average family income and average family disposable income. Gains have been particularly significant among the two lowest-income provinces – Newfoundland and Prince Edward Island. The average family in Newfoundland earned, after income tax, about 85 per cent of the national figure in 1981, compared to 75 per cent in 1971. For both family income indicators, Quebec has retreated the most, followed by Ontario.

TABLE 1

Earned income per capita, by province and territories, selected years 1961–81: relationship to national average (Canada = 100)

	1961	1966	1971	1976	1981
Newfoundland	53.2	52.5	54.8	56.1	53.4
Prince Edward Island	53.5	53.6	57.0	60.2	59.0
Nova Scotia	75.0	71.5	74.2	74.2	73.4
New Brunswick	64.1	65.1	68.1	69.0	64.9
Quebec	89.5	89.2	87.8	90.4	89.9
Ontario	121.1	118.3	119.2	112.5	110.6
Manitoba	93.5	91.0	93.7	93.9	92.9
Saskatchewan	67.2	92.3	78.7	99.5	98.9
Alberta	100.3	99.0	98.6	105.0	114.4
British Columbia	113.7	111.0	109.5	109.5	109.7
Yukon and Northwest Territories	103.1	85.1	91.9	94.7	105.3
Disparity gap (ratio of highest to lowest)	2.27	2.25	2.17	2.00	2.14
Canada (1961 = $1,494 = 100; current dollars)	100	140.8	203.2	396.6	679.2

SOURCE: Statistics Canada, *Provincial Economic Accounts*, Catalogue 13-213 Annual

TABLE 2

Personal income per capita, by province and territories, selected years 1961–81: relationship to national average (Canada = 100)

	1961	1966	1971	1976	1981
Newfoundland	58.2	59.9	63.8	68.1	64.9
Prince Edward Island	58.8	60.1	63.7	68.2	67.4
Nova Scotia	77.8	74.8	77.5	78.4	77.9
New Brunswick	68.0	68.9	72.3	75.3	71.3
Quebec	90.1	89.2	88.7	93.2	93.3
Ontario	118.4	116.4	117.0	109.6	107.7
Manitoba	94.3	91.9	94.1	93.1	93.0
Saskatchewan	71.0	93.1	80.3	98.8	99.5
Alberta	100.0	100.1	99.0	102.4	110.2
British Columbia	114.9	111.6	109.0	108.8	101.7
Yukon and Northwest Territories	96.6	80.8	86.8	91.4	101.7
Disparity gap (ratio of highest to lowest)	2.03	1.94	1.83	1.60	1.69
Canada (1961 = $1,494 = 100; current dollars)	100	139.8	208.0	412.1	704.6

SOURCE: Statistics Canada, *National Income and Expenditure Accounts*, Catalogue 13-201

Greater disparities are observed in gross domestic product (GDP) per capita in current dollars. Table 3 shows that during the period 1961–81 Ontario moved from first place to fourth, behind Alberta, British Columbia, and even Saskatchewan. Saskatchewan achieved the fastest growth rate in GDP per capita among all the provinces, repeating its performance observed in income. However, Saskatchewan also displayed the most erratic performance, because of its narrow economic base. In 1981, New Brunswick had supplanted Nova Scotia as the strongest Atlantic province in GDP per capita. Quebec and Manitoba have been moving further below the average, though not as rapidly as Ontario, which has been slowly converging toward the national average since 1961.

In unemployment, regional disparities are as persistent as in income per capita, and they favour the same regions. As the study by the Economic Council of Canada, *Living Together*, pointed out, there is one exception. British Columbia has had higher unemployment than the three prairie provinces over the past thirty years, even though it traditionally leads the same three provinces in per capita income.[2]

The Atlantic provinces, followed by Quebec, have consistently led the nation in unemployment levels, as Table 4 indicates. The table also reveals that disparities in unemployment have converged, though they are larger than a straightforward comparison of conventional statistics would indicate. The Economic Council of Canada found that inclusion of discouraged workers (those who want to work, but have given up looking for employment) made unemployment in Newfoundland 50 per cent higher in 1978 than the official rate showed.[3]

SUB-REGIONAL DISPARITIES

Sub-regional differences in economic well-being in Canada are substantial. Income disparities within the Atlantic region, for example, are greater than those between that area and other parts of Canada. Some counties in Nova Scotia have an average per capita income less than 70 per cent of the provincial average, while others have an average of 110 per cent. The same is true also in Newfoundland, New Brunswick, and Prince Edward Island, where some counties also have an average per capita income of less than 70 per cent of the provincial average.

Even the wealthiest regions of Canada have areas that do not share in the overall economic prosperity. Ontario, for example, has areas with an average per capita income below the national average, below the Quebec average, and below some areas of Atlantic Canada. Ontario's low-income areas are in Manitoulin, with its large native population, and Haliburton, with one of the oldest age profiles in Canada.

Manitoba and Saskatchewan are provinces of extremes. There, census divisions with a large native population constitute some of the poorest regions in Canada in

TABLE 3
Provincial gross domestic product at market prices, per person, by province and territories, selected years 1961–81: relationship to national average (Canada = 100)

	1961	1966	1971	1976	1981
Newfoundland	50.0	52.1	56.2	53.6	52.0
Prince Edward Island	49.4	48.4	52.3	52.2	50.5
Nova Scotia	65.3	63.0	67.9	66.0	61.3
New Brunswick	60.5	61.3	63.7	63.8	63.1
Quebec	91.1	89.9	88.9	88.1	86.0
Ontario	119.9	117.4	117.3	109.4	106.5
Manitoba	90.4	87.1	90.7	91.4	88.1
Saskatchewan	77.3	99.6	86.9	101.2	108.8
Alberta	108.8	109.3	110.8	137.1	146.0
British Columbia	111.1	109.2	106.8	108.6	109.4
Yukon and Northwest Territories	99.9	105.8	97.7	88.9	112.1
Disparity gap (ratio of highest to lowest)	2.42	2.42	2.24	2.62	2.89
Canada (1961 = $1,494 = 100; current dollars)	100	142.2	200.1	385.3	642.5

SOURCE: Statistics Canada, *Provincial Economic Accounts*, Catalogue 13-213 Annual

TABLE 4
Provincial unemployment rate, selected years 1961–81: relationship to national average (Canada = 100)

	1961	1966	1971	1976	1981
Newfoundland	275	171	135	189	186
Prince Edward Island	–	–	–	135	150
Nova Scotia	114	138	113	134	134
New Brunswick	148	156	98	155	154
Quebec	130	121	118	123	137
Ontario	77	76	87	87	87
Manitoba	70	82	92	66	79
Saskatchewan	58	44	56	55	61
Alberta	66	74	92	56	50
British Columbia	120	135	116	121	88
Disparity gap (ratio of highest to lowest)	4.74	3.88	2.41	3.43	3.72
Canada (1961 = $1,494 = 100; current dollars)	100	47.8	87.3	100	107

SOURCE: Statistics Canada, *The Labour Force*, Catalogue 71-001 Monthly

terms of per capita income. Yet census divisions that include Regina, Saskatoon, and Brandon have very high per capita income, when compared with the national level. Some areas in the Atlantic provinces, notably the counties in which Moncton, Saint John, Fredericton, and Halifax are found, have incomes higher than the Canadian average. However, counties along the north coast in Newfoundland and in northern New Brunswick have particularly low incomes. Kent County in New Brunwick, for example, has the fourth-lowest income in all of Canada.

Similar differences in economic well-being exist at the sub-regional level when unemployment rates are the indicator. Work is much scarcer in northern New Brunswick, northern Newfoundland, and eastern Nova Scotia than in central or southern New Brunswick, St John's, or Halifax County. Again, there are large areas in the wealthy regions of Ontario and western Canada that offer fewer employment opportunities than some areas in less developed provinces. A graphic illustration of sub-regional disparities is presented in Figure 1, which illustrates the relative positions of sub-regions in Ontario and the four Atlantic provinces, compared to their provincial averages.

INDICATORS OF DISPARITIES IN REGIONAL GROWTH

Levels of income and employment do not tell the whole story about the economic health of Canada's regions. Other indicators also measure economic strength, and they too reveal significant differences among regions.

Population has grown at different rates in various regions. The past twenty years have witnessed a marked turn-about in migratory movements among provinces. In the 1960s, only Ontario, British Columbia, and Alberta enjoyed an inflow of population; in the 1970s they were joined by the Atlantic provinces and Saskatchewan. This latter development represented a departure from Canada's usual migratory pattern: there was an exodus from the central provinces and a net inflow to the Maritime provinces and also to Alberta and British Columbia. The extent of the reversal was quite dramatic for the Maritimes which in the 1960s lost about 118,000 people but in the 1970s gained 37,000. By 1981, however, the Atlantic provinces were again experiencing a net loss in population.

Table 5 indicates that between 1961 and 1981 only three provinces – Alberta, British Columbia, and Ontario – showed an increase in their population gained from inter-provincial population movements. However, Ontario's share started to decline in 1975. the largest decline in overall population share occurred in Saskatchewan, despite its having one of the highest rates of natural population increase of any province.

Migration patterns are much more pronounced at the sub-provincial level. It is unusual for a province to change its share of Canada's population by more than 1 per cent in a ten-year period; the same is not true of census divisions. For example,

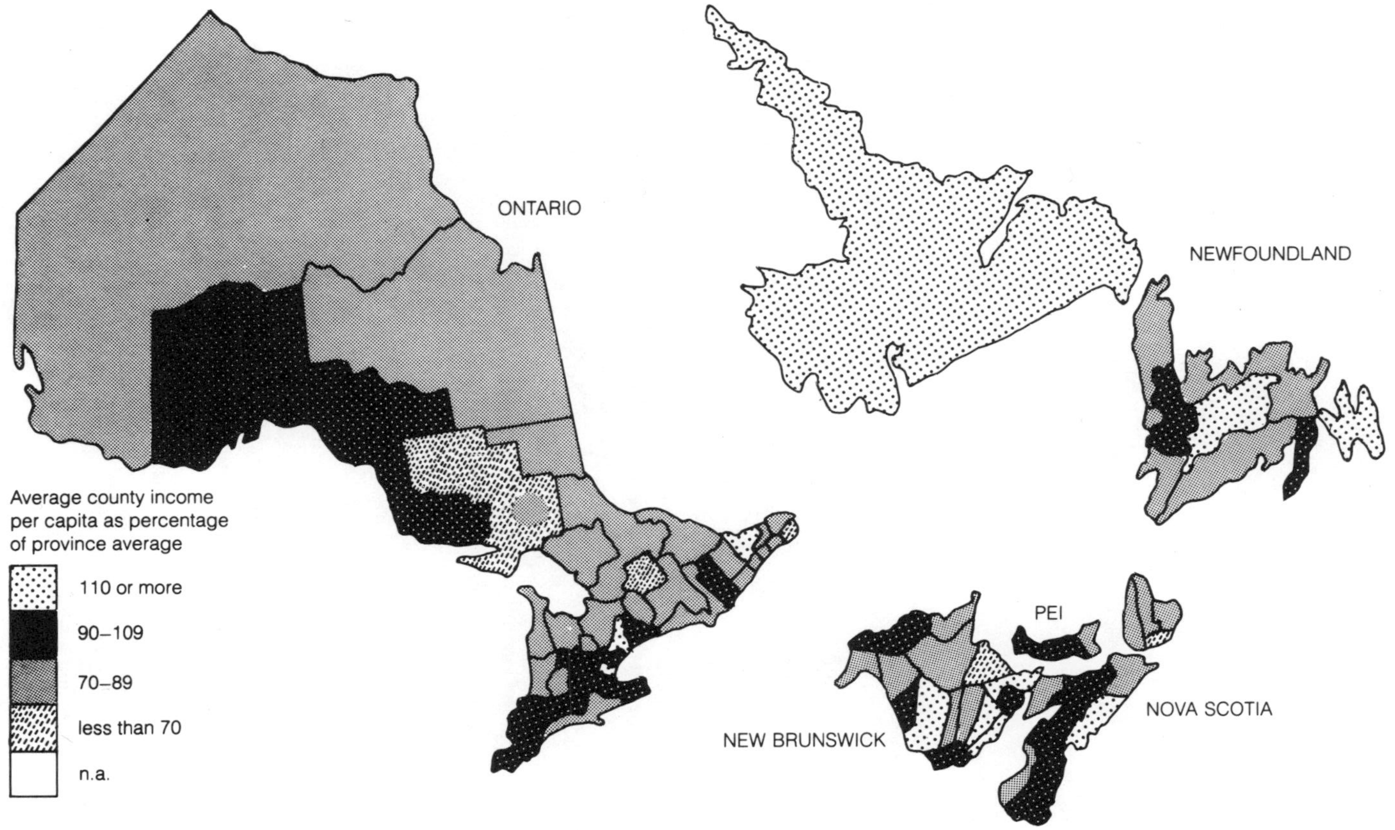

FIGURE 1 Sub-regional income distribution, 1978 (Atlantic provinces and Ontario)

Average county income
per capita as percentage
of province average

110 or more

90—109

70—89

less than 70

n.a.

ONTARIO

NEW BRUNSWICK

PEI

NOVA SCOTIA

NEWFOUNDLAND

TABLE 5
Net interprovincial migration, by province and territory, selected years 1961–81 (in thousands)

	1961–66	1966–71	1971–76	1976–81
Newfoundland	−15.2	−19.3	−1.8	−18.9
Prince Edward Island	−2.9	−2.7	3.7	−0.8
Nova Scotia	−27.1	−16.3	11.3	−7.1
New Brunswick	−25.6	−19.5	16.8	−10.3
Quebec	−19.8	−122.7	−77.6	−156.4
Ontario	85.3	150.7	−38.5	−57.8
Manitoba	−23.4	−40.6	−26.8	−42.2
Saskatchewan	−42.0	−81.3	−40.7	−9.7
Alberta	−1.9	32.0	58.5	186.3
British Columbia	77.7	114.9	92.2	122.6
Yukon	−1.3	1.1	0.9	−0.9
Northwest Territories	−1.9	2.0	1.9	−4.4

SOURCE: Statistics Canada, *International and Interprovincial Migration in Canada*, Catalogue 91-208 Annual

between 1971 and 1976, the average annual population growth ranged from −2.7 per cent in Saskatchewan's Assiniboia area to 8.65 per cent in British Columbia's Central Fraser Valley.

During the 1970s and early 1980s all provinces except Newfoundland, Prince Edward Island, and Saskatchewan had regions of rapid growth and regions of strong decline. In the Maritime provinces, the arc from Halifax through Moncton to Saint John has experienced strong growth.[4] Meanwhile, Cape Breton, including Sydney and the western extremity of Nova Scotia, witnessed a sharp decline. In Quebec, most of the Gaspé peninsula and the Eastern Townships, the North Shore, and the west saw decline or growth less rapid than the median for Canada's census divisions. Growth has been concentrated around the three counties in the Hull area and the suburban counties and satellite cities around Montreal.

In Ontario, the contrast between the rapidly growing south and the declining north stands out clearly. Similarly, growth in Manitoba has been centred around Winnipeg and Brandon. In Saskatchewan, the census divisions containing Regina and Saskatoon registered growth over a ten-year period. In Alberta, growth rates were generally higher, with decline restricted to the two census divisions east of Drumheller. British Columbia saw 18 of its 29 census divisions register particularly substantial growth; the only census divisions declining were in the central coast region.[5]

Another indicator of economic health is the ratio of transfer payments to total income. A province, for example, in which residents derived 15 per cent of their income from government transfer payments has less favourable economic circumstances and a weaker economic structure than one in which such payments

TABLE 6

Personal transfers from governments as a percentage of personal income, by province and territory, selected years 1961–81

	1961	1966	1971	1976	1981
Canada	9.0	8.1	11.1	12.5	12.3
Newfoundland	16.3	19.1	23.3	27.7	27.7
Prince Edward Island	17.6	17.8	20.1	22.4	23.0
Nova Scotia	12.0	12.1	14.8	17.0	17.3
New Brunswick	14.1	12.9	16.0	19.6	20.1
Quebec	9.7	8.2	11.9	15.1	15.5
Ontario	7.0	6.7	9.6	10.2	10.0
Manitoba	9.8	9.0	11.4	11.7	12.5
Saskatchewan	13.6	8.8	12.8	12.0	12.9
Alberta	8.8	9.1	11.4	10.3	9.1
British Columbia	10.0	8.7	10.8	12.0	11.2
Yukon and Northwest Territories	3.3	3.7	6.3	9.2	9.3

SOURCE: Statistics Canada, *Provincial Economic Accounts, System of National Accounts*, Catalogue 13-213 Annual

comprised only 5 per cent of income. Table 6 reveals substantial differences at the provincial level in the importance of government transfer payments as a source of income. For example, in 1976, the percentage of total income derived from unemployment/employment benefits was nine times as high in Newfoundland as in Alberta. In 1981, the average Newfoundlander received 27.7 per cent of his or her personal income in the form of government transfers – or 2.2 times the national average – compared to 16.3 per cent, or 1.8 times the national average, in 1961.

Heavy reliance on transfer payments also probably indicates widespread poverty.[6] The average after-tax income of families and unattached individuals whose major source of income is transfer payments is only approximately one-third of the Canadian average.

Some provincial governments may have grown dependent on federal transfer payments. Figure 2 illustrates the importance of federal transfers to some province,[7] particularly the four Atlantic provinces. In Prince Edward Island, for example, federal transfers represented 56 per cent of provincial revenues for 1980–81. Compare this with only 12 per cent in Alberta. Of course, federal transfers have given provincial governments and individuals in slow-growth regions money to spend. This capacity has served to narrow regional disparities on a number of fronts, as we shall see.

A CAPACITY TO SPEND: ITS IMPLICATIONS

Federal transfer payments to slow-growth regions have been substantial over the

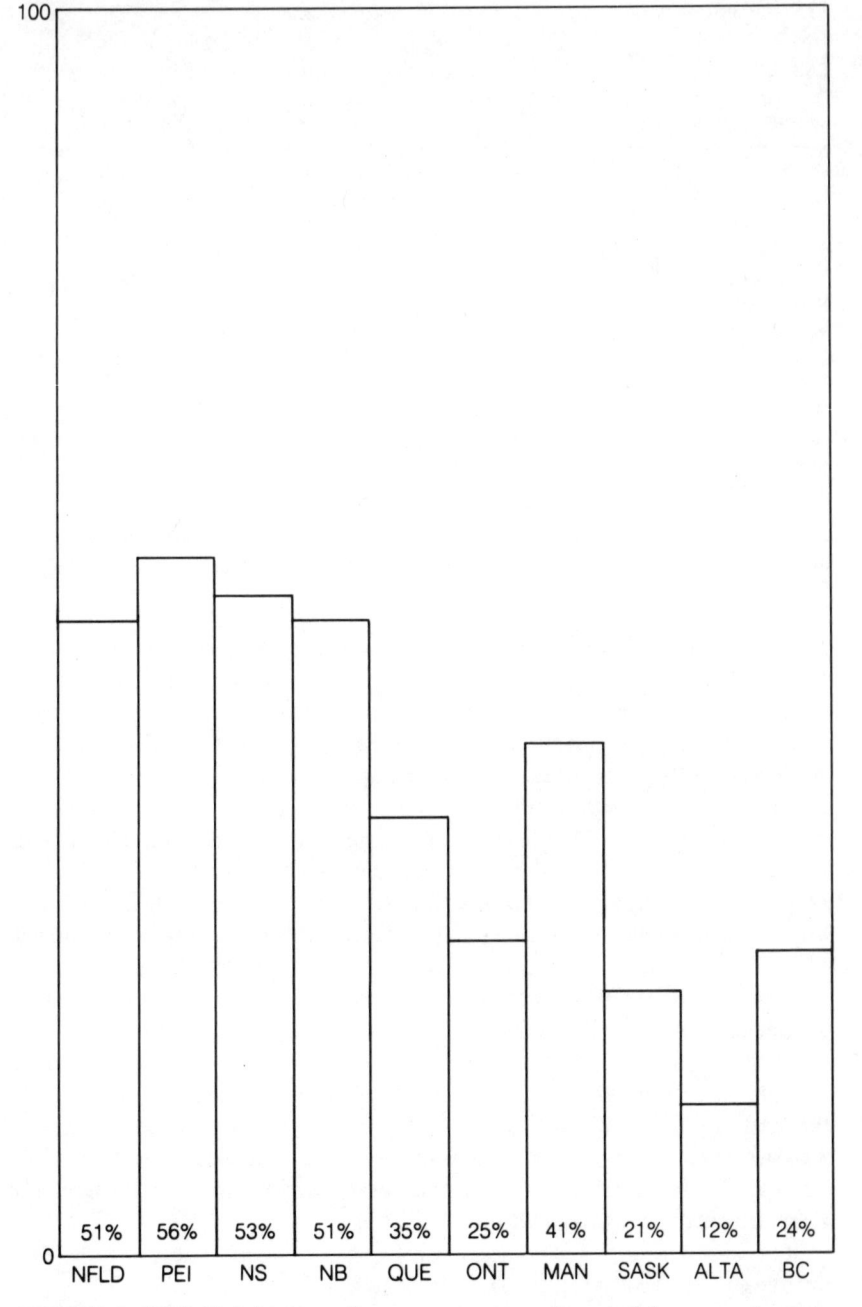

FIGURE 2 1980–81 federal transfers as a percentage of provincial revenues (source: Statistics Canada, *Provincial Economic Accounts*, Catalogue 13-213)

past twenty years. Net regional incidence of federal expenditures (expenditures in a region less federal revenues accruing in the region) jumped in the four Atlantic provinces and Quebec between 1961 and 1981. Federal expenditures, including investments in public infrastructure, transfer payments, and the provision of government services, are all included in this calculation. The jump in net federal regional expenditures in constant 1971 dollars for the four Atlantic provinces amounted to close to $400 per capita. This compares with a decrease for three of the four western provinces and little change for Ontario.[8]

Between 1975 and 1979, the four Atlantic provinces saw a substantial increase in UI benefits paid relative to contributions made. In Prince Edward Island and Nova Scotia, the increase was nearly 100 per cent. Between 1961 and 1981, federal transfers to persons, as a percentage of total personal income, went up by 9 percentage points in the Atlantic provinces, and 3 points in Ontario.

Federal transfers to provincial governments and to individuals enabled the 'have-not' regions to close the gap with the other regions on a number of points. By 1979–80, the total fiscal capacity of eight provinces fell within a relatively narrow range, 85–99 per cent of the national average. This brought the four Atlantic provinces much closer to the national average of provincial expenditures per capita in 1979 than they were in 1962.

Increased provincial expenditures can indicate better public services, as has probably occurred in the 'have-not' regions. Between 1962 and 1979 the Atlantic provinces moved considerably closer to the national average in health and education expenditures. The disparity in provincial education expenditure per capita has narrowed considerably, with Newfoundland, for example, now within 7 percentage points of the national average. In health, Newfoundland moved from 46 per cent of the national average to 81 per cent in the same period. In provincial hospital bed capacity per capita, the most disparate province was within 15 percentage points of the national average in 1981, compared with 26 percentage points in 1961.

Federal transfer payments have not only increased the capacity of provincial governments to provide services to their residents but have also enabled individual Canadians in 'have-not' regions to acquire basic household necessities. Regional disparities in this respect, extremely wide twenty years ago, are now virtually non-existent. For example, Newfoundland moved from 38.3 per cent in 1961 to 97.1 per cent of the national average for the indicator 'households with refrigerator.' For 'households with telephone,' Prince Edward Island moved from 64 per cent in 1961 to 94 per cent in 1981. Ontario, meanwhile, declined from 109 in 1961 to 100.6 in 1981. For 'households with exclusive use of installed bath facilities,' New Brunswick moved from 78.8 per cent in 1961 to 99.6 per cent of the national average in 1981; Ontario went from 112.8 per cent to 100.6 per cent.

Clearly, then, federal transfer payments have contributed to the virtual elimination of regional disparities in basic household necessities. They have helped greatly to narrow the regional gap in family income and in individual spending power. In its study *Living Together*, the Economic Council of Canada estimated the effect on income disparities of federal transfers by comparing the actual distribution of transfers (1974–75) with a hypothetical even distribution. Income disparities would have been greater, the study revealed, had the federal government transferred money in proportion to population only. The reduction was greatest for the Atlantic region, in the order of 20 per cent of the income gap.[9]

DISPARITIES IN ECONOMIC GROWTH

Federal transfer payments have lessened regional disparities in public services and individual purchasing power. They have not, however, reduced regional disparities in employment opportunities, in earned income per capita, and in the economic weight of each region, as measured by gross provincial product. But they were not intended to do this.

Other regional development measures were designed to bring employment to slow-growth regions. The most important in recent years have been DREE. However, a comprehensive evaluation of its success is impossible. DREE expenditures have not been large enough for us to be able to assess their impact in relation to other economic forces, such as interest rates, the value of the Canadian dollar, and even other federal expenditures, such as transfer payments to provincial governments and individuals.

There is another major stumbling block in evaluating DREE efforts. DREE was not very clear about its objectives and kept changing its policy framework. At one point, the growth-pole concept held sway. Then DREE sought to tie its efforts to a development opportunities concept. This in turn was followed by an attempt to assess initiatives in terms of their relevance to a region's natural economic strength. Toward the end, senior DREE officials frequently spoke about local or community development concepts. Even when a particular theory was in vogue, it did not prevent the department from sponsoring a variety of initiatives that did not readily fit in with that theory. The one possible exception was in the early days, when Jean Marchand and Tom Kent held firm to the growth-pole concept and by and large resisted initiatives that did not correspond with that approach. But even then there were exceptions, as evidenced by DREE's involvement in highways construction outside the designated growth-pole areas.

With the introduction of the General Development Agreements (GDAS), however, came an all-embracing and unexceptionable theoretical framework, essentially non-selective and hardly a guide for action. The department had, in the words of a DREE economist, 'ten policies – one for each province.' Viewed from the regions, DREE funds represented a 'B' budget fund for provincial governments, from which they would seek funding for new economic development. Provincial governments came forward with proposals, and, if these proved unacceptable, they simply came back with a new set. The result is that DREE funded a variety of projects, not always mutually supportive.

The goals and objectives of the GDAs were extremely broad and of little benefit even as a checklist against which to assess proposed projects. New Brunswick's GDA did not, for example, prevent DREE from providing assistance for the construction of a marina for local pleasure-boat owners, for highway construction, and for the establishment of a community college. Such a variety of theoretical and policy frameworks makes it impossible to evaluate the effect of DREE expenditures. Even evaluating the impact of individual GDAs is very difficult, if at all possible.

The frequent changes of policy and organizational direction posed yet another difficulty. Before a thorough assessment of one approach could be initiated, a new one would take its place. Insufficient time had elapsed to determine the effect of a particular program on a given sector. With a new policy announced, officials had little interest in assessing a program that was now history.

New policies were introduced for a number of reasons, not simply because existing ones were no longer effective. In fact, federal-provincial competition appears to have been largely responsible for at least two of the three major policy reviews. In 1973, the federal government sought to establish closer links with provincial governments by introducing the GDAs. By 1981, Ottawa concluded that it was not getting the credit to which it was entitled and decided to scrap these agreements. Since the principal motive behind the two last policy reviews was federal-provincial tension, it may well be more appropriate to assess them from this perspective rather than from one of regional development. Certainly, the 1973 policy review placed the provinces in a favoured position in shaping new regional development initiatives. The 1982 review appears to have made it much more difficult for provinces to do so, with the federal government now having the option of delivering certain projects directly.

Notwithstanding the above, there have been attempts to evaluate the effect of GDA-sponsored initiatives. The conclusions of some of these were presented in earlier chapters. The evaluations were incomplete, and almost all concluded that more time was required. The evaluations were carried out either by federal-provincial committees of officials or by outside consultants.

One regional development program evaluated by numerous government officials, outside consultants, and outside critics was the Regional Development Industrial Incentives Act (RDIA). The fact that it was a continuing, self-contained program, supporting easily identifiable projects, probably explains why it was so often evaluated. It took up only 20 per cent of DREE's budget, compared with about 80 per cent for the GDAs. Evaluations led to a variety of conclusions, favourable and unfavourable.

The Economic Council of Canada found that the incrementality of projects under RDIA was between 25 and 59 per cent and that of jobs between 35 and 68 per cent. An investment project is considered incremental if the firm, without assistance, would not have undertaken the project or would have undertaken it outside the designated region. The lower rates, 25 and 35 per cent, represent, according to the Council, a very conservative estimate of DREE's success. On the whole, the Council found the program beneficial, with a benefit-to-costs ratio of between 3 and 19 to 1. The Council concluded: 'The subsidies ... seem successful enough to be a paying proposition. The value of the jobs created appears to outweigh the inefficiency involved in locating production inappropriately.'[10]

David Springate found that regional incentives grants had relatively little influence on the investment decisions of large firms. He concluded that the grants produced few changes in timing, size, or technology of the project. Carleton Dudley suggested that the grants were not sufficiently generous to offset the added operating cost of locating in slow-growth regions. He estimated the potential of grants for reducing the operating cost of a firm to be between 1 and 5 per cent of sales, substantially less than the added cost of operating in designated regions, estimated to be between 5 and 20 per cent.[11]

Some studies of RDIA have attempted to identify various characteristics associated with the type and degree of incrementality. According to LeGoffe and Rosenfield, incrementality tended to be higher when the projects involved small, new products; equipment had been modernized; an element of high risk and high profitability existed; and foreign competition was high. Incrementality tended to be lower for larger projects undertaken by firms that had experience with similar projects; projects that were necessary for the normal continuation of a firm's operations; and projects showing a high profit/investment ratio.[12]

However, incrementality is a controversial issue. The lack of consensus about it may well stem from the difficulty of measuring it reliably. Dan Usher explained the difficulty: 'Normally one is taxed or subsidized for doing something regardless of whether one would do it or not in the absence of the tax or subsidy. It is as though the family allowances were restricted to children who would not have been conceived, in its absence, or Crow's Nest Pass rates restricted to grain that would not have been grown if freight rates were higher.[13]

Others have suggested that the RDIA program had a built-in capital bias that ran counter to its objective of job creation. An RDIA grant, it was pointed out, lowered the cost of capital by a greater percentage than it lowered the costs of labour. Firms were encouraged, in other words, to emphasize new plants and equipment rather than new jobs. Robert Woodward concluded: 'DREE fails to achieve the greatest number of new jobs, and incurs a higher cost per new job created, by continuing with the subsidies which are inconsistent with their goals.[14]

Several important considerations have been largely overlooked in evaluations of the regional incentives program. The first DREE minister, Jean Marchand, warned that regional development programs, such as special-areas and regional incentives, must have a limited geographical application or their value would be severely diluted. By the time that DREE was disbanded, the regional incentives program had been extended to include all four Atlantic provinces; all of Quebec; northern Ontario south to and including Parry Sound, Nipissing, Renfrew, and Pembroke; all of Manitoba and Saskatchewan; northern Alberta; northern British Columbia; and the territories. All in all, the regional incentives program covered 93 per cent of Canada's land mass and over 50 per cent of the population.

Clearer objectives would have focused the program. Its objectives kept evolving or changing, more to justify new area designations than as a result of changing economic circumstances. In the early years its principal aim was promotion of new employment opportunities in slow-growth regions, notably Atlantic Canada and eastern Quebec. In 1971, and again in 1977, Montreal was designated under DREE's regional incentives program to encourage rapid-growth manufacturing industries.

The criteria for area designation were particularly loose and ill-defined. All that was required to designate a new area was an order-in-council. Criteria such as earned income per capita or unemployment rates were never established. The Industrial and Labour Adjustment Program (ILAP) offered assistance to attract new manufacturing activities especially to designated communities, a number of which were located in non-DREE areas of southern Ontario. In the end, practically the only regions not designated for special 'regional' assistance were the Toronto area, Edmonton, Calgary, and Vancouver.

Experience has shown, notably with ILAP and the Montreal special area, that incentives in the more developed areas attract many more applicants than for the traditional 'have-not' regions. We saw, for example, that the ILAP program in Windsor, Ontario, generated substantially more interest and applicants than the same program in Sydney, Nova Scotia. In the case of the regional incentives programs, the Montreal area generated 1,241 approved and accepted grants in a 5-year period. It took the four Atlantic provinces 12 years to achieve 421 approved grants and the Lower St Lawrence and Gaspé regions 10 years to reach 134. Over 36,000 jobs were expected to be created in the Montreal area over the 5 years of the regional grants approved there, compared with 20,000 for the Atlantic provinces over the 12-year period.[15]

Such wide geographical application of the regional incentives program invariably diluted its impact on the traditionally slow-growth regions. The program was not as promising for the Gaspé and the Atlantic regions as for such major urban centres as Montreal and Windsor, and, with major urban centres designated, the Gaspé and Atlantic regions lost some of their appeal under RDIA.

Other industrialized countries have been much more successful in limiting the geographical application of regional incentives. Some make public an explicit and objective system for designating regions. West Germany, for example, identifies labour market areas and ranks them according to three weighted criteria: a measure of unemployment ($w-1$), income per capita ($w-1$), and an index of infrastructure provision ($w-0.5$). Major OECD regional incentives, except those available in Canada, cover between 27 and 46 per cent of the population and 31 to 77 per cent of the land surface. In the case of the European Community (EC), a norm appears to have developed in terms of population coverage, so that between one-quarter and one-third of the national population falls into designated regions.[16]

DREE's regional incentives program remained largely 'responsive.' Officials simply responded to applications from entrepreneurs who were proposing to initiate projects. There was no provision made 'to market' the program. Only toward the end of DREE's existence were some efforts made to have officials meet with the private sector to identify jointly economic opportunities that might meet regional development objectives. But before this approach was given a chance to prove itself, it was tossed aside with the government reorganization.

From the inception of the incentives program, on 1 July 1969, to 31 March 1981, over $1 billion in grants were committed. They were expected to generate investments in eligible assets of over $5 billion and to help in the direct creation of 167,691 jobs. The cost for each job created for the life of the program came to approximately $5,000. By 1981, inflation had increased the average cost per job to close to $11,000, which compares favourably with other federal job-creating incentives schemes. Programs in the former Department of Industry, Trade and Commerce and in the Employment and Immigration Commission had a cost per job of between $8,200 and $11,700.[17]

From an administrative point of view, the regional incentives program was more solid than it appeared. Although the Bricklin and Clairtone failures received wide public exposure, and numerous newspaper articles were subsequently highly critical of the program, fewer than 10 per cent of approved projects were discontinued or were not in commercial production three years after the initial grant payment was made.[18]

A REVIEW OF OTHER FEDERAL DEPARTMENTS

Politicians from all parties have argued that the federal government has not established a government-wide policy on regional development; DREE had been left alone in the field.

Others have made the same observation. The Economic Council of Canada, for example, pointed out that RDIA expenditures, or total DREE transfers to the private sector, amounted to only about 3 per cent of total federal grants and subsidies to the private sector. The Council concluded also that non-DREE transfers to the private sector favoured the more developed regions. The Council noted that the Department of Agriculture spent 60 per cent of its resources in Ontario and Quebec in the mid-1970s. Meanwhile, the four Atlantic provinces received $7.3 million, or just slightly over 2 per cent of total agricultural subsidies.[19]

The former Department of Industry, Trade and Commerce directed the great majority of its development efforts, 1973–78, to Ontario and Quebec.[20] Under the Defence Industry Productivity Program (DIPP), it allocated 59.7 per cent of the funds to Quebec and 35.4 per cent to Ontario. It virtually ignored Newfoundland, Prince Edward Island, Saskatchewan, New Brunswick, and Alberta. Moreover, while Ontario and Quebec benefited from all its programs, New Brunswick, Nova Scotia, Prince Edward Island, and Newfoundland had limited or no activities in the following: the General Adjustment Assistance Program (GAAP); the Industrial Design Assistance Program (IDAP); the Fashion Design Assistance Program (FDAP); Adjustment Assistance, Promotional Projects Board (PPB); the Footwear and Tanning Industry Assistance Program (FTIAP); and the Enterprise Development Program (EDP).

Industry, Trade and Commerce did little to involve the peripheral regions even in its later years. Its report on the industrial benefits derived from new fighter aircraft angered western and Atlantic governments. The lion's share of the industrial benefits were earmarked for the two central provinces, which received about 90 per cent of projected expenditures, and the department had assessed the project 'in terms of [its] likely impact upon Quebec, Ontario and *the rest of Canada.*'[21]

In 1980–81, Industry, Trade and Commerce had a total expenditure budget of $298,987,833, excluding the Western Grain Stabilization program. Ontario was allocated $93,537,543 or 31.3 per cent, of the budget, and Quebec $86,709,504, or 29 per cent. The remaining $118,704,786 was allocated among the other provinces and territories, and to offices and programs outside Canada. The four Atlantic provinces got $33 million, or 11.4 per cent. Over $27 million of this came from the ship-building industry assistance program.[22]

The expenditure patterns of federal departments prompted leaders in the Atlantic provinces to argue that DREE was not truly a regional development agency, but one that sought to balance Ottawa's economic development funds directed toward the established areas. Introduction of ILAP reinforced this view. Its community and sector designations clearly favoured southern Ontario; over 80 per cent of ILAP spending went to Ontario communities.[23]

THE FEDERAL RELOCATION PROGRAM

A brief assessment of Ottawa's program to relocate government units is also required. The program was designed to promote economic activity in the less-advantaged regions of the country. Historically, Ontario and Nova Scotia have had a large number of federal public servants relative to their proportion of the total population. Ontario, with approximately 35 per cent of the population, has over 45 per cent of federal employees. About 27 per cent of federal public servants work in the National Capital Region. (Only about 12 per cent of us federal government employees are located in the Washington, DC, area.)[24]

To correct the imbalance and to promote regional development, Ottawa embarked on a decentralization program in the mid-1970s. Under the program, some 5,100 permanent positions and close to 6,000 casual or temporary positions were actually transferred out of Ottawa, mostly to slow-growth areas.

It is difficult to determine the cost of the program. Sinclair Stevens claimed that he was saving the government at least $76 million when he cancelled ten relocating projects, involving about 850 permanent positions and an undetermined number of causual positions. With these figures, the cost per permanent job created would be $89,411.[25] This figure can be misleading, in that it includes capital construction cost of new buildings in receiving communities. A corresponding adjustment should have been made for rental cost of existing accommodation in the Ottawa region.

In 1981 the task force on decentralization calculated the cost of jobs created under its program at $26,000 each (1977 dollars). This figure is an average of all jobs actually transferred under the program and accounts for rental cost in Ottawa, had a particular unit not been transferred. Some units were relocated at substantially lower cost. For example, Rigaud, Quebec, was chosen as the site for a new training centre for Revenue Canada, with over 100 new positions. The task force estimated that the total additional cost for locating the facility in Rigaud, as opposed to Ottawa, amounted to only $100,000 a year, for added travel costs.[26]

Even the figure of $26,000 per job created set by the task force needs further comment. The amount is considerably higher than the figure for jobs created under DREE's RDIA program. But the $11,000 figure for DREE should be adjusted to reflect the overhead costs involved in administering RDIA. The figure needs to be adjusted to reflect incrementality as well: if 30 per cent of the new jobs would have been created anyway, then the RDIA estimate is inaccurate. These two revisions would add about $7,000 to the figure.

There are other factors that also need to be considered in assessing the decentralization program. There are strong indications that the decentralized units are functioning more efficiently in the regions than if they were located in Ottawa. The cheque redemption control unit of the Department of Supply and Services, located in Matane, in the economically depressed Gaspé region, processes the same number of cheques with 275 employees that it processed with 300 employees when it was in Ottawa. The director of the unit explained that one reason for the increased productivity was that he was able to select the 275 employees from 3,500 applicants, while in Ottawa he had considerably fewer applicants to choose from. He added that staff turnover at Matane is practically non-existent, compared to the high turnover experienced earlier in Ottawa. The director of the Supply and Services unit in Shediac, New Brunswick, reported similar findings and also claimed that his unit was far more efficient there than when it was located in Ottawa.[27]

These considerations were overlooked when Sinclair Stevens put a hold on the program and when Donald Johnston effectively terminated it. Johnston disbanded the task force and transferred responsibility for identifying potential units for decentralization to line departments and agencies. Since then, few new developments have surfaced or units actually been decentralized.

REGIONAL DEVELOPMENT EFFORTS AT THE SUB-PROVINCIAL LEVEL

It is impossible to assess the impact of federal and provincial expenditures on sub-provincial economic development simply because the necessary data are not available. Some information, however, is available for joint DREE-province spending between 1960 and 1980 in sub-provincial areas.[28] It reveals that the more developed areas within slow-growth provinces received the greater part of the funding. For instance, spending was substantially higher in the Halifax-Dartmouth area than in western Nova Scotia or even Cape Breton Island. In per capita terms, however, Cape Breton did slightly better than other regions of the province.

A similar spending pattern is evident in New Brunswick, where the more developed and industrialized Saint John area received more funding than the economically depressed Miramichi area. The resources allocated to Saint John were triple those received by Miramichi. This imbalance is true for other depressed areas of the province, including the southwest and northwest. The one exception was in the underdeveloped northeast: Gloucester and Restigouche counties received more funding than Saint John in both absolute and per capita terms.

In Quebec, Greater Montreal and cities within a 100-mile radius of the city did remarkably well in comparison to other areas of the province. The Montreal special-area designation enabled a number of nearby communities to obtain twice as much funding as other areas of Quebec in half the time. For instance, Sherbrooke, Trois-Rivières, and Ste-Hyacinthe received more funding than the economically depressed areas of Lac St-Jean and the Gaspé.

A different spending pattern held for Newfoundland, Ontario, and the west. In Newfoundland, St John's did not do as well as other areas of the province. In the other provinces, the developed regions of Calgary, Edmonton, Toronto, and Vancouver benefited very little from province-DREE programs.

The 50 per cent investment tax credit benefited exclusively sub-provincial slow-growth areas, but there is no way of knowing to what extent firms took advantage of the program.

Information for sub-provincial areas is also available under the former industrial incentives program (RDIA). The largest number of jobs created under this program occurred in the Montreal area. The more developed areas in slow-growth provinces also did remarkably well. In Nova Scotia, for example, Halifax led all other areas, with almost twice as many jobs created. The same was true for Newfoundland, in the case of St John's; for Manitoba, in the case of Winnipeg; and for Saskatchewan, in the case of Regina and Saskatoon. The one exception is New Brunswick, where jobs created were pretty well evenly distributed among all areas.

THE NEW FEDERAL ORGANIZATION FOR ECONOMIC DEVELOPMENT

The federal government's organization for economic development, put in place in 1982, has already been described. It remains to assess its likely effect on regional economic development.

It is hardly possible to overemphasize the importance of government organization for regional economic development. Recognizing this, a former DREE minister remarked that 'certain areas of this problem [i.e., regional disparities] do not necessarily deal with economics but rather with the government machinery itself.'[29] Prime Minister Trudeau and DREE's first minister, Jean Marchand, spent considerable time reviewing different organizational options before establishing DREE in 1968. To give regional economic development priority status is easy; to adopt a structure that will provide the basis to develop concrete measures is considerably more difficult.

Before assessing the new structure for regional development, we will take another brief look at the new policy that led to the government reorganization and the forces that shaped this new policy. Clearly, the main preoccupation of Ottawa officials in the early 1980s was the 'softening' of Canada's industrial heartland and the required adjustment. There were promising prospects for the future development of energy-related mega projects, some of them in the 'have not' regions. The perceived challenge was to manage these projects so that the benefits from them would remain in Canada and assist in the necessary industrial adjustment. Canada's regional problem was thus seen as having changed a great deal, with the 'have-not' regions facing excellent development prospects, while the industrial heartland grappled with considerable problems of adjustment.

Meanwhile, the main preoccupation of the prime minister and cabinet was federal-provincial relations. It was felt in Ottawa that the pendulum had swung much too far in favour of the provinces and that measures were required to restore Ottawa's ascendancy. DREE spending was seen as geared toward the provinces, with provincial governments not only shaping new initiatives, but also able to claim most of the credit for them.

The federal presence therefore needed to be reasserted and made more visible. In the words of Bruce Doern, 'Federal ministers were increasingly tired of provincial governments and of being perceived as a mismanaged, debt-ridden and remote government, while the provincial governments basked for most of the 1970s in the political glory of balanced budgets, perceived competence, and sensitivity and closeness to their people.'[30] The federal cabinet sought to re-establish the identification of Canadians with their national institutions. The federal government would deal directly with individuals, firms, and institutions, rather than funnel its support through provincial governments.

Pierre De Bané, as minister of DREE, had warned departmental officials that the status quo was unacceptable and that he was not prepared to support it. Many Atlantic and Quebec MPs had asked him to adjust DREE programs to give the federal government more visibility. Some suggested that if this could not be done then the department should be disbanded. De Bané suggested to the prime minister a complete review of Ottawa's regional development policy.

The convergence of interests critical of DREE led to the new government structure. Like DREE had for some thirteen years, the new structure was to influence greatly the scope and pace of Ottawa's work in regional development in the years to come. It sought to make regional development central to policy- and decision-making in Ottawa. However, there were strong reasons to believe that it would not succeed.

The policy that inspired the new organization presumed that the regional problem in Canada had changed dramatically because of the economic prospects associated with mega projects in the west, the north, and the east and because of the far-reaching adjustments required in Canada's industrial heartland. It is now clear that Ottawa overestimated the impact of these projects on economic development. Alsands, Sable Island, Hibernia, the Beaufort Sea, the High Arctic, Cold Lake, and even lesser-known projects, such as Point Lepreau II, are still on the drawing board or fading further and further from Canada's economic landscape. They simply have not delivered what was envisaged. Even if they all had proceeded as planned, they still would not have lived up to their high expectations. Including all the mega projects identified in the Report of the Blair-Carr task force, total public investment would have amounted to $400 billion. Though impressive in absolute terms, this figure represents only 10 per cent of total projected capital investments in Canada in the 1980s and 1990s.

As it happened, they did not all materialize. Mega projects have since been described as the ET of Canadian politics. 'Like the ugly but lovable "extra terrestrial" beast of the Spielberg movie, mega projects landed for a brief visit, were befriended by a few, attracted much attention, and then left – or so it seemed.'[31] When they will return as a force in the Canadian economy is unclear, as is the importance they will have when they do return. Even if they do return in full force, the most that they can do from a regional development perspective is generate new revenues for the provincial governments of Nova Scotia and Newfoundland and provide new development opportunities for the larger urban centres of Halifax and St John's. Their importance for New Brunswick and Prince Edward Island is anything but clear. As for northern New Brunswick, the Gaspé, rural Newfoundland, and Cape Breton, their possible effect is even less certain.

Again, even if the various mega projects had proceeded as originally envisaged, there is considerable doubt that the new organization would have been able to deliver what the prime minister said it would. Directing industrial benefits from mega-projects implies the ability to locate spin-off activities in designated areas. Yet the current organization for economic development in Ottawa has locational or regional considerations pushed well down in the bureaucracy. The reorganization left no department or agency able to go beyond narrow sectoral mandates, and no single minister to speak on behalf of the regions when new economic activities from mega-projects or from other initiatives surfaced.

The leading department for regional consideration became the Ministry of State for Economic and Regional Development (MSERD). But the mandate of its minister encompassed both national and regional economic concerns. Moreover, it was a central agency with all the limitations that entails, some of which have been described in this study. Central agencies are best known for their ability to stop policy or program initiatives, rather than coming forward with them. Their role is goal-keeping, simply because to maintain credibility in the bureaucratic system they must be seen as objective and detached, with the capacity to evaluate initiatives.

It was difficult to imagine MSERD making proposals for the slow-growth areas. If it had, who in Ottawa would have evaluated them? Where would it have gotten the necessary funding? The only logical places are the economic envelope and the regional fund, both of which were managed by MSERD. Yet, surely if it had sought funding from these sources, line departments would have argued that MSERD held an unfair advantage in reviewing their proposals for possible funding.

Shortly after the reorganization was announced, a Privy Council Office official declared that under the new structure public debates such as that between De Bané and Gray over the location of a new Volkswagen plant could not take place today. He explained: 'It [public debate between two ministers] will never happen again ... DREE had its own ideas on VW and IT&C had different ideas. There was a lot of squabbling. Now that they're together, they'll have to resolve their differences internally and then go to cabinet.'[32] The point here is not whether national or even regional considerations should decide the location of the Volkswagen parts plant.

Rather, it is that with the reorganization, there would no longer be anyone in the cabinet bringing regional considerations into discussions whenever new economic activities were proposed.

Regional trade-offs were now to be resolved at the official level. This gave cause for concern. Officials in Ottawa are quite naturally purpose-oriented, preoccupied with sectors and programs. To promote a regional perspective in Ottawa, in the words of a former senior DREE official, is like pulling against gravity. Tom Kent described the situation in this fashion: 'From the point of view of almost all conventional wisdom in Ottawa, the idea of regional development was a rather improper one that some otherwise quite reasonable politician brought in like a baby on a doorstep from an election campaign.[33]

Quite naturally, cabinet ministers think of economic decisions in terms of their effect on the regions and constituencies they represent. Ministers have a basic 'feel' for regional issues which the bureaucracy, even with the best of intentions, is incapable of grasping. It is not uncommon to see ministers fight it out in the cabinet on behalf of their regions. It is unusual to see senior public servants drawing battle lines over regional issues. They are much more likely to disagree on sectoral matters, on whether or not the government should intervene in a given situation, and on the program interests of their departments, as opposed to those of other departments. In any event, economists in Ottawa are like 'most economists'; they 'have a prejudice against regional 'growth' policy on the grounds that such policies compromise efficiency in resource allocations.'[34]

Regionalism in Ottawa is, thus, sustained by its political constituency. For regional development to be at the forefront of cabinet deliberations it needs an advocate at the political level, supported by a group of dedicated officials with a clear mandate. This may well give rise to uncomfortable debates between cabinet colleagues on the appropriate location of potential economic activities, but at least debates would be engaged. And the regional advocacy function in the cabinet requires more than ten 'regional' ministers pawing the cabinet table to direct to their regions whatever new initiatives come along. It requires a minister with a distinct mandate to speak on behalf of the regional dimension in policy-making, supported by permanent officials with responsibility to define and articulate regional circumstances. In short, promoting regional development in Ottawa and coming forward with specific measures will not automatically occur simply because federal politicians stress their importance to national unity at election time.

The government reorganization of 1982 and the current organization in Ottawa have also left no one to address economic development issues at the sub-provincial level. In the past, DREE had been active in a number of economically depressed areas. It had sponsored a number of special regional development plans for such areas as coastal Labrador, northeastern New Brunswick, and the Manitoba northlands. These plans were negotiated by DREE and the relevant provincial government. That mandate was missing in the new order of things. MSERD, a central agency managing the economic expenditure envelope, could hardly have been an advocate and brought forward, with the co-operation of the provinces, initiatives for sub-provincial regions. As well, DRIE has a much narrower mandate than DREE had. It is a sectoral department with a program orientation that also does not readily accommodate sub-provincial development. At best, it can deliver some industrial and tourism initiatives to certain areas.

Experience confirmed that sub-provincial planning was missing. Neither MSERD nor DRIE has come forward with such plans. More important, existing subsidiary agreements negotiated by DREE with the provinces under the various GDAS were either not renewed or were replaced with nothing resembling what the depressed regions had previously had, going back to ARDA programs.

The 1982 reorganization sought to solve political and administrative problems posed by the GDAS and provincialism. No attempt was made to design new instruments to deal with regional development. Further, and more important, the nature of the problem was not addressed. Nowhere in the government announcement was reference made to 'regional disparities,' to the nature of economic disparities, and to the kinds of program required for their solution. No reference was made to appropriate regional development goals. Similarly, the subsequent decision to do away with MSERD was based on the need to streamline government operations, not on any intention to redirect regional development efforts.

THE NEW ORGANIZATION IN REAL LIFE

The new policy for economic development and the new organization are now over three years old. Subsequent changes to the organization have simply done away with MSERD. There have been no major alterations to the federal regional development policy unveiled in 1982, notwithstanding two changes of government. Sufficient time has elapsed for us to look at actual performance, particularly with respect to the 1982 reorganization. The central purpose of the new policy and organization was to make regional development central to policy- and decision-making in Ottawa in order to give them the kind of priority they never had under DREE.

If one equates priority status with funding levels, then the new policy and the new structure fell short of expectations. Spending under the GDAS and, of late, under the ERDAS has fallen dramatically, even in absolute terms, from the levels attained in the late 1970s. In the case of Newfoundland, GDA spending in 1978–80 was over $67 million, but then fell to about $25 million in 1982–83. For New Brunswick, the fall was from $52 million in 1979–80 to less than $40 million in 1982–83.[35] The sharp decline in spending is evident in every province except

Manitoba. This decline will probably continue even if allowance is made for spending under federal direct-delivery initiatives. Fewer and fewer subsidiary agreements are now being signed under the ERDAS – not nearly as many as was the case for the GDAS. From 1978 to 1981 an average of ten subsidiary agreements were signed annually with provincial governments. In 1982 and 1983, the average stood at five.

Federal line departments are now delivering programs under the ERDAS. This might lead one to believe that they are more present in regional development matters than they were under DREE. However, where they are delivering projects under the various subsidiary agreements, they have simply nudged provincial governments aside and are now delivering initiatives that are similar to those delivered by provincial governments under the GDAS. Little else appears to have been accomplished. The initiatives are essentially similar; only the implementors have changed.

There is no evidence to suggest that the 'A' base of the ongoing programs of federal line departments has been tailored to reflect different regional circumstances. In short, federal line departments have simply carried on with 'business as usual,' notwithstanding the new government organization and Prime Minister Trudeau's directive that all departments should shoulder responsibility for regional development.

This unwillingness to follow new policy directions will come as no surprise to at least some students of public policy. Pressman and Wildawsky, in their study of program implementation, discovered that even when major new policy directions are announced, things will keep on being done just as before and 'old patterns of behavior are often retrospectively rationalized to fit new notions about appropriate objectives ... [That is] the ordinary condition of administration.'[36]

DRIE is a sectoral department concerned with Canada's industrial performance. Its program is national in scope, and possibilities exist for government funding for projects, even in Toronto. It is true that the program is more generous for slow-growth regions, but the kind of funding for tier 4 assistance is the maximum, and certainly not all projects are able to obtain that level of funding.

For the first full year of operation, the program was more successful in the Windsor–Quebec corridor than elsewhere. The estimated number of jobs to be created or maintained under tier 1 is well over twice the number of jobs estimated for tier 3 and tier 4 combined in the first year of operation. In terms of financial resources, DRIE funds earmarked for tier 1 projects alone amount to over $229 million, compared with $23 million for tier 4, $46 million for tier 3, and $74 million for tier 2.[37]

DRIE regional officials report that over time the program will favour even more tier 1 regions, or the more developed regions of the country. The reason, they point out, is two-fold. First, DRIE will invariably focus on sectoral problems and assess all new initiatives from a sectoral perspective without attaching sufficient importance to regional considerations. Specifically, they maintain that initiatives from northern New Brunswick will be assessed from the same perspective as those from southern Ontario. Risks for investors in remote slow-growth areas are much greater than in, say, southern Ontario, and potential development initiatives are not as evident in slow-growth regions. This, it is pointed out, calls for the kind of flexibility that the new DRIE organization and program do not provide.

Second, DRIE never provides the maximum level of assistance available under tier 4. The most that DRIE has agreed to grant thus far under tier 4 is 60 per cent of the maximum allowed. Again, that the sectoral perspective should gain ascendancy over the regional in DRIE should come as no surprise. Michael Jenkin remarked: 'In large measure, IT&C industrial sector branch organizational structure has been maintained [in DRIE] as well as its emphasis on the functional, as distinct from the regional dimension of industrial policy.'[38]

Perhaps the biggest disappointment of the new approach has been the regional fund. There is an inherent contradiction between the objectives of the new organization and the regional fund concept. Prime Minister Trudeau argued that DREE was being disbanded because sectoral departments in Ottawa tended to point to it whenever a regional problem surfaced. DREE had, as a by-product, absolved other departments of any concern they might have had about regional considerations. The same logic, potentially at least, holds true for the regional fund. Sectoral departments may be tempted to continue with their regular programs and turn to the regional fund whenever they have to deal with regional problems.

In any event, the regional fund has had little effect on federal policies and programs. It is not possible to determine either the exact size of the fund or the criteria employed to assess projects. More important, we know virtually nothing of the kind of projects supported by it.

This leads one to ask what became of the DREE expenditure budget. In announcing the regional fund, the prime minister explained that funds freed up from the DREE budget would provide the financial resources to establish the regional fund. He also stated that the fund should reach $200 million by 1984– 85.[39] No one seems to know even if that objective has been met.

CONCLUSION

The new policy and organization for economic development established in 1982 made several incorrect assumptions. The energy mega projects did not justify the promise seen in them for the Atlantic coast or for the western provinces. The regional problem has not shifted to southern Ontario and Quebec, as envisaged. The new government organization had little chance of meeting the stated objectives of making regional economic development central to Ottawa's policy-making and decision-making processes. Many observers would agree that federal line departments and agencies have not contributed to regional development as much as they could have by adjusting their policies and programs to make them more sensitive to regional circumstances. There is no convincing evidence, however, to suggest that the reason for this was directly related to DREE's existence. To do away with DREE, the one federal agency with at least the potential to be sensitive to regional circumstances, in the belief that that change will make all federal departments more sensitive to them appears naïve.

That said, DREE was not without its problems. The first was the lack of central purpose in its spending. DREE was not able to turn the GDAs into something more than enabling documents. They remained the miscellaneous program instruments of both levels of government, funding everything from schools to industrial parks. Certainly, DREE could have gone much further in assessing the economic factors of the lagging regional economies and making more selective interventions. It is impossible to assess the economic impact of DREE's spending simply because clear objectives were never defined. The regional industrial incentives program was evaluated on numerous occasions, but there is no agreement on whether or not it was a success. While much criticism of DREE is valid, one can question the wisdom of doing away with the department. In my view, it would have been more appropriate if DREE's objectives had been reoriented and its program instruments updated.

The government reorganization and subsequent changes offer little more than what already existed – minus, of course, DREE. Government transfer payments to slow-growth areas will probably continue unchallenged from within the federal government. If there is any change, it will be simply to reduce them. No one will be coming forward in cabinet to identify self-sustaining economic activities in slow-growth areas. In outlining his priority areas, the new minister of DRIE in the Mulroney cabinet, Sinclair Stevens, spoke about 'international trade, the competitiveness of Canadian industry, the need to rekindle business confidence, and attracting foreign investment to Canada.'[40] Nothing was said about regional development.

10

Regional economic development reconsidered

This study has shown that the problem of Canada's regional development remains a complex puzzle to policy-makers. New policy directions, government reorganizations, and substantial public funds have all been tried. Yet regional disparities persist. Further, with sluggish or non-existent economic growth and with a turbulent world economy, the bias toward national economic growth and away from interregional equity is becoming much stronger. There is a growing tendency to stress total development in the national economy at the expense of the less obvious benefits of interregional balance.

But federal politicians are not giving up, if one is to take their rhetoric at face value. Senior spokesmen of all major political parties continue to stress the importance of regional development for national cohesion. And provincial governments in slow-growth regions still talk about regional disparities in essentially the same terms as they did in the late 1960s. Much as the Liberal government before, the Conservative government in Ottawa has stressed the importance of regional development to national unity. And much like the Liberal government had done in the late 1960s, the Conservative government talks about the need to alleviate regional disparities.

This chapter looks at the problem of regional disparities after twenty years of federal attempts to alleviate them and also in light of new economic circumstances. It seeks also to shed new light on the problem and considers the appropriateness of past and present regional development objectives.

THEORY AND PRACTICE

In an earlier chapter, we noted the confusion as to the most appropriate approach to regional disparities. No general theory has emerged, and no comprehensive solution has been defined. The Economic Council of Canada suggested that Canada, much like other countries, is 'trying this and that, and doing what they can in a difficult situation.'[1]

In DREE's early years, the growth-pole approach held sway, and Canada applied the concept to its regional development planning. The federal government limited the number of communities designated as special areas. It considered this vital to the success of the growth-pole approach. Substantial amounts of public funds were quickly committed by the federal government and the provinces to spur economic development in selected urban areas. Yet only a few years after its introduction, the growth-pole approach was rejected outright. This rather sudden rejection was based not so much on empirical evidence as on an intuitive belief that something else, a new approach, would be much better. The growth-pole concept was too 'narrow' and 'too restricted' for Canada.

The main reason for the disappointment with growth poles, however, may be that too much was expected. They were to give rise to strong and vibrant urban centres that would attract new economic activities. They would also 'alleviate' regional disparities between Canada's regions, with strong urban centres attracting surplus labour from surrounding rural areas and with new, more sophisticated economic activities contributing to higher per capita incomes. Before sufficient time had elapsed to assess the results of the approach, the concept was abandoned.

But we also learned from social scientists not only in Canada but abroad as well, that the growth-pole concept was only one of a series of 'fashions and fads' that was seized upon 'only to be abandoned ... when it turned out that it was not a unique or complete solution after all.' Social scientists now insist that 'perhaps never in the history of economic thought has so much government activity taken place and so much money been invested on the foundation of so confused a concept as the growth pole became in the late 1960s and early 1970s.'[2]

The growth pole gave way to the 'comprehensive' GDA approach, which in turn gave way to the equally comprehensive ERDA approach. Putting aside the issue of political visibility, ERDAs thus far have offered little that is new in terms of regional development programs. Like the GDAs, they are essentially enabling instruments for governments to 'cost-share' projects or put in place special measures under the broad label of regional development. Governments in Canada have described this process as 'pursuit of development opportunities.'

It is difficult to discern the theoretical framework behind past and present GDA and ERDA programs. The variety of projects sponsored is so wide that no conceivable theory could possibly cover all initiatives. The development approach provided for a 'multi-dimensional' view and a 'host' of policy and program instruments, but it had fallen out of favour among students and practitioners of regional development in Canada by the 1970s. It was viewed as dated and better suited to underdeveloped countries than to Canada's slow-growth regions.

Certainly by the late 1970s, senior federal spokesmen were pointing to the regional comparative approach as the guiding principle for future initiatives. DREE was not a welfare agency, and the department would seek to build upon the economic strengths of the different regions. A region's comparative advantage would signal which projects would secure government funding. Recent press releases on ERDA-sponsored initiatives indicate that the comparative advantage is still favoured by governments.

One would be hard-pressed, however, to demonstrate that GDA and ERDA initiatives conform to the requirements of the comparative advantage approach. A cursory look at the mix of subsidiary agreements sponsored even within a single province under GDAS and ERDAS reveals that program formulation is guided more by a 'B' budget process than by a regional development theory. Government officials know approximate budgetary levels for their respective provinces and put together subsidiary agreements of one kind or another so as to spend the allocated funds. Every effort is made to commit all funds earmarked for their provinces on the basis of a priority list. Subsidiary agreements are ranked according to the anticipated benefits they can bring to selected sectors of the economy or sub-provincial regions. There are always unsigned subsidiary agreements on the shelf to be brought out whenever funds become available. Occasionally, politicians push through high-profile agreements on highway construction and the like, but, here again, the guiding principle is not a particular theory of regional development.

Other more recent theories of regional development have had little effect on government planning and programs. Neo-marxist and neo-classical models and recent literature on regional dependency exude an aura of other-worldliness to those in government departments planning regional development initiatives. Consequently, they have had very little effect. One keen student of regional development remarked: 'There is no manual for dependency theory planning.'[3]

Richard Lipsey probably was correct when he stated: 'For all the concern about regional area development and regional problems in Canada, we don't really have an underlying theory. We don't know what we would have to do.' The problem, it would appear, is not peculiar to Canada. Other countries are experiencing considerable difficulty in establishing a theoretical framework for regional development initiatives. According to the chairman of the advisory committee of the United Nations Centre for Regional Development, we may have 'to admit to ourselves that there is no general theory at hand which will enable us to deal with all cases and all objectives, and that there is not likely to be one in the near future.' He added recently: 'If we have learned anything about the development process during the past thirty years, it is surely that there are *no* panaceas for development.'[4]

However, we need not abandon completely the search for new theories or dismiss out of hand all theoretical considerations. What we perhaps need is a new 'clinical approach' to regional development problems. With the realization that the various approaches tried thus far have not lived up to expectations, perhaps we ought 'to go back to the laboratory.' Herbert Simon recently pleaded for the replacement of physics by biology as the main methodological model for the social sciences.[5] Such an approach would be particularly well suited for regional development planning, provided we recognize that there are no wonder-drugs.

A central feature of the clinical approach is that what is required in one region may not be required in another. This could be true on most fronts, ranging from the nature of initiatives to be supported to methods of delivery (for example, local development agency as opposed to regular government programs). Certain regions might have to resort to more drastic measures than we have employed in the past (for example, lowering the minimum wage). Just like medical doctors do, regional planners should look to case histories to diagnose the ills of the different regions and prescribe treatments. They should not expect that the same treatments will produce the same results always and everywhere. Equally important, regional planners 'had better keep [their] eyes on the patient as treatment proceeds and be prepared to change it if it appears not to work.'[6]

A clinical approach would also permit more realism about what we can accomplish and also help us establish firm criteria to guide governments in supporting projects for regional development. It would also encourage us to hang a question mark on everything done or planned in the name of regional development.

ARE REGIONAL DEVELOPMENT MEASURES NECESSARY?

The first question that should be asked about Canada's regional development policy is whether special measures are necessary. Presumably, if one allowed the forces of change to have full play, then the necessary adjustments would take place. Once the adjustments were complete, the real product of the regions would be higher, and labour and capital would be in a more productive arrangement.

Those who support this approach can argue that after twenty years of efforts and the spending of billions of dollars the problem of regional disparities is still very much with us. They can argue also that past measures may have blunted economic adjustment and hindered regional growth and self-reliance. From the view-point of economic efficiency, they can point to a variety of reasons why governments should do away with special regional development measures. However, an unrelenting pursuit of national efficiency is simply not acceptable in Canada. The cost in adjustment and in personal hardship would be prohibitive. Canada's interregional tensions could well become unmanageable.

This would be so not simply from a federal-provincial perspective, but also within the federal government. Regional tensions within the federal government often pose serious difficulties. Regional ministers frequently square off in cabinet and in caucus in bitter debates over the location of new economic activities. From time to time, these debates will erupt in full public view through the press, as they did in 1982 over the industrial benefits from the F-18 fighter plane.[7] Anyone sitting in on a regular basis in cabinet committee meetings will confirm that regional tensions will spark bitter rows far more often than language issues and ideological considerations.

It is difficult to imagine regional ministers and MPs from slow-growth regions supporting pure national efficiency, either publicly or in caucus, even if long-term benefits would accrue not only to the national economy but also to his or her own region. The political mandate of politicians in Canada is such that the long-term perspective holds little appeal. This no doubt explains Thomas Courchene's observation that governments will intervene and will not 'stand idly by and allow the unfettered market to call the adjustment tune.'[8]

It is also unlikely that provincial governments would accept the national efficiency option. Province-building is now widespread, and much has been said of late about the growing economic prowess of the provinces. Slow-growth provinces remain convinced that 'discriminatory' federal policies have obstructed their development. It is hardly possible to imagine them turning their economic fate over to the national efficiency model. Such a model could well prompt provincial governments to initiate actions that in themselves would bring about economic inefficiencies.

There are many occasions in which the competitive actions of several provinces can harm the national and provincial economies. The classic example is found with common resources, such as the fisheries industry, where competitive over-exploitation leads to lower total catches. There are other examples. If all provinces set up competing incentive schemes, the resulting distribution of investment might not be greatly changed, but the overall government cost could be greatly increased. A similar situation could surface if provincial governments were to compete for markets. If the amount of Canadian pulp and paper products sold is more or less fixed during a given period, and one province then offers incentives to its producers to capture a bigger share of the market, the effect will spill over to the other provinces. These, in turn, will be confronted with the choice of losing jobs and earned income or providing compensatory incentives to their own producers. Another example of the overspill problem is found in a variety of government actions that serve to erect barriers to trade within Canada. A classic example here is discriminatory procurement policies on the part of provincial governments, which tend to view economic development as a 'zero-sum game' in which the winners are identified on a case-by-case basis and in highly regional terms. Provinces have come to expect Ottawa to work toward a fair distribution of economic activity throughout the country, with some smaller provincial governments claiming that this is in fact the federal government's main responsibility.

There are thus important reasons of economic efficiency for the federal government to be directly involved in promoting regional economic development. For Ottawa to vacate the field completely would provoke bitter regional tensions and probably give rise to all kinds of 'Me first' provincial economic initiatives. The national efficiency model would thus not be given a chance to prove itself, and costly interprovincial competitive measures would probably result.

There is another reason for the federal government to intervene in the field. Regional economic development, it has been argued, is consistent with the aim of creating a national identity. There is a connection between regional disparities and the strains on our national unity. The Royal Commission on the Economic Union and Development Prospects for Canada declared in its interim report that 'a fundamental tenet of the Canadian federation has been to spread economic and social opportunities among all regions.' In short, the sharing of prosperity among Canadians wherever they live has been part of the bargain of Confederation. For the federal government to wash its hands of this responsibility and to unleash market forces on the national economy, ignoring the part played by national institutions for over 100 years, could well lead some provincial governments (notably, those that would stand to lose the most) to break the Confederation bargain. Premier Peckford put it in blunt terms when he said: 'Canada as a nation cannot survive if there are permanently rich and permanently poor provinces.'[9]

The notion of regional balance in Canada's economic development remains an important concern to the country's political leaders, notwithstanding the difficult economic conditions of recent years. The point continues to be made by all players at every federal-provincial conference on the economy. More significant, a separate section was inserted in the Constitution Act, 1982, on 'equalization and regional disparities.' The section commits both levels of government to 'promoting equal opportunities ... and further economic development to reduce disparity in opportunities.'[10]

REDEFINING THE REGIONAL PROBLEM

During the late 1960s, Ottawa declared war on regional disparity. 'Economic equality,' declared Prime Minister Trudeau, 'is just as important as equality of language rights.' No doubt this has become the most-quoted phrase in newspaper editorials in Atlantic Canada during the past fifteen years. Conventional thinking has it that a large part of the regional problem was and is to be found in eastern Quebec and the Atlantic provinces.

Certainly, expectations were raised, and there was a degree of optimism that regional disparities would be alleviated. Two indicators of economic well-being have historically measured regional disparities – per capita income and unemployment rates. These two indicators would tell us when regional disparities had finally been alleviated. They have not yet lost their appeal. The Atlantic Provinces

Economic Council (APEC), for example, recently issued a report that called on Ottawa to set regional development goals tied to income and employment indicators. It concluded that 'goals and objectives for regional economic development must be defined for slow-growth regions in terms of moving them closer to the Canadian average of certain measures or indicators.' A special discussion paper released by Premier Peckford spoke of 'real disparities between Newfoundland and the rest of the nation.' The 'real disparities' were described in terms of income and unemployment rates.[11]

Other than the federal transfer payments to individuals which have narrowed the regional gap in per capita income, little progress has been made in earned income per capita and in unemployment rates over the past twenty-five years. This is so despite the various attempts at promoting regional development described in this study. Are we employing realistic indicators?

Disparities in unemployment and per capita income are interrelated. Higher unemployment will result in lower per capita income, even if the regional income disparity for those with a job is relatively small. Over the past twenty years, for example, the earned income per employed person in the Atlantic provinces has trailed the national average by less than 15 percentage points, while income per capita has been more like 30 percentage points behind the national average.

Thus, two highly interrelated indicators have been employed time and again to tell the whole story of regional disparities in Canada. Although they are easy to grasp and have been useful in focusing public attention on the problem, they have serious shortcomings. We need other indicators to assess regional differences. Essentially, the two traditional indicators give an incomplete picture of regional economic conditions and establish unrealistic targets.

In basic household necessities, regional differences no longer exist in Canada. Twenty-five years ago, they were substantial. The disparity in provincial health and education expenditures per capita fell by almost half between 1962 and 1979. Health care, as measured by hospital beds and physicians per capita, is now 'of reasonable quality to all Canadians.' The same can be claimed for education. In fact, no systematic and significant regional disparities exist in terms of such basic indicators as life expectancy at birth, student-teacher ratios, the availability of police and fire protection, or the provision of public utilities.

Other indicators suggest a different regional picture than that revealed by per capita income and unemployment rates. The percentage of owner-occupied dwellings in the Atlantic provinces is substantially higher than elsewhere in the country, standing at 120 per cent of the national average, which compares with 102.7 per cent for Ontario. Residents of the Atlantic provinces lead in owner-occupied dwellings without mortgages: about 150 per cent of the national average. Compare this with 92 per cent for Ontario, 86 per cent for Alberta, and 91 per cent for British Columbia, three of Canada's wealthiest provinces.[12]

Although quality-of-life indicators are very difficult to measure and to interpret, it is nevertheless possible to say that a great number of these indicators clearly favour the traditionally have-not regions. There is a price to pay, it appears, for regions witnessing rapid economic growth, strong in-migration, urbanization. During the mid- to late 1970s, the three westernmost provinces saw tremendous economic growth. At the same time, they led the way in violent crime, divorce, death due to alcoholism, and suicide. Alberta's divorce rate was an average of 50 percentage points higher than the national average, while the four Atlantic provinces all had averages of below 30 per cent of the national average. The suicide rate was also considerably higher in the more developed regions, with a difference of some 60 percentage points between British Columbia and Prince Edward Island. Even the use of tranquillizers is much more widespread in Ontario, Alberta, and British Columbia than in New Brunswick, Prince Edward Island, and Newfoundland.

Again, regional income and employment indicators overlook these important considerations, concentrating as they do exclusively on one aspect of the economic health of a given region. Certainly these indicators point to the economic strength of southern Ontario, Alberta, British Columbia, and Saskatchewan. As the Economic Council of Canada observed, 'no amount of legitimate tinkering' will make regional differences disappear.[13]

These differences exist, however, for a variety of reasons. A quick look at the country's natural resource endowment, for example, reveals that Alberta, British Columbia, Saskatchewan, and Ontario are highly favoured both in terms of total resource base and resource base per capita. Figures 3–6 trace the regional shares of value added in four primary sectors. Although the data are plotted only at ten-year intervals, the points actually represent five-year averages centred on the years beginning in 1936. This smooths out the frequent wide annual swing in primary output and provides a better perspective on longer-term trends. The four easternmost provinces have witnessed a rather steady decline in their share of national output as the new resources were developed further west. The one exception is fisheries, where the Atlantic share has increased.

Ontario's relative decline in primary resources has been counterbalanced by steady performance in the manufacturing sector, where, especially since the Second World War, it has gradually increased its share of output. With 35 per cent of Canada's population, Ontario has more than 50 per cent of the country's manufacturing sector and 41 per cent of the national domestic product.[14]

A region's human resources can shape the economic structure and play a pivotal role in attracting development projects. For one thing, age structure reveals the size of a region's labour resource. For potential productivity, the important determinant is not total population but population of working age. Perhaps surprisingly, the portion of the population of working age, usually considered to be

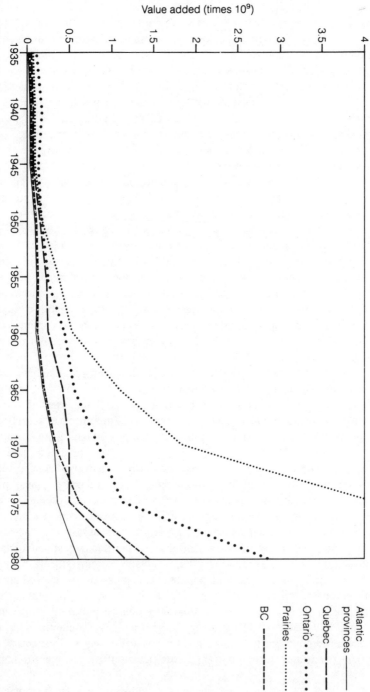

MINING – value added by region

Value added (times 10^9)

Atlantic
provinces ————

Quebec ———

Ontario ••••••

Prairies ••••••••••

BC ––––––

FIGURE 3 Resources – regional shares of value added (source: Statistics Canada, *Provincial Gross Domestic Product by Industry System of National Accounts*, Catalogue 61-202 Annual)

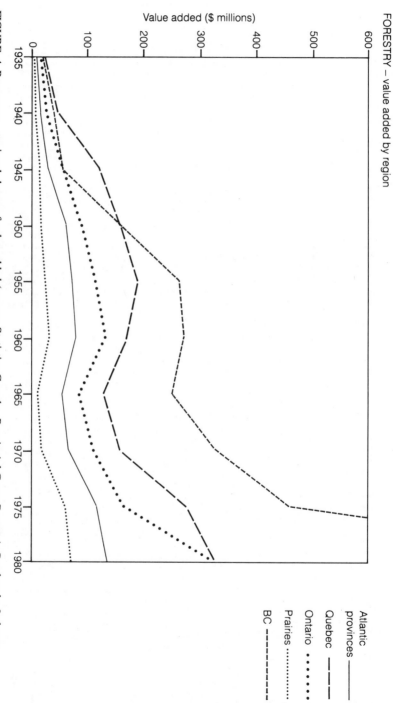

FIGURE 4 Resources – regional shares of value added (source: Statistics Canada, *Provincial Gross Domestic Product by Industry*, Catalogue 61-202 Annual)

AGRICULTURE – value added by region

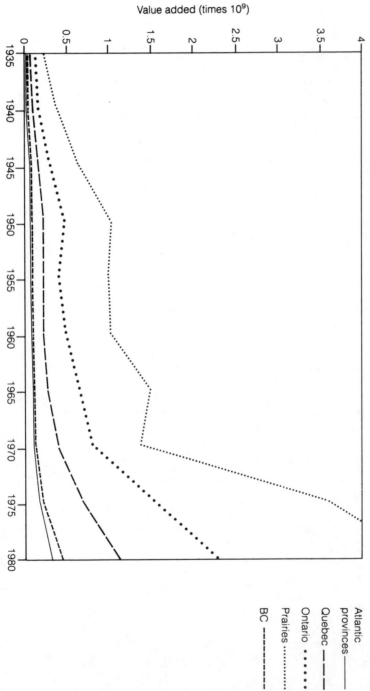

Value added (times 10⁹)

Atlantic
provinces ─────
Quebec ── ── ──
Ontario • • • • • •
Prairies ••••••••
BC ── — ── — ──

FIGURE 5 Resources – regional shares of value added (source: Statistics Canada, *Provincial Gross Domestic Product by Industry*, Catalogue 61-202 Annual)

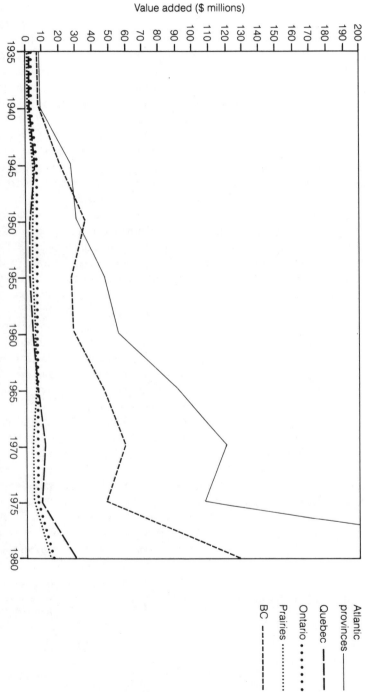

FISHERIES – value added by region

Value added ($ millions)

Atlantic
provinces ————

Quebec — — —

Ontario • • • • •

Prairies ••••••••

BC – – – – – – –

FIGURE 6 Resources – regional shares of value added (source: Statistics Canada, *Provincial Gross Domestic Product by Industry*, Catalogue 61-202 Annual)

between 15 and 65, differs significantly among the regions. Figure 7 illustrates that, in 1981, this fraction varied from 64.5 per cent in the Atlantic provinces to over 69.4 per cent in Quebec.

The four Atlantic provinces, Manitoba, and Saskatchewan have smaller fractions of their population in the 15-to-65 age bracket, largely because of decades of out-migration of young job-seekers. A lower share of productive population implies that a region's economic indicators calculated per capita will be relatively less favourable than the same indicators calculated per worker. Perhaps the most important consequence of a relatively high concentration of population in the dependent age brackets (under 15 or over 65) is the relatively high 'overhead' burden this places on an economy as a whole, particularly for education and health facilities.

In more recent years, many observers have pointed to urbanization as one of the key factors influencing economic growth, earned per capita income, and employment opportunities. One of the reasons for this view is that many of the service functions in a modern economy – financial administration, research and development, and headquarters' activities – take place in cities. Many service functions, in turn, are among the fastest growing sectors of the economy. Therefore regions with population concentrated in large urban centres will receive more than their share of this growth. The Economic Council of Canada observed: 'The most populous urban centres everywhere have had high rates of growth. Their growth rate was more than double that for the total regional population in the Atlantic and Prairie regions, and this was all the more notable because both experienced large net outmigration and relatively weak population growth.'[15]

Major Canadian urban centres often show less disparity than do the regions. Halifax's unemployment and personal income statistics are closer to Hamilton's than Nova Scotia's are to Ontario's. Further, urban size does have a positive influence on income and on participation rates in the labour force, which indicates greater diversity of available jobs in larger urban areas.

Ontario has the most mature urban structure of any region in Canada. Cities such as Ottawa, Hamilton, London, Windsor, St Catharines, Kitchener-Waterloo, and Thunder Bay, with populations ranging from 100,000 to 500,000, provide an urbanized and highly developed hinterland to support the position of Toronto. The dramatic rise of Alberta's energy-based economy in the late 1970s, coupled with the emergence of Vancouver, Calgary, and Edmonton as important corporate and financial centres, has spurred a 'second Canadian economic heartland.' But the 700-mile corridor stretching from Windsor to Quebec City has not lost its economic importance and still accounts for about 70 per cent of Canada's manufacturing employment. The region is also home to most corporate head-quarters in the country.

Quebec's urban structure is weaker, mainly because Montreal has only Quebec

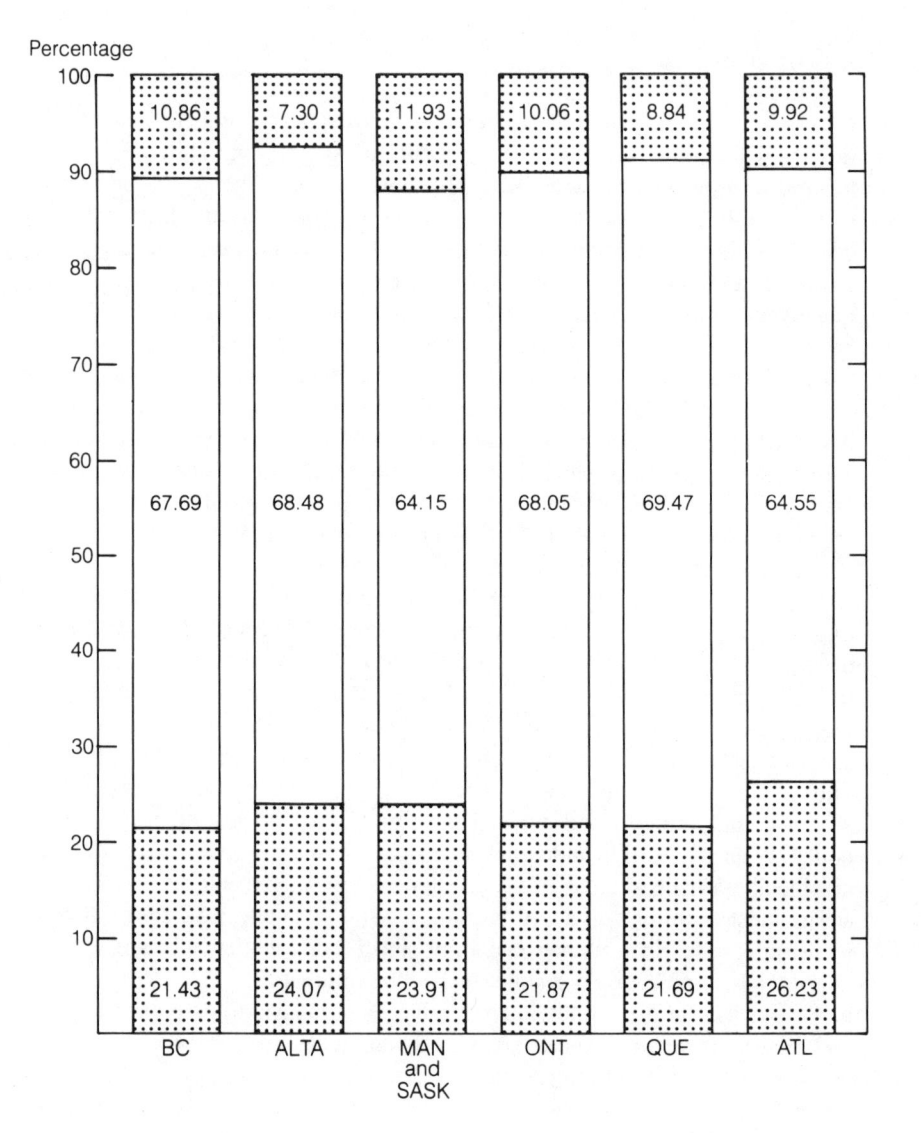

FIGURE 7 Fraction of population of working age, 1981 (source: Statistics Canada, *1981 Census of Canada*, Population Catalogue 92-901, vol 1)

City as an important urban centre from which to draw support. The four Atlantic provinces have the weakest urban structure of any region. They have only a handful of urban centres with 100,000 people or more. The Economic Council of Canada believes that the region's economy would benefit from a greater concentration of population. Notwithstanding transportation subsidies amounting to 50 per cent of transportation cost for most manufacturing items, Atlantic manufacturers have developed little strength in industries that are not resource-based or closely linked to local markets.

Can Canada realistically hope to alleviate regional disparities, as defined by income and employment levels? The economic forces that have led to existing development patterns are strong, and it would take extremely powerful and costly countervailing forces to change that pattern to abolish regional disparities. In fact, the burden that would be imposed on the 'have' regions would be so large that it might well be unacceptable and could threaten national unity quite as much as would persistent and pronounced regional disparities.

A review of federal regional development efforts points to the conclusion that differences in regional growth rates are caused more by economic factors and less by institutional factors than many in slow-growth regions tend to believe. The relative lack of manufacturing in the west and the Atlantic provinces and the perennial labour surplus in the Maritimes and eastern Quebec cannot be attributed substantially to federal policies, such as the customs tariffs and the auto pact. Allan Tupper points out in his study: 'There is some evidence which suggests that provinces may have over-estimated the significance of discriminatory federal policy as an obstacle to industrial development.' Ken Norrie adds: 'The geographically peripheral areas of the country are just not feasible sites to naturally attract most types of secondary industry ... Hinterland regions do not become industrial centres in a market economy and the distribution of manufacturing industries across Canada is a simple reflection of this fact.'[16]

A close look at the economic circumstances of the Maritime provinces in the mid-nineteenth century reveals signs of economic decline. The post-Confederation decline, which continued into the next century, appears the result of the regional economy's inability to adjust. Roy George suggests that 'shipbuilding was perhaps the best example. The province's [Nova Scotia's] pre-eminence in building wooden sailing ships was undermined by technical developments and called for a change to steam driven steel ships. But the industry continued in the old way, making no concession to progress, and died.'[17] In turn, lumbering in the region suffered from the decline in ship-building. Agriculture also suffered following an inflow of less expensive foodstuffs from other parts of Canada, and fishing slipped badly when world markets for saltfish dwindled. In short, Confederation is not responsible for all the economic ills of the Atlantic provinces and eastern Quebec. Further, regional development policies and programs cannot now turn the tide and alleviate regional disparities.

The urban structure of a region is regarded as a key determinant of earned per capita income, participation rate in the labour force, and overall economic growth. Southern Ontario's urban structure clearly leads the way. But duplicating that structure in all regions of the country is hardly a realistic goal, nor is re-creating, even on a smaller scale, the industrial structure of Ontario.

THE NEED FOR CLEAR OBJECTIVES

We must assess regional disparities in Canada in a manner that goes well beyond the standard income and employment indicators. A more comprehensive method should bring together a wide-ranging set of measurements of economic and social well-being. Quality-of-life indicators should be included, even though they will never be as neat and tidy as the other bench-marks. The assessment should lead to a new set of regional development objectives, more realistic than those advanced in the late 1960s and still regarded as valid and appropriate by provincial governments, economic think tanks, and many residents of slow-growth regions.

The notion that regional disparities could actually be alleviated emerged under far different circumstances than those of today. In the late 1960s, governments were expanding into virtually every sector and were not confronted with large deficits. They had resources at hand to launch such ambitious undertakings as the US 'war on poverty' and the establishment of a 'just society.' The revolution of rising expectations and improved communications had also taken hold. One region knew very quickly the development performance of another region, and this knowledge influenced governments' goals. Expectations were such that things had to be accomplished quickly, and standards of performance were set very high.

In regional development, only limited research had been undertaken, and new concepts were barely off the drawing board. No one knew what was possible. There was little literature or practical experience in the area. Although virtually no research had been undertaken on the concept, the Canadian government embraced growth poles and announced ambitious regional development objectives.

It is now clear that the goal of alleviating regional disparities is unrealistic, and new objectives should be established. A restatement of objectives is urgently required, not simply because existing ones are unrealistic, but also to strengthen national unity. Unrealistic goals create excessive expectations and ultimately lead to bitterness and disillusionment. Premier Peckford said recently: 'If Newfoundland is to even equal the national average earned income by the year 2000, a growth rate of double the national average will be required each year ... [Even then] Newfoundland will still not catch the three leading provinces by the year

2000.'[18] The sheer futility of such an objective is made evident by the fact that between 1946 and 1979 Alberta's earned income did not increase at anywhere near that pace, despite intense energy-related economic activity.

A sustainable national consensus must be based on a realistic perception by Canadians as to what they can expect from their national institutions. Unrealistic expectations can erode that consensus. Ottawa has a responsibility to state clearly that it does not have the capacity to alleviate regional disparities, as traditionally defined. What Ottawa should state is that it will pursue a policy of economic development for all regions but cannot guarantee that any one region's relative share, as measured by employment levels and earned income, will not decline. Realistic development objectives should then be defined for each region. These should be clear and precise, so as to assist in creating comprehensive strategies. Though there are political advantages to vague and imprecise objectives, leaders from slow-growth regions should realize that imprecise objectives do not normally contribute to well-designed policies and programs and certainly make it difficult to assess their success or failure.

It looks, however, as if the federal government and the provinces are not adjusting their objectives to correspond to the economic potential of each region. New Brunswick's recently signed ERDA has retained the objective of closing the gap in earned per capita income with the national average. Other ERDAS lack rigour and purpose or simply restate what was said some ten years earlier. In Prince Edward Island, for instance, the federal government and the province have agreed 'to better utilize the human resources of the province in order to provide its economy with increased flexibility to meet changing economic conditions and to maximize employment opportunities.'[19] Such wide-sweeping objectives serve little purpose in planning new initiatives, in serving as a guide to assess proposals, or in gauging the progress made in developing the economic potential of the province. The Nova Scotia ERDA has, as its first objective, 'to enhance the economic development of Nova Scotia throughout all areas of the province.'[20] Practically any conceivable project of 'economic development' could be approved under such an objective.

The importance of defining clear and realistic regional development objectives can hardly be overemphasized. Yet clear objectives would no doubt necessitate some difficult policy choices. If, for example, Ottawa and Prince Edward Island or New Brunswick agree that the overriding regional development goal is to create self-sustaining economic activity, then decisions will be required that may well prove painful to some. For instance, the federal government may have to set public-service wages more in line with the wages for comparable work in the private sector in the region. The benefits of higher wages for the employed federal public servant would then be considered against the zero wages obtained by the unemployed. Similarly, affected provincial governments might lower the provincial minimum wage in order to lower unemployment.[21] Obviously, both these measures might be seen as politically unacceptable. This view, however, should be considered against the backdrop of the continuing dependence of certain regional economies on federal transfer payments.

There are other reasons why regional development objectives should be stated more clearly. Government resources for regional development, as for other policy fields, are becoming more and more difficult to obtain. Clear objectives can pave the way for strategic development plans that can move regional development programs away from enabling documents, which, as this study makes clear, give rise to a virtually insatiable appetite for any kind of project in practically any place in Canada.

Clearer and move realistic objectives could also make it easier to encourage federal departments and agencies to contribute to overall regional development efforts. There has been little reason in the past for them to add to the hodge-podge of initiatives called regional development. One more project thrown in might contribute to pump-prime a region that much more, but would serve little other obvious purpose. Lastly, clearer objectives can permit more realistic assessment of the economic foundations of lagging regional economies and help identify where selective interventions would provide the basis for self-sustaining economic activity.

11

Prospects

It is relatively easy to achieve a consensus that something should be done to promote regional development. It is also easy to get agreement that DREE and other such past federal initiatives were less successful than initially envisaged. It is more difficult to come forward with measures that will contribute to regional development, bearing in mind the limited resources of governments for that purpose. In this chapter, we will look at regional development instruments used in the past and consider possible new ones.

FEDERAL-PROVINCIAL CO-OPERATION AND REGIONAL DEVELOPMENT STRATEGIES

The importance of close federal-provincial co-operation in regional economic development was made evident in chapter 4. Yet such considerations are a two-edged sword, having both the capacity to frustrate any development effort on the part of one level of government if they are not promoted with care, or the capacity to pursue effectively development opportunities if they are.

One indispensable ingredient of federal-provincial co-operation is a clear understanding of the responsibilities of both levels of government. This understanding has not always been evident. During DREE's early years, we saw a 'take it or leave it' approach on the part of the federal government. This was followed by a period under the GDA approach when the federal government, through DREE, reacted to provincially designed initiatives. Later came a preoccupation by Ottawa with public visibility for its regional development efforts. One thing remained constant throughout, however. All efforts were developed in relation to their effect on a given provincial economy. Projects were defined and implemented essentially from a provincial perspective.

Both the federal government and the provinces, especially those in disadvantaged regions, have been preoccupied with what is good for the province or, perhaps, for a particular sub-provincial area. There has been virtually no effort to determine what a province or an area can do efficiently in relation to other regions. The GDAS, the Prince Edward Island comprehensive plan, and now the ten ERDAS appear to present ten separate and autonomous policies. Yet it is anything but certain that simply 'pump-priming' a regional economy is the most effective way of achieving growth targets. In the words of economist N.H. Lithwick, 'If you look at DREE's series of provincial reports, there is one interesting problem and that is that the numbers do not add up. If you take ten separate regional policies or sets of forecasts that are under no obligation to relate one to the other, you end up with the aggregrate being rather different from the components. The sum of the components do not make a sensible aggregate.'[1]

This policy orientation holds two major drawbacks. It can give rise to costly interprovincial competition, as it has, in fact, done; the resulting harm to the national economy is obvious. It can also prevent integration of the regional economy within the national economy. Linking peripheral economies with the national economy holds considerable promise as a means of spurring development in slow-growth regions. Much as developing countries prefer trade with and access to the world economy over foreign aid, slow-growth regions would benefit from integration with the national economy and access to a larger market. The regional economy least integrated with the national economy – that of the Maritimes – is also the least developed. Trade between the Atlantic provinces and the other regions is at nowhere near the level of that among other regions.[2]

The federal government should approach federal-provincial negotiations with the purpose of putting in place measures to integrate regional economies. It should seek to place regional development efforts in a context considerably larger than individual provinces. In addition, the federal government should go to the negotiating table only after it has developed a clear set of objectives for national economic development and a corresponding set for the regional level. Only then should a series of development strategies be formulated. Each strategy should entail an evaluation of top-priority projects and explicit trade-offs between regions or sub-regions. For example, a decision to promote development in one sector could require a firm decision not to support similar initiatives in another region.

In negotiating with provincial governments, Ottawa should be prepared to offer incentives to integrate the provincial economies more fully with the national one. Federal funds should also be conditional on a province opening up its market to another region. An excellent example is Ontario's decision to increase the price of wine from British Columbia to protect its own Niagara wine industry. Federal funds should also be employed to counter destructive interprovincial bidding for new industrial plants.

Provincial governments meanwhile would approach negotiations much as they have done in the past. They too would come to the table with a development strategy in hand, no doubt with a clearer understanding of the local economy than the federal government and greater awareness of what would work and what would not. They certainly can deliver initiatives more quickly and efficiently than Ottawa. Recent experience has shown that federal direct-delivery initiatives are not implemented as efficiently as those of provincial governments under the various GDAs,[3] probably because of the large and rather cumbersome federal bureaucracy. The provinces, however, may not appreciate national economic priorities and the need for better integration of the national and regional economies.

One issue that should not be overlooked is that of federal visibility. Provincial governments have rarely complained about lack of credit for their efforts. They are on-site, closer to the community level, and able to gain favourable public exposure. The same is not the case for the federal government, and it should get proper credit for its efforts. Unless this happens, federal cabinet ministers and MPs will never give regional development the political legitimacy and support that it requires.

There are many examples of the federal government's not receiving the political credit it deserves in this area. There are, of course, the standard complaints over the lack of recognition of federal support for the various provincial public services through the equalization program and shared-cost programs in health and post-secondary education. But there are more striking examples. When the federal government announced that it would close the Canadian Forces Base in Chatham, New Brunswick's government, over two years, criticized Ottawa for pulling out 1,500 permanent jobs in an economically depressed area. Ottawa finally announced in May 1984 that it would locate a low-level air defence training school in Chatham that would secure at least 1,400 permanent jobs for the area. The following day the provincial minister of development issued a statement claiming that 'the province had found the answer to CFB-Chatham.' He was also critical of the federal government for leaving 'several employees in the cold to wait until the changeover is complete in 1988.'[4] Such statements do not enhance federal-provincial co-operation and are likely to do little more than arouse the ire of federal politicians. In addition, government MPs in Ottawa insist that provincial governments will invariably suggest a mid-week date for official opening ceremonies for joint projects, knowing full well that a Friday or Saturday would be much more convenient for travel to and from Ottawa.

Federal visibility is viewed by many as a messy and somewhat senseless issue. Provincial politicians dismiss it as simply another example of federal paranoia, and students of regional development view it as irrelevant to the problem at hand. Yet it cannot be so easily dismissed, and provincial governments, in particular, should be more open to the issue. They should appreciate the fact that it is far easier for them to be viewed in the local press as being on the side of provincial and community-level interests and promoting specific initiatives than it is for the federal government, which is often asked to decide between provinces and regions.

The development of regional development strategies could increase Ottawa's visibility and accountability. The federal government would be able to announce a strategy, state clearly where it stands on development issues, and provide an agenda for discussion with a number of interest groups. In short, the public would know the position of the federal government before it is completely lost in intergovernmental negotiations.

POLICY AND PROGRAM INITIATIVES

The regional strategies would provide the means to frame regional development objectives and priorities for each region. These efforts should go beyond the present practice of having provincial governments compete vigorously against each other for projects. A decision-making pattern has emerged in which regions grab whatever project is around, with little regard for the most appropriate location from an economic and overall development perspective. Federally sponsored initiatives, notably under the GDAs, have reinforced this pattern.

To be effective, these regional strategies must also go beyond a simple transfer of federal funds. Richard Higgins, a specialist in regional planning, has described what a development strategy should contain:

(i) a clear statement of the nature and dimensions of the problems of regional disparity and regional development in Canada:
(ii) a presentation and discussion of the various alternatives available in confronting these problems;
(iii) a discussion and summary of the various alternatives in terms of the roles and responsibilities of individuals, the private sector of the economy and the different levels of government in confronting regional disparity and regional development;
(iv) a statement of the role and responsibility which is actually accepted by the Government of Canada when dealing with regional development;
(v) a clear, precise and realistic set of objectives and targets;
(vi) a statement of the overall strategy to be employed in meeting the objectives. This should be a total strategy and should indicate the strategic role for individual transfer payments and block funding to the provinces as well as specific federal development initiatives, federal-provincial development initiatives and where possible, provincial initiatives;
(vii) a summary of the implementation strategy to be followed, including an outline of how the overall federal administration would be required to respond to directly assist in meeting the objectives; and
(viii) a process for continually reviewing the strategy and for modifying it as necessary.[5]

These strategies should seek to enhance interregional linkages on the one hand and create production and self-sustaining employment opportunities on the other. Past preoccupation with closing gaps between regions should give way to a new focus on reducing the gap between the potential and actual economic growth of each region. The important test would be whether these strategies could go beyond being simply an instrument to transfer federal funds to a grab bag of provincially inspired development initiatives and succeed in integrating the regional perspective into federal policies. A word of clarification regarding the regional perspective in federal policies is in order. Regional perspective is frequently contrasted with a sectoral perspective, where the national economy is viewed both as a collection of industrial sectors with total output that equals the Canadian GNP in the same way as the total output of the regional economy equals GNP.

How can the regional perspective be integrated into federal policies? Should a series of national sectoral policies be developed and then modified to fit the regional strategies, or should regional strategies be developed and subsequently modified to incorporate sectoral considerations? Both should be developed simultaneously so that neither has the upper hand. The federal government has traditionally started with a sectoral strategy. Yet this approach has contributed little to national economic cohesion or to easing of interregional tensions. Attempts at defining a national industrial strategy have always been viewed as helping the Windsor-Quebec corridor. If the regional perspective were given precedence, then federal policy-making could well produce the kind of economic decision-making that evolved under the GDA approach – inward-looking, with little potential for integrating the various regional economies.

The formulation of federal policies incorporating both sectoral and regional perspectives at the outset would permit a comprehensive pulling together of both concerns early in the process. Such an approach might encourage officials to analyse regional comparative advantages and development opportunities in ways that made interregional and intersectoral trade-offs as clear as possible. Failure to go beyond a regional 'add-on' approach will only invite inappropriate and counterproductive provincial action and the creation of ad hoc measures by the federal government. Better integration of national and regional policies could assist the development process.

REGIONAL DEVELOPMENT INSTRUMENTS AND PROGRAMS

Regional strategies must be supported by a series of instruments and programs. Some of these already exist but need revision, others are dormant and need to be reactivated, and still others should be introduced.

A regional development fund was introduced in the 1982 government reorganization. Little has been said about the fund since it was established. A regional fund, properly financed, offers important advantages.[6] It can introduce flexibility and discretion to a regional development package. Flexibility, however, can lead to the introduction of unrelated initiatives, with unpredictable impact on other regions or indeed other initiatives in the designated region. There is a strong tendency to revert to 'one-shot' projects at the end of the government fiscal year when budgets must be spent if the money is not to be lost. To avoid this kind of spending, provision could be made for the unspent portion of the annual allocation of the regional fund to be brought forward to the next fiscal year.

The success of a regional fund depends on clearly defined criteria for screening applications. Another important consideration is geographical application. Presumably a regional fund deals with the more permanent or structural regional problems. Thus, the fund should apply to most of Atlantic Canada, northern Quebec, and Ontario, the western northlands, and the British Columbia interior.

Eligibility should be tied to two regional development goals: potential for long term self-sustaining economic activity, and ability to integrate into the regional economies. The aim of the fund would be to lessen the dependence of economically disadvantaged regions on transfer payments and to ensure that new economic activities do not conflict or compete with others in other regions of the country.

Industrial incentives remain one of the most widely employed instruments to influence location or expansion of industry in certain regions. Both the United States and Canada offer such incentives, as do thirteen European countries, Japan, and Australia.[7] Despite difficulties in measuring the cost benefits of incentive programs or even determining their relative influence, such programs continue. A British government report sums up the situation: 'The most our witnesses could say was that although the imbalance persisted between assisted and non-assisted areas, they thought that the situation was better than it would have been without the incentives.'[8] The Canadian experience is similar: uncertainty about effectiveness, but a widespread feeling that things would be much worse had the program not existed. It is essentially on that basis that Canada's incentives program remains the cornerstone of the federal government's involvement in regional development.

Having had one sort or another of regional industrial incentives over the past twenty years, Canadians might expect more tangible evidence of support for them than a simple feeling that things could have been much worse. If they are not able to demonstrate the importance and viability of their programs with the information available to them, not to mention that it is clearly in their interest to do so, there is little hope others will be able to or even inclined to attempt it. The onus is on the supporters of the programs to show that they have had a positive impact. On this point, however, DREE produced 'confusing and irrelevant statistics.'[9] Nor was the research of others who supported the program convincing. Of course, there are always good reasons why certain economic activities are found where they are, and moving them is not always cheap, easy, or even possible.

Outside firms lured into a region solely on the basis of incentives may not have performed as well as initially envisaged. One survey reveals: 'Some $30 million were poured out over a four-year period mainly to American firms to induce them to set up factories in Cape Breton. By the end of the period, virtually all had failed and almost nothing remained.'[10] Although they could not support their claim with empirical data, field officials operating DREE's former RDIA program insist that the best bet for long-term success was, typically, a local company, growing to meet expanding markets, or an entrepreneur with a new business venture.

Thus the federal government should retain some form of regional industrial incentives, but with changes. A substantial reduction in the expenditure budget allocated to regional incentives would force the government to be more selective in approving grants and give priority to projects that are clearly most deserving from a regional development perspective. Further, the budget should be increased only when it is demonstrated that incentives encourage regional development.

There are several possible incentive tools available to the federal government, the most popular being the cash grant. Cash grants hold advantages over other incentives schemes, particularly for small and medium-size businesses. Cash is provided in the first years of operation when it is most needed and most difficult to obtain. For smaller single-plant firms, such grants are more attractive than tax allowances, which depend on the company being in a taxable position. Because of start-up costs and general tax allowances, most smaller firms are not in a taxable position for at least two years, and frequently up to six years. Also, cash grants are more easily understood by small and medium-sized businesses than are fiscal concessions.

One area where tax incentives could replace cash grants is for modernization and expansion of existing firms. At present, firms with such plans can apply for a federal cash grant. A firm wishing to expand does not face the same difficulties as a firm about to get started in business. It has no start-up cost, an established cash flow, and presumably a mature organization from which to expand. A tax concession could facilitate modernization or expansion, if an incentive is at all required. Cash grants provide the federal government greater visibility than tax incentives, but then administrative cost is considerably higher than that for tax incentives.

There are sufficient reasons to retain a cash grant incentives program for regional development purposes for new businesses in designated regions. The question that must now be addressed is: how limited an area should cash grants cover, and on what basis should an area be designated? Too wide a coverage diffuses efforts. When the program covers over 50 per cent of the population, as RDIA did, most observers and many DREE officials consider it much too extended.

However, limiting the program to, say, only 15 per cent of the population would assist the most economically disadvantaged areas, but it would also have limited impact because of the scarcity of private-sector development opportunities and initiatives likely to surface. A DREE study revealed in the early 1980s that the right mix between needy areas and private-sector initiatives would lead to a program that covered about 25 per cent of the Canadian population, and I have no reason to disagree with this conclusion. Census divisions should be employed to establish boundaries, if only because defining new special boundaries would be too costly, since it would require the collection of primary data. Evaluation criteria for the program should be tied to the creation of employment and movement away from dependence on transfer payments.

The program's administrative procedures should be streamlined and more flexible than those used in the past. Small businessmen just starting up do not always have access to advice on the elaborate application procedures to obtain a government grant. Their needs are different from larger businesses; for example, they may require advance grant payments on construction costs.

The program should cover manufacturing and processing industries and primary resource processing and service facilities that correspond to a region's economic circumstances. The 'shot-gun' approach of the past, where any company in any type of manufacturing activity would be urged to enter a slow-growth region if it meant new jobs, should be dropped for a more sober assessment of what would have the best chances of long-term success in any given region. Once this has been determined, officials should have considerable flexibility in bringing new activities to the region. It is far better to risk grants to small and medium-sized businesses in these areas than to rely on transfer payments which may avoid the embarrassment of supporting businesses that have gone bankrupt, but which are neither an efficient allocation of public funds nor likely to support much self-sustaining economic activity.

Administratively, the program should be guided by a 'pro-active' capacity, as opposed to the largely 'responsive' regional incentive programs of the past. A capacity should be developed, either inside the federal government or through ongoing federal-provincial co-ordination, to identify investment opportunities through import substitution and export analysis, industry profiles, and corporate industrial and economic intelligence.

There is also still considerable scope for governments, especially the federal government, to promote slow-growth regions to the business community. Firms tend to overlook such regions as a matter of course, even though they often hold distinct advantages, either because of quality surplus labour or available resources.[11] Once such an opportunity is identified, a program package could be offered to a particular firm. However, if, after consultation, and despite a possible incentive package, it was determined that a particular manufacturing activity is better suited to southern Ontario, then the company should be encouraged to locate there, without any government assistance unless specific linkages or spin-off activities in slow-growth areas could be proved.

It is no longer wise to retain an inflexible view of interregional equity in new jobs created in the manufacturing sector.[12] International competition for new manufacturing jobs is far more intense now than at any time in the past. It is no longer so much Moncton in competition with Toronto as it is the Canadian economy in competition with South Korea, western Europe, and, of course, the United States. Industrial development in Canada in the 1980s is also being shaped by ever-increasing competition from newly industrialized countries and by the seemingly limitless applications of the microprocessor in such areas as machine tools and automated assembly. In short, future competition for 'footloose' industrial development will involve pushing and pulling not so much between regions in Canada but rather between Canada and other nations.

In Canada, as elsewhere, industrial growth will be more dependent on investment in innovation and less on investment in new productive capacity. A shift in emphasis will also occur from competitiveness in terms of price to competitiveness in terms of novelty and quality. In turn, this will require a concentration on research, development, design, and engineering.

How are slow-growth areas likely to fare against established areas under such conditions? To the extent that Canada can compete in the international marketplace, economic factors are likely to favour larger, more sophisticated urban centres. Halifax is likely to do much better than Cape Breton, and Montreal better than the Gaspé. It may be unwise, both from a national and regional perspective, to scatter our high technology all across the country and, by doing so, ignore the interactive requirements of the industry.

This is not to suggest that governments should not pursue industrial development for slow-growth regions. However, industrial development for these regions will probably be more difficult than in the past, and governments should not raise expectations unduly. Large industrial incentives to big businesses may no longer constitute the appropriate cornerstone for Canada's regional economic development policy. They can no doubt still play a significant role, but in more isolated instances, where designated regions would clearly benefit and where they would contribute to the national economy rather than fragmenting an already weakened industrial sector.

Special measures for slow-growth regions should go beyond standard cash grants to large businesses. More attention should be paid to local strengths and local entrepreneurs than in the past, when solutions for slow-growth regions were pinned on the hope of attracting footloose industrial activities from elsewhere. In North America and western Europe, large industrial enterprises are shedding jobs at a rapid rate as a result of a concentration on productivity and the world-wide redistribution of manufacturing. With severe shrinkage of employment in existing industries the likely pattern for the next decade, slow-growth regions should look to new enterprises for promoting economic development. New enterprises or companies five years old or less now account for some 33 per cent of net growth in employment.[13] Slow-growth regions, like others, should foster local entrepreneurial initiative or the creation of new enterprises.

One route that should be explored is community enterprise. Such an enterprise can foster the capacity of local entrepreneurs, whether the community itself or an individual. Such an approach can spur development with a small amount of start-up money and can be more effective than capital-intensive works or large industrial subsidies.[14] It is also less likely to entail the kind of interregional conflict associated with large, regionally biased industrial incentives.

Former DREE deputy minister Tom Kent recently described the potential of this approach: 'While there have been some disappointments, there have been a great many small successes, exploiting a wide range of opportunities – in fishing, in fish farming, in fish processing, in sheep farming, in vegetable growing, in a great variety of craft activities, in tourist accommodations of unconventional kinds, in tourist facilities and restaurants, in the lumber industry, in modular home manufacturing, in a number of metal fabricating and similar small industries. I could go on ... I can't resist adding that the cost per job has been modest.'[15] Community-level enterprises can provide training for owner-managers and management training in rural areas and sponsor small-scale marketing studies, among other things. Such community-level enterprises need to be developed in close co-operation with the relevant provincial government.

Community-based development projects do not have the glamour or offer the massive number of new jobs that some high-technology manufacturing facilities can bring to communities. However, some community-based enterprises have been very successful and have created self-sustaining economic activity. The federal government introduced in the early 1980s, through DREE and CEIC, the LEDA program (Local Economic Development Agency). This initiative sought to involve local interests, particularly businesses, in managing the program.[16] The program was not costly, and in some communities it created productive employment opportunities. It also motivated local businesses to take an active interest in the economic health of their community.

An interesting example is the Kent-LEDA initiative, a federally funded local economic development agency. With a total annual funding of $350,000, the Kent-LEDA organization has made debt and equity investments in numerous small projects and has provided counselling and technical assistance to local entrepreneurs. The organization is directed by a group of local Kent-area business people and invests, on average, in twelve new or expanding businesses a year. Thus far, its success rate compares favourably with DREE's former RDIA program; 90 per cent of the firms in which it invested are still operating. It has created approximately fifty new jobs a year. There are also reasons to believe that this fact is a more accurate assessment of jobs created than those claimed under the RDIA program. In many instances, LEDA represents the lender of last resort, so that the new businesses would not have gone ahead without its financing. Decisions on proposed projects have been removed from government departments and turned over to an independent board of directors. Frequently, businessmen sitting on the board will approve a project, not because of the applicant's sound financial statement, but because he or she is well known in the community and has established credibility as 'a solid citizen.' This approach might appear awkward in larger centres, but in small rural communities it is working. Equally important is the contribution the organization has made to the business climate in the area. It regularly organizes workshops for the local business community, business-week activities, and the like.[17]

Governments might organize training courses on how to start and operate a small business. They should stress management training and upgrading for small and medium-sized businesses in slow-growth regions. Being isolated from large urban areas, such firms are often not able to take advantage of new technology, new business knowledge, or emerging markets for their products. This problem has long been identified, but little has been done about it. Such measures would not be as politically attractive as a grant creating new jobs, but they hold promise for solid growth.[18]

Such local initiatives involve issues of government organization and of power. In identifying and evaluating small local projects, the planner should be in the field working with local people, providing the necessary expert knowledge on the basis of which they can make decisions. Transferring authority to the field forces planners to the community level, where they perform not only a managerial but also an entrepreneurial function. One cannot predict in advance what new investment opportunities will be found, but one can predict that some will be found.

This approach calls for devolution of decision-making power to unofficial and non-governmental local organizations. Government officials will invariably argue, however, that control must remain in their hands, because otherwise chaos might result. As one observer remarked, 'It is hard to persuade a tiger to part with its stripes.'[19] If the objective is to promote local entrepreneurial initiatives, then governments must have sufficient confidence in the would-be entrepreneurs to let them create a favourable local environment. Different communities will need different measures, and federal and even provincial public servants cannot always respond to local circumstances because of national and provincial standards or criteria. Field offices are subject to the same kind of administration and financial controls as are head offices.

If decision-making and responsibility remains in government hands, then there will invariably be pressure to centralize operations, even if at first departments accept the need to decentralize operations to the field. There will always be a head office with central planners using models requiring specialized skills and technical manipulation. These planners can help plan regional development, but not local community efforts. They tend to mistrust people in the field and often fail to see that officials in regional offices can plan. Central-government officials often do not like the discomforts of trying to reach remote and peripheral communities and visit them infrequently. Decentralization usually leaves systems of hiring and supervision intact so that agents of influence tend to reinforce the sectoral perspective. Government officials operating in the field are thus not always free to 'push, probe, and cajole' local élites and communities into trying 'this and that' for stimulating economic development.[20]

In certain instances chaos may result and government funds will be wasted if decision-making authority is turned over to local non-government agencies. However, the limited experience we have tells us that locally designed measures to promote new businesses, such as the Kent-LEDA project, do not involve large amounts of public funds. Questions still remain about the effectiveness of a number of costly regional development efforts sponsored by GDAS and Ottawa's regional industrial incentives program. In addition, the cost of maintaining a government bureaucratic structure, either federal or provincial, for delivering an incentives program to the private sector is high when compared with the administrative or overhead cost of local development agencies. DRIE's operating budget for 1984–85 amounts to $220 million. This figure represents only administrative costs, such as salaries and travel expenses of permanent officials. To put this in perspective, total DREE spending for RDIA grants to business never amounted to more than $118 million annually, even in the early 1980s when the program covered 50 per cent of the population.[21]

Tax measures, for reasons described earlier, have a limited effect on small and medium-sized businesses in disadvantaged areas. There is one possible exception, however, that the federal government should consider. Just as individuals used to be able to put aside tax-free capital for the purchase of a home (the Registered Home Ownership Program), so individuals in slow-growth regions might be allowed to accumulate capital tax-free for business purposes. Guidelines could be established to direct the accumulated capital to designated regions.

Another measure to spur development in severely demand-deficient communities is Ottawa's relocation program; it will be recalled that some units proved more productive when moved to slow-growth areas.

STRUCTURING GOVERNMENT FOR REGIONAL ECONOMIC DEVELOPMENT

How should the federal government organize itself to emphasize regional economic development? Regional development should have an advocate at the cabinet table – a minister with a clear and unencumbered mandate for promoting regional economic development. Should that minister head a central agency or a line department? General theory on central agencies holds that they should be neutral and objective and should not compete for resources available to line departments. The theory provides for a neat and tidy division of responsibility, with central agencies acting as the 'honest broker' among competing line departments.[22] For managing an expenditure envelope in an orderly fashion, the theory has proved quite successful in practice.

Where the theory runs into difficulty is with problems requiring flexibility and a capacity to cut across sectoral or jurisdictional lines. Incremental change in the operation of line departments, where there is an entrenched tradition of doing things a certain way, is slow and often comes about only after strong pressure from outside the organization. These routines are frustrating to someone who has to react quickly to emerging opportunities, as frequently occurs in regional development.

How can the federal government combine a flexible approach and co-ordination of various line departments – in short, a central agency capacity? One option would be to establish an agency or department that cuts across jurisdictional lines, that has solely a regional development mandate, and that manages only the regional development fund. The agency would define strategies, negotiate them with provincial governments, and ensure a regional dimension in federal policies and programs. But the agency's capacity would go beyond that. It could play a DREE-type role by providing money from the regional fund to line departments as an incentive to do new and needed things.

Such an agency should be entrepreneurial and should avoid falling into routines or established patterns of activity. In the absence of proposals from line departments, it should develop them internally. It should be able to initiate new programs, as required, when line departments are unable to respond quickly. It should transfer such new initiatives to line departments as soon as the initiatives are mature enough to stand on their own and the department understands the objective of the program, so that it would not choke it with tradition.

Such an agency could launch a variety of initiatives immediately. It could, for example, reactivate the government's relocation program. To do this, it ought to assess the efficiency of the units already relocated and carry out a detailed cost analysis of potential units for decentralization. It could look at community-level development agencies as a means of stimulating low-cost development in particularly hard-pressed areas. It might transfer or divert funds from the Unemployment Insurance Program to finance such community-based enterprises and create jobs. It could also reactivate DREE's Bureau of Business and Economic Development, which was established shortly before the department was disbanded. The bureau's approach was innovative and energetic, in search of new investment projects for

DREE-designated regions. Its import-replacement analysis helped identify possible new dynamic sectors. There was some optimism that productive job-creating projects could be identified by this means, considering that Canada imported 12,000 commodities in 1979, with a value of about $62 billion.

The agency could launch a host of research projects. It could monitor and evaluate the regional performance of federal departments and agencies. It could initiate research to identify the advantages and means of integrating the economies of slow-growth regions more fully into the national economy. It could regularly assess federal expenditures, including tax expenditures by regions, and report its findings to Parliament.

The new organization would thus depart from tradition, in combining the capacities of a central agency with that of a program and research body. It would avoid potential conflict with line departments, in that it would not manage the overall expenditure envelopes. In contrast to existing central agencies, the bias of the new organization's policy and program would favour regional development. It would thus be able to avoid the central agency syndrome of developing a superb 'gatekeeper's' capacity – that is, the ability to stop things – but being unable to come up with creative and workable solutions. Conversely, it would also avoid the tendency of line departments to fall into established patterns of doing things and thus being unable to respond quickly enough to changing economic circumstances and opportunities.

Maximum financial provisions of signed sub-agreements as of 1 July 1982

	Total ($)	Federal share ($)	Provincial share ($)	Other ($)
Newfoundland				
Forestry	66,522,155	58,178,500	8,343,655	
Labrador Interim	22,097,000	19,662,300	2,434,700	
Tourism	13,264,600	11,938,140	1,326,460	
Agriculture	16,341,300	14,707,170	1,634,130	
Rural	14,580,000	13,122,000	1,458,000	
Industrial	26,650,000	23,985,000	2,665,000	
Forestry 1981–85	52,093,000	46,883,700	5,209,300	
Coastal Labrador	38,996,000	33,800,000	5,196,000	
Pulp and Paper	33,000,000	30,000,000	3,000,000	
Nova Scotia				
Halifax-Dartmouth	109,299,786	79,997,000	29,302,786	
Canso	30,057,500	22,503,400	7,554,100	
Industrial	23,789,000	19,031,200	4,757,800	
Tourism	13,750,000	11,000,000	2,750,000	
Energy	24,875,000	19,000,000	5,875,000	
Panamax Dry Dock	57,600,000	43,900,000	13,700,000	
Michelin	56,000,000	42,000,000	14,000,000	
Pulp and Paper	21,250,000	17,000,000	4,250,000	
sysco II	96,250,000	77,000,000	19,250,000	
Ocean Industry	35,000,000	22,950,000	12,050,000	
New Brunswick				
Saint John and Moncton	51,200,000	35,840,000	15,360,000	
Northeast	95,500,000	67,175,000	28,325,000	
Agricultural II	34,622,500	27,698,000	6,924,500	
Developing Regions	26,274,000	20,401,500	5,872,500	
Pulp and Paper	42,250,000	33,800,000	8,450,000	
Market Square	10,107,300	8,085,800	2,021,500	
Forestry II	37,500,000	30,000,000	7,500,000	

ACTIVE (concluded)

	Total ($)	Federal share ($)	Provincial share ($)	Other ($)
Quebec				
Transport	454,775,000	209,105,000	245,670,000	
Forestry	322,333,000	193,400,000	128,933,000	
Industrial Infrastructure	137,670,000	82,602,000	55,068,000	
Agriculture	103,266,000	61,960,000	41,306,000	
Water Treatment	200,000,000	120,000,000	80,000,000	
Tourism	136,000,000	69,600,000	66,400,000	
Public Infrastructure	34,876,000	23,261,000	11,615,000	
Pulp and Paper	240,000,000	135,000,000	105,000,000	
Amos	42,500,000	25,500,000	17,000,000	
Inter-Port	9,250,000	5,550,000	3,700,000	
Ontario				
Northeastern	30,602,000	15,301,000	15,301,000	
Single-Industry	19,800,000	10,215,000	9,585,000	
Community and Rural	9,456,650	4,728,325	4,728,325	
Forest	82,236,500	41,118,250	41,118,250	
Pulp and Paper	180,000,000	60,000,000	120,000,000	
Eastern	50,350,000	25,175,000	25,175,000	
Northern Rural	18,500,000	10,000,000	8,500,000	
Sault Ste Marie	69,600,000	21,000,000	24,300,000	24,300,000
Manitoba				
Industrial	44,000,000	26,400,000	17,600,000	
Value-Added Crops	18,500,000	11,100,000	7,400,000	
Tourism	20,000,000	12,000,000	8,000,000	
Winnipeg Core	96,000,000	32,000,000	32,000,000	32,000,000
Saskatchewan				
Qu'Appelle	33,700,000	17,960,000	15,740,000	
Northlands	127,000,000	87,000,000	40,000,000	
Interim Water	15,250,000	7,900,000	7,350,000	
Planning 1979–84	1,500,000	750,000	750,000	
Alberta				
Nutritive II	28,000,000	14,000,000	14,000,000	
British Columbia				
Industrial	70,000,000	35,000,000	35,000,000	
Agriculture	86,750,000	30,000,000	30,000,000	26,750,000
Travel	50,000,000	25,000,000	25,000,000	
Intensive Forest	50,000,000	25,000,000	25,000,000	
Ridley Island	9,600,000	4,800,000	4,800,000	
Yukon				
Renewable Resources	6,600,000	4,520,000	2,080,000	
Interim Tourism	6,000,000	5,100,000	900,000	
Total	3,852,984,291	2,281,704,285	1,488,230,006	83,050,000

EXPIRED

	Total ($)	Federal share ($)	Provincial share ($)	Other ($)
Newfoundland				
Gros Morne	22,935,200	20,641,680	2,293,520	
Highways 1974–75	13,864,444	12,478,000	1,386,444	
Fisheries Marine	12,000,000	10,800,000	1,200,000	
Special Fish	6,130,000	5,517,000	613,000	
NORDCO	4,910,080	4,419,072	491,008	
Highways 1975–76	22,222,000	20,000,000	2,222,000	
St John's Urban	68,000,000	51,000,000	17,000,000	
Highways 1976–81	101,435,556	88,244,000	13,191,556	
Planning	6,385,000	4,000,000	2,385,000	
Inshore Fisheries	11,761,000	10,584,900	1,176,100	
Mineral	12,458,000	11,212,200	1,245,800	
Stephenville	15,000,000	13,500,000	1,500,000	
Nova Scotia				
Mineral	19,838,000	15,870,400	3,967,600	
Agriculture	48,217,000	29,980,000	18,237,000	
Planning	5,000,000	2,500,000	2,500,000	
Interim Cape Breton	4,300,000	3,010,000	1,290,000	
Forestry	57,776,000	36,142,000	21,634,000	
SYSCO	19,500,000	15,156,000	4,344,000	
New Brunswick				
Highways 1974–75	13,335,000	10,000,000	3,335,000	
Agricultural	11,840,975	9,472,780	2,368,195	
Forestry	74,228,500	58,902,800	15,325,700	
Industrial	30,227,750	24,182,200	6,045,550	
Kent Region	7,751,000	6,200,800	1,550,200	
King's Landing	4,393,000	3,514,400	878,600	
Miramichi	351,440	263,580	87,860	
Highways 1975–76	11,690,000	8,767,500	2,922,500	
Planning	4,875,000	2,437,500	2,437,500	
Tourism	14,743,000	11,794,400	2,948,600	
Minerals and Fuels	11,313,125	9,050,500	2,262,625	
Highways 1976–77	12,000,000	9,000,000	3,000,000	
Highways 1977–81	56,000,000	42,000,000	14,000,000	
Quebec				
SIDBEC	243,716,000	30,000,000	8,608,000	205,108,000
Industrial Studies	2,000,000	1,000,000	1,000,000	
Mineral	28,600,000	17,160,000	11,440,000	
St-Félicien	298,000,000	30,000,000	20,000,000	248,000,000
PICA	13,292,000	7,975,200	5,316,800	

EXPIRED (concluded)

	Total ($)	Federal share ($)	Provincial share ($)	Other ($)
Ontario				
Cornwall	16,255,000	8,127,500	8,127,500	
Northwestern	50,888,650	25,444,325	25,444,325	
Dryden	3,200,996	1,600,498	1,600,498	
Interim Northlands	427,500	213,750	213,750	
Manitoba				
Interim Northlands	43,813,850	26,288,310	17,525,540	
Planning	2,600,000	1,300,000	1,300,000	
Mineral	8,500,000	4,250,000	4,250,000	
Northlands	162,916,000	110,509,000	52,407,000	
Interim Water	8,950,000	5,350,000	3,600,000	
Saskatchewan				
Mineral	4,350,000	2,175,000	2,175,000	
Steel	182,800,000	35,000,000	10,000,000	137,800,000
Interim Northlands	63,300,000	39,980,000	23,320,000	
Planning	2,600,000	1,300,000	1,300,000	
Agribition	1,700,000	850,000	850,000	
Interim Mineral	2,469,500	1,234,750	1,234,750	
Forestry	24,000,000	12,000,000	12,000,000	
Agriculture	15,320,000	7,660,000	7,660,000	
Alberta				
1974–75 Transportation	14,314,000	5,000,000	9,314,000	
Interim North	14,423,728	7,211,864	7,211,864	
Nutritive	17,000,000	8,500,000	8,500,000	
1975–76 Transportation	16,046,000	5,000,000	11,046,000	
1976–79 Transportation	30,000,000	15,000,000	15,000,000	
North	55,000,000	32,500,000	22,500,000	
British Columbia				
1974–75 Highways	16,000,000	5,000,000	11,000,000	
Fort Nelson	7,000,000	3,000,000	3,000,000	1,000,000
1975–76 Highways	10,000,000	5,000,000	5,000,000	
Coal	3,000,000	1,500,000	1,500,000	
1976–79 Highways	30,000,000	15,000,000	15,000,000	
Coal – 1977–81	10,000,000	5,000,000	5,000,000	
Northwest Territories				
Interim Community	3,833,000	2,460,000	1,373,000	
Total	2,110,797,294	1,030,231,909	488,657,385	591,908,000
Grand total (active and expired)	5,963,781,585	3,311,936,194	1,976,887,391	674,958,000

Industrial and Regional Development Program (IRDP)

PROGRAM ELEMENTS

1) INDUSTRIAL DEVELOPMENT CLIMATE

a) Assistance may be made available to economic, business or technological institutes for studies and specialized common services having significant and direct benefits for regional industrial development.

   All Tiers are eligible

b) Assistance may be available for the establishment of non-profit centres or institutions that are expected to become financially self-supporting if the centre or institution carries on or supports work related to industrial development.

   All Tiers are eligible

c) Infrastructure directly related to regional industrial development may be supported on a shared cost basis with provinces.

   Availability
   Tier II
   Tier III
   Tier IV

2 INNOVATION

a) *Studies* Assistance may be made available toward the cost of hiring qualified consultants for studies on project feasibility, technology transfer, market research and venture capital search associated with prospective innovation projects.

Availability	Maximum Sharing Ratios
Tier I	50%
Tier II	60%
Tier III	75%
Tier IV	75%

b) *Developing New Products or Processes* Assistance may be provided for projects to develop or demonstrate new or improved products or processes. These must be scientifically feasible, entail significant technical risk and represent attractive prospects for commercial exploitation.

Availability	Maximum Sharing Ratios
Tier I	50%
Tier II	60%
Tier III	75%
Tier IV	75%

c) *Developing Technological Capability* Projects for the improvement or expansion of technological capability which do not lead directly to identifiable sales may be supported if the technological capability is of strategic importance to the firm and the regional industrial development priorities of the government.

Availability	Maximum Sharing Ratios
Tier I	50%
Tier II	60%
Tier III	75%
Tier IV	75%

d) *Development and Demonstration* Projects to develop or demonstrate new products or processes, but which *do not* entail significant technological risk may be supported in a way similar to those in section b) above. However, this assistance will be repayable upon successful commercial exploitation of the resulting product or process.

Availability	Maximum Sharing Ratios
Tier I	50%
Tier II	60%
Tier III	75%
Tier IV	75%

e) *Industrial Design* Assistance may be made available for the design of a new, durable product, capable of being mass produced, that offers good prospects for commercial exploitation subject to certain conditions.

Availability	Maximum Sharing Ratios
Tier I	50%
Tier II	60%
Tier III	75%
Tier IV	75%

3) ESTABLISHMENT

a) *Studies* Funding may be provided toward the cost of hiring qualified consultants for studies of project feasibility, market research or venture capital search associated with a prospective establishment project.

Availability	Maximum Sharing Ratios
Tier I	50%
Tier II	60%
Tier III	75%
Tier IV	75%

b) *Plant Establishment* Funding may be made available for the establishment of new production facilities for manufacturing or processing, selected service sectors related to industry or tourism operations.

Availability	Maximum Cost Sharing Ratios	Minimum Approved Capital Costs
Tier I	Not eligible	N/A
Special Tier I*	35%	$100,000
Tier II	35%	100,000
Tier III	50%	50,000
Tier IV	60%	25,000

*If the unemployment to labour force ratio for a Tier I region exceeds the national average by one percentage point for any consecutive six-month period, that region will be eligible to apply for Tier II assistance for one year.

4) MODERNIZATION/EXPANSION

a) *Studies* Assistance may be provided toward the cost of hiring qualified consultants for project feasibility studies, market research and venture capital search for projects associated with modernization, productivity improvement or expansion.

Availability	Maximum Sharing Ratios
Tier I	50%
Tier II	60%
Tier III	75%
Tier IV	75%

b) *Modernization* Assistance may be made available for the acquisition of new, advanced machinery and equipment which significantly enhances the productivity of existing activities in manufacturing and processing, selected services related to industry and tourism operations.

Availability	Maximum Sharing Ratios	Minimum Approved Capital Costs
Tier I	25%	$250,000
Tier II	35%	100,000
Tier III	50%	50,000
Tier IV	50%	25,000

c) *Expansion* Assistance may be made available for the expansion of existing manufacturing or processing production facilities, as well as those in selected service sectors related to industry or tourism operations.

Availability	Maximum Sharing Ratios	Minimum Approved Capital Costs
Tier I	25%	$250,000
Tier II	35%	100,000
Tier III	50%	50,000
Tier IV	50%	25,000

Note: In Tier I, assistance will be targeted to the most promising areas of industrial potential and comparative advantage.

d) *Adaptation of Microelectronics/Electronics Technology* Funding may be provided to manufacturers and processors for the first installation of microelectronic devices in their products and operations, for the design of custom microelectronic devices, and for incorporation or application of electronic dependent products or systems in products, processes, production methods or facilities.

Availability	Maximum Sharing Ratios
Tier I	50%
Tier II	60%
Tier III	75%
Tier IV	75%

5) MARKETING

a) Assistance may be made available to persons carrying on or about to carry on a tourism operation for the collection and dissemination of information for the purpose of developing the domestic market, for arranging a special event likely to attract tourists and for organizing conferences likely to result in a substantial increase in tourists or visitors.

Availability	Maximum Sharing Ratios
Tier I	50%
Tier II	60%
Tier III	75%
Tier IV	75%

b) Assistance may be available to non-profit organizations for activities promoting the acceptance of Canadian standards and product specifications, for market research and analysis, advertising, trade shows or other events or for the publication of and dissemination of catalogues to promote Canadian products if the purpose of these activities is to increase the marketing of products or services.

All Tiers are eligible

c) *Studies* Funding may be available toward the cost of hiring qualified consultants for feasibility studies for the above as well as for market research or marketing strategies studies for a) preceding.

Availability	Maximum Sharing Ratios
Tier I	50%
Tier II	60%
Tier III	75%
Tier IV	75%

d) *Program for Export Market Development* (PEMD) Although not part of IRDP, PEMD will be delivered by ITC/DREE on behalf of the Department of External Affairs in support of ITC/DREE's continuing responsibilities for trade promotion in Canada.

All Tiers are eligible

6) RESTRUCTURING

a) *Studies* Assistance may be provided toward the cost of hiring consultants for studies of project feasibility, market research, and venture capital search associated with prospective restructuring projects.

Availability	Maximum Sharing Ratios
Tier I	50%
Tier II	60%
Tier III	75%
Tier IV	75%

b) *Restructuring* Loan guarantees up to 90% may be provided on a last resort basis. An annual insurance fee will be levied. (Projects involving loans of less than $500,000 will normally be referred to the Federal Business Development Bank (FBDB) which can better serve this level of business clientele through its direct lending activities).

For some companies, which do not find loan guarantees sufficiently useful, repayable contributions of up to 25% may be provided for capital costs.

All Tiers are eligible

Participation loans are available in Tiers II, III, and IV.

GENERAL PROGRAM CRITERIA

Incrementality No project may be supported unless it would likely not proceed, insofar as location, scope or timing are concerned, unless support is provided.

Commercial and Economic Viability The project and persons undertaking the project must be considered to be economically and commercially viable within reasonable bounds of risk.

Significant Economic Benefits to Canada The project and exploitation of the results of the project must represent significant net economic or social benefit to Canada within reasonable bounds of risk.

Eligible Applicants Individuals, associations, partnerships, cooperatives, bodies corporate, and non-profit organizations are eligible provided the project or activity is undertaken in Canada. Eligibility of the applicant will be dependent on the type of project or activity applied for.

Amount and Conditions of Programs Support Eligible projects will not necessarily be supported at the maximum levels. The minimum amount of financial support required for the project to proceed and for economic benefits to be maximized will be provided.

Targeting Program Support Priorities will be set after consultations with the private sector and other interested persons. Project proposals will be given a ranking in accordance with priorities and the economic benefits of the project. Regional development considerations will be of paramount importance.

The Development Index for the Industrial
and Regional Development Programs (IRDP)

THE DEVELOPMENT INDEX

To establish which areas are eligible for the various levels of assistance, an index has been designed. The index, which will ensure an equitable and objective ranking of areas in Canada, is based on 260 of Canada's census districts. These districts are the smallest discrete areas for which sufficient historical data are available on a nationally consistent basis.

Three measurable factors are used to calculate the formula for the development index. They are:

a) the level of unemployment in a census district (based on three-year averages using the most recent years for which data are available);
b) the level of income per person in a census district (based on three-year averages using the most recent years for which data are available);
c) the fiscal capacity of the province in which the census district is located (based on averaging annual available data for two years now; three years when data are available.)

Each of the factors is assigned a different weight to reflect their different importance. The unemployment factor has a 50% influence weight; the income factor, 40%; the provincial fiscal capacity, 10%. Weightings were chosen to reflect the traditionally accepted measurements of economic hardship.

THE TIERS

The IRDP provides differing levels of assistance over four tiers. The regions designated in the tiers will not remain static as the tier designations will be evaluated annually against changes in the statistical data.

The cut-off points between the tiers themselves is:

0–5%	Tier IV	those regions in which the 5% of Canadians most in need of economic assistance reside;
5–20%	Tier III	those regions in which the next 15% in terms of economic development need reside as well as the NWT and the Yukon;
20–50%	Tier II	those regions in which the next 30% of the population reside; and,
50–100%	Tier I	those regions in which the remaining 50% of the population reside.

SHORT-TERM ADJUSTMENT PROVISION

Provision has also been made to deal with Tier I districts that find their economic and employment bases suddenly eroded due to a cyclical and temporary downturn in the economy. Therefore, if the unemployment to labour force ratio for a Tier I region exceeds the national average by one percentage point for any consecutive six-month period, that region will be eligible for Tier II assistance for establishment for one year.

Notes

CHAPTER ONE: INTRODUCTION

1 The following constitute some of the most important published works on regional
development in Canada: T.N. Brewis, *Regional Economic Policies in Canada*; N.H.
Lithwick ed, *Regional Economic Policy*. See also T.N. Brewis and G. Paquet,
'Regional Development and Planning in Canada,' 123; Thomas J. Courchene,
'Avenues of Adjustment,' 145–84. The Economic Council of Canada has published a
number of excellent studies on regional disparities, including *Living Together: A
Study of Regional Disparities*; L. Copithorne, *Natural Resources and Regional Dis-
parities* (Ottawa: Minister of Supply and Services, 1979); and Neil Swan and Paul
J.E. Kovacs, *Empirical Testing of Newfoundland Data of a Theory of Regional
Disparities*.
2 Pierre E. Trudeau, quoted in Richard W. Phidd and G. Bruce Doern, *The Politics and
Management of Canadian Economic Policy*, 324
3 Brewis, *Regional Economic Policies in Canada*
4 Allan Fotheringham, *Malice in Blunderland, or How the Grits Stole Christmas*
(Toronto: Porter Books, 1982), 24; 'Towards an Economic Strategy for Canada: The
British Columbia Position,' a statement by William R. Bennett, February 1978; 'Notes
for an Opening Statement to the Conference of the First Ministers on the Economy –
Hon. William Davis,' 27–29 November 1978. Specifically, Premier Davis said: 'To
trade off competitive industrial development so as to achieve a better regional distribution of incomes is a terribly expensive strategy which we can no longer
afford.'
5 Canada, *Preceedings of the Standing Senate Committee on National Finance* (4
December 1980), issue no. 18, 19 and 22
6 Grant L. Reuber, *Canada's Political Economy*, 61–2
7 G. Bruce Doern, 'The Mega-Project Episode and the Formulation of Canadian
Economic Development Policy,' 237; Brewis, *Regional Economic Policies in
Canada*, 7

8 Quoted in André Raynauld ed, *Seminar on Regional Development in Canada: Transcript of the Proceedings* (Montreal: Le Centre de recherche en développement économique de l'Université de Montréal, 24 October 1980), 105

9 Economic Council of Canada, *Living Together*, 215–16

10 François Perroux, *L'Economie du xxe siècle*, 179

11 See J.R. Boudeville ed, *L'Espace et les poles de croissance* and *Problems of Regional Economic Planning*, 11

12 J. Paelinck, 'Programming a Viable Minimal Investment Industrial Complex for a Growth Center,' in N.M. Hansen ed, *Growth Centres in Regional Economic Development* (New York: Random House, 1972), 139–59

13 See J. Friedmann and W. Alonso eds, *Regional Policy*, chapters 2, 3, 8, 13, 16–19, and 25.

14 See, among others, Economic Council of Canada, *Living Together*, chapter 3.

15 Donald Jamieson stressed this point in a major address outlining the Department of Regional Economic Expansion's new policy orientation. See DREE, 'Notes for a General Statement by the Honourable Donald Jamieson to the Standing Committee on Regional Development Concerning the Policy Review,' April 1973, 11, mimeo.

16 See, for example, A. Scott, 'Policy for Declining Regions,' 46–67.

17 See, among many others, Thomas J. Courchene, 'Avenues of Adjustment,' 145–84.

18 Thomas J. Courchene, 'A Market Perspective on Regional Disparities,' 515

19 Ralph Matthews, *The Creation of Regional Dependency*, 15; David Alexander, 'New Notions of Happiness,' 29; Richard Simeon, 'Regionalism and Canadian Political Institutions,' paper presented to a graduate seminar at the University of Saskatchewan in January 1975, mimeo, 19

20 Thomas J. Courchene, 'A Market Perspective on Regional Disparities,' 513

21 Economic Council of Canada, *Living Together*, 215– 16

CHAPTER TWO: REGIONAL ECONOMIC DEVELOPMENT AND FEDERAL-PROVINCIAL RELATIONS

1 See, among others, Donald J. Savoie, 'Cooperative Federalism with Democracy,' 54–8.

2 During this period, Pierre De Bané declared: 'Successful regional development ... depends on a collective effort ... This applies equally to all levels of government.' See Department of Regional Economic Expansion, 'Notes for an Address by the Honourable Pierre De Bané, Minister of Regional Economic Expansion, to the Canadian Regional Science Association, 23 May 1981,' 4.

3 See Allan Tupper, *Public Money in the Private Sector*, chapters 2–5.

4 Richard Simeon, *Federal-Provincial Diplomacy*, 185

5 The province-building concept and its significance were first demonstrated by E.R. Black and Alan Cairns in 'A Different Perspective on Canadian Federalism,' 27–44.

6 Ottawa, *Background Paper on Federal-Provincial Fiscal Arrangements* (Department of Finance: Federal-Provincial Relations and Social Policy Branch, 1980), 9–54

7 Alan Cairns, 'The Governments and Societies of Canadian Federalism,' 700

8 Tupper, *Public Money in the Private Sector,* 11–24, 41–68

9 'Provinces Must Fit Programs to Ottawa's,' *Globe and Mail*, Toronto, 13 August 1981, 1

10 Ottawa, Office of the Prime Minister, press release (untitled), 18 July 1975, 1

11 Department of Finance, *Federal-Provincial Fiscal Arrangements in the Eighties*, A Submission to the Parliamentary Task Force on the Federal-Provincial Fiscal Arrangements by the Honourable Allen J. MacEachen, Deputy Prime Minister and Minister of Finance, 23 April 1981, 10–11

12 Ottawa, *Government Policy and Regional Development*, 79

13 See Anthony Careless, *Initiative and Response*, 60

14 See, for example, various comments by provincial premiers in Ottawa, Secrétariat des conférences intergouvernementales canadiennes, *Conférence fédérale-provinciale des Premiers Ministres, les 13–15 février 1978*, 298–384.

15 See Careless, *Initiative and Response*, 60–5. See also Donald J. Savoie, *Federal-Provincial Collaboration*, chapters 3, 8, and 9.

16 Interview with a former DREE official

17 See Cairns, *Governments and Societies*. See also Savoie, *Federal-Provincial Collaboration*, chapters 8 and 9.

18 Savoie, 'Cooperative Federalism with Democracy,' 56

19 Simeon, *Federal-Provincial Diplomacy*, 187

20 See DREE: various planning subsidiary agreements with provincial governments were signed, including with Newfoundland in 1976, with Nova Scotia in 1976, and with New Brunswick, Manitoba, and Saskatchewan in 1975. The Canada–Prince Edward Island Comprehensive Development Plan also provided funds for provincial public servants. See also 'Decision Coming within 10 days on Job Losses,' *The Guardian* (Charlottetown), 8 October 1981, 1.

21 See Savoie, *Federal-Provincial Collaboration*, chapter 8.

22 Quoted in 'De Bané Advice to Fall in Step Rubs Premiers the Wrong Way,' *Globe and Mail* (Toronto), 14 August 1981, 12

CHAPTER THREE: SHAPING DREE

1 Canada, *Report of the Royal Commission on Maritime Claims*, 1926

2 Based on a presentation by Benjamin Higgins at the Canadian Institute for Research on Regional Development, Moncton, New Brunswick, in November 1984. Professor Higgins was employed by the federal government to work on the reconstruction conference.

3 Canada, *Report of the Royal Commission on Dominion-Provincial Relations*, 1940, 269–76

4 There are numerous studies on Ottawa's equalization program. Canada, *Fiscal Federalism in Canada*, 157–76. See also Douglas H. Clark, 'Federal-Provincial Fiscal Arrangements for the 1972–76 Fiscal Period,' 206–14.
5 Canada, *Report of the Royal Commission on Canada's Economic Prospects*, 1957, 404
6 See Anthony Careless, *Initiative and Response*, 39–88.
7 Frank Walton, 'Canada's Atlantic Region,' 44
8 See, among others, Careless, *Initiative and Response*, 71–99.
9 See, among others, Thomas N. Brewis, 'Regional Development in Canada in Historical Perspective,' 220.
10 Canada, *Department of Regional Economic Expansion Annual Report, 1969–1970*, 12–16
11 Walton, 'Canada's Atlantic Region,' 44
12 Re Pickersgill, see Careless, *Initiative and Response*, 113–16; reasons for failure based in interview with a former DREE official
13 See Careless, *Initiative and Response*, 91–108.
14 Ibid, chapter 4
15 Ibid, chapters 2 and 3
16 Donald J. Savoie, *Federal-Provincial Collaboration*, chapter 2
17 Ibid
18 See, among many others, Canada, *Fiscal Federalism in Canada*, chapters 3–6.
19 Canada, *Report of the Royal Commission on Bilingualism and Biculturalism – Book 1*, 1967, xliv
20 Economic Council of Canada, *Third Annual Review* (Ottawa, 1966), 265
21 Quoted in Richard W. Phidd and G. Bruce Doern, *The Politics and Management of Canadian Economic Policy*, 324
22 Marchand declared: 'Because things are boiling over in central Canada, monetary conditions have to be tightened in order to head off inflation; the restraint may be felt here [Atlantic Canada] even though, far from the economy boiling over, there is persistent and severe unemployment.' See DREE, Atlantic Conference '68, 'Address by the Honourable Jean Marchand: A New Policy for Regional Development,' 29 October 1968, mimeo, 7.
23 See DREE, *Regional Policy in the Canadian Context*, policy discussion document published by DREE in 1978, 6. See also J.P. Francis and N.G. Pillai, 'Regional Economic Disparities and Federal Regional Development Policies in Canada,' 135–9.
24 Canada, *House of Commons Debates*, 20 March 1969, 6893–5
25 Interview with former DREE officials
26 For an assessment of the French experience, see Jérôme Monod and P. de Castelbajae, *L'Amènagement du territoire*.
27 Interviews with Jean Marchand and a former official of the Privy Council Office
28 The account that comprises the rest of this chapter is based on the interview with Jean Marchand.

CHAPTER FOUR: DREE – THE EARLY YEARS

1 See Anthony Careless, *Initiative and Response*, 60–121.
2 See Geoffrey Stevens, *Stanfield* (Toronto: McClelland and Stewart, 1973), 3–11.
   Canada, *Commons Debates*, 27 February 1969, Stanfield: 6020; Douglas: 6024
3 Canada, *Commons Debates* 27 February 1969, Trudeau: 6016; Marchand: 6894
4 Interview with a member of Parliament
5 Canada, Government Organization Act, *Statutes of Canada*, 1969, part IV, subsequently consolidated in the Department of Regional Economic Expansion Act, *Revised Statutes of Canada*, 1970, ch. R-4.
6 Richard Higgins suggests that perhaps 'the failure to achieve objectives in public life often results in severe criticism from the press, opposition parties and others. The rewards are usually meagre, to say the least, for a well-prepared and hard-fought initiative which falls short of expectations.' See Canada, *Proceedings of the Standing Senate Committee on Finance*, issue no. 3, 21 November 1978, 6.
7 Canada, House of Commons, Standing Committee on Regional Development, *Minutes of Proceedings*, 1970, 2:27
8 Interview with officials; see also Careless, *Initiative and Response*, 87–9.
9 DREE, *Annual Report 1971–1972*, 33. For a detailed assessment of the program in Manitoba, see Rural Community Resource Centre, *The Socioeconomic Impact of the Special ARDA Program in Manitoba* (Brandon University, 1981).
10 DREE, *Annual Report 1981–1982*, 29–39.
11 Careless, *Initiative and Response*, chapters 5–10. See also Donald J. Savoie, *Federal-Provincial Collaboration*, 18–19.
12 Canada, House of Commons, Standing Committee on Regional Development, *Minutes of Proceedings*, 1970, 2:62
13 Interview with officials. See also DREE, *Annual Report 1971–1972*, 16.
14 See, among many others, J.P. Francis and N.G. Pillai, 'Regional Economic Disparities and Federal Regional Development Policies in Canada,' 136–7.
15 DREE, *Annual Report*, various dates
16 Interview with officials. See also Careless, *Initiative and Response*.
17 Interview with officials. See also DREE, *Annual Report 1970–1971, Annual Report 1971–1972*.
18 Robert S. Woodward, 'The Effectiveness of DREE's New Location Subsidies,' 244–51
19 DREE, *Annual Report 1969–1970*, 10–12
20 Commenting on planning in his new department, Marchand spoke of 'planning to attract new industries, to stimulate and aid the modernization and expansion of existing industries, to find customers outside the region, ... the kind of growth that is reproductive in the sense that one thing leads to another'; DREE, Atlantic Conference '68, 'Address by the Honourable Jean Marchand: A New Policy for Regional Development,' 29 October 1968, mimeo, 14.

21 Interview with former DREE officials. See also DREE, *Annual Report 1971–1972*, 21.
22 Ibid, 14, 22
23 DREE, *The Loan Guarantee Programme*, undated, 1
24 Interview with former DREE officials
25 Ibid

CHAPTER FIVE: DREE AND THE GENERAL DEVELOPMENT AGREEMENTS

1 Pierre Normandin ed, *The Canadian Parliamentary Guide* (Ottawa, 1973), 512
2 Donald J. Savoie, *Federal-Provincial Collaboration*, 26. J.P. Francis later became acting deputy minister of the department for one year while Love was on special leave.
3 DREE, *The New Approach*
4 DREE, 'Province ... Economic Circumstances and Opportunities,' Yellow Book, April 1973
5 DREE, *Atlantic Region, Economic Circumstances and Opportunities*, Yellow Book, April 1973
6 DREE, *New Brunswick, Economic Circumstances and Opportunities*, Yellow Book, April 1973
7 DREE, *Quebec, Economic Circumstances and Prospects*, Yellow Book, April 1973
8 DREE, *Ontario, Economic Circumstances and Prospects*, Yellow Book, April 1973
9 DREE, *Western Region, Economic Circumstances and Prospects*, Yellow Book, April 1973
10 DREE expenditures did fall in the four Atlantic provinces and increased elsewhere. See Canada, Department of Regional Economic Expansion, *Annual Reports*, 1971–1972 and 1979–1980.
11 DREE, 'Notes for a General Statement by the Honourable Donald Jamieson to the Standing Committee on Regional Development Concerning the Policy Review,' April 1973, mimeo, 11
12 See, for example, DREE, *Canada-Saskatchewan General Development Agreement* (Ottawa; Information Canada, 11 February 1974).
13 DREE, *The New Approach*, 21; DREE, *A Better Way to Grow*, 6
14 See Savoie, *Federal-Provincial Collaboration*, chapter 6.
15 DREE, *Canada–New Brunswick General Development Agreement* (Ottawa: Information Canada, 23 April 1974), 8
16 See, for example, DREE, *Canada–Nova Scotia Industrial Development* (22 June 1976), 5.
17 Savoie, *Federal-Provincial Collaboration*, chapters 4, 5
18 Ibid
19 Ibid
20 Canada, House of Commons, Standing Committee on Regional Development *Minutes of Proceedings* (Ottawa, 1973), 12:4–12:5

21 See DREE, *Les Ententes de développement du* MEER, various dates. The last such report was issued in 1981 by the Department of Supply and Services.

22 DREE, *Annual Report 1978–1979* (Ottawa), 47

23 DREE, *Atlantic Region Industrial Parks: An Assessment of Economic Impact* (Ottawa, undated), 18–72

24 See N.H. Lithwick, 'Regional Policy: The Embodiment of Contradictions,' 135–40.

25 Interview with a former MSERD official. This view was fairly widespread in Ottawa, notably in central agencies, but also to some extent even in DREE head office.

26 Interview with a former DREE Atlantic regional official

27 Canada, Proceedings of the Senate Standing Committee on Agriculture, *Minutes of Proceedings* (Ottawa, 1977), 11–19

28 Savoie, *Federal-Provincial Collaboration*, chapter 7

29 Ibid, 48–52 and chapter 7

30 'No Fisheries Accord – LeBlanc,' *Moncton Times*, 11 February 1977, 1

31 See Donald J. Savoie, 'The GDA Approach and the Bureaucratization of Provincial Governments in the Atlantic Provinces,' 116–31.

32 DREE, *Atlantic Region Industrial Parks: An Assessment of Economic Impact* (Ottawa, undated), 18–72

33 Canada, *The New Approach*, 25

34 See, for example, B. Higgins, F. Martin, and A. Raynauld, *Les Orientations du développement économique régional de la province du Québec* (Ottawa: MEER, 1970).

35 DREE, *Montreal Special Area* (Ottawa, undated).

36 This commitment led to the signing of a subsidiary agreement for eastern Ontario. See DREE, *Canada–Ontario Subsidiary Agreement–Eastern Ontario*, 20 December 1979.

CHAPTER SIX: THREE ABORTED POLICY REVIEWS

1 See Donald J. Savoie, 'The GDA Approach and the Bureaucratization of Provincial Governments in the Atlantic Provinces,' 116–31.

2 See Richard Simeon ed., *Must Canada Fail?* (Montreal: McGill-Queen's University Press, 1977), chapters 2, 13, 16, and 17.

3 Canada, Conseil économique du Canada – *Treizième Exposé annuel* (Ottawa: Supply and Services, 1976). This annual report dealt at length with the problem of inflation.

4 Thomas J. Courchene, 'Avenues of Adjustment,' 145–77

5 DREE, *Annual Report, 1978–1979*, 3, 2

6 Ibid 3

7 Canada, *Proceedings of the Standing Senate Committee on National Finance* (21 February 1978), issue no. 3, A:7 and A:8

8 The review discussed in this and the three following paragraphs is DREE, *Economic Development Prospects in the Atlantic Region* (December 1979)

9 DREE, *Economic Development Prospects in Quebec* (December 1979)

10 DREE, *Economic Development Prospects in Ontario* (December 1979)·, 2

11 Ibid 1–14, 58–9

12 Ibid 2

13 DREE, *Economic Development Prospect in the Western Region* (December 1979)

14 See DREE, *Canada-Manitoba Industrial Development Subsidiary Agreement*, 1 April 1978

15 DREE, *Economic Development Prospects in the Western Region* (December 1979)

16 DREE minister Marcel Lessard declared: 'Clearly, one of the principal advantages of the GDA mechanism is its flexibility, a characteristic which ... is absolutely essential in a country with such diverse economic regions'; Canada, *Proceedings of the Standing Senate Committee on National Finance* (21 February 1978), issue no. 3, A:17.

17 See, among others, Savoie, *Federal-Provincial Collaboration*, chapter 7.

18 Interview with Marcel Lessard

19 Quoted in *Atlantic Insight* (Halifax), 1 2, 19

20 Ibid, 12. See also Mike Forestall, MP for Dartmouth–Halifax East, *Regional Development: A Failed and Forgotten Commitment* (undated), mimeo. Interview with former DREE officials and with Elmer MacKay

21 Ian McAllister, 'How to Re-Make DREE', 42

22 'A Maverick in the Liberal Ranks,' *Ottawa Journal*, 23 July 1980, 4; Pierre de Bané,' A New Regional Development Policy' (undated), mimeo

23 Interview with Pierre De Bané. See also 'Pierre De Bané a eu le seul ministère qui l'intéressait – Des chances égales pour tous,' *Le Droit* (Ottawa), 20 August 1980, 1

24 As note 23

25 DREE, *Senior Staff Conference, 17 and 18 June 1980*, 22

26 Ibid, 23–4

27 DREE, 'Statement of Intent – Hon. Pierre De Bané and Hon. Prof. Claudio Signorile,' 17 November 1981. See also DREE, 'Canadian and Italian Ministers Discuss Economic Development' (news release), 17 November 1981.

28 'A Maverick in the Liberal Ranks,' 4

29 'Provinces Must Fit Programs to Ottawa's, De Bané Says,' *Globe and Mail* (Toronto), 13 August 1981, 1

30 'De Bané's Future Appears Bright despite New Post,' *Gazette* (Montreal), 13 January 1982, 13

31 DREE, *The Prince Edward Island Comprehensive Plan*, 1969; 'Federal Activity to Remain Strong – De Bané,' *The Guardian* (Charlottetown), 8 October 1981, 3

32 'Cabinet to Meet PSA on Impending Layoffs,' *The Guardian* (Charlottetown), 10 October 1981, 3.

33 DREE, '$10 million in Harbours Work Slated for Quebec' (news release), 17 August 1981

34 DREE, 'Notes for an Address by the Honourable Pierre De Bané to the Standing Committee on Regional Development,' 17 March 1981, 5

35 DREE, 'Notes for an Address by the Honourable Pierre De Bané to the Standing Committee on Regional Development,' undated, 1

36 Canada, *The Credit Is Yours 50%* (Ottawa: Supply and Services, 1981)

37 DREE, 'Notes for a Speech by Russell MacLellan, M.P., Parliamentary Secretary to the Honourable Pierre De Bané, Federal Minister of Regional Economic Expansion, to the 13th Annual Conference of the Industrial Developers Association of Canada, Quebec,' 21 September 1981, 5.

38 'La venue de 2 usines à Bouctouche, créera 1,000 emplois dans Kent,' *L'Evangéline* (Moncton), 17 July 1981, 3

39 See 'Bickering over Car Plant Led to Cabinet Shake-up,' *Sunday Star* (Toronto), 17 January 1982, 1.

40 The controversy led to a series of charges and counter-charges between Ottawa and Quebec City. See DREE, 'Statement by the Honourable Pierre De Bané on the Decision by Volkswagen,' 13 October 1981, p. 5.

41 Statement by Bruno Rubess, president of Volkswagen Canada, 13 October 1981, 1

CHAPTER SEVEN: NEW POLICIES, STRUCTURES, AND PROGRAMS

1 Ottawa, Office of the Prime Minister, 'Reorganization for Economic Development (release), 12 January 1982

2 Ottawa, Department of Finance, *Economic Development for Canada in the 1980's* (November 1981), 11

3 Ottawa, Department of Energy, Mines and Resources, 'Notes for an Address by the Honourable Marc Lalonde, Minister of Energy, Mines and Resources, to the Second Atlantic Outlook Conference,' Halifax, 18 February 1982, mimeo, 2

4 Finance, *Economic Development for Canada in the 1980's*, 17, 3; MSED, 'Notes for an Address by the Honourable Bud Olson, Minister of State for Economic Development – Mega Projects,' undated, mimeo, 2–3

5 'Reorganization for Economic Development' (release)

6 See, among others, Ronald W. Crowley, 'A New Power Focus in Ottawa,' 5–16.

7 MSERD, 'Contacts in Federal Economic and Regional Development Departments,' January 1984, 2

8 Ottawa, Ministry of State for Economic Development, 'Notes for an Address by the Honourable Bud Olson, Minister of State of Economic Development – A FEDC for PEI,' undated

9 Media Tapes and Transcripts Ltd (Ottawa), *As It Happens*, 24 February 1982, 5–6

10 Canada, The House of Commons of Canada, Bill C-152, An Act Respecting the Organization of the Government of Canada and Matters Related to or Incidental Thereto – As Passed by the House of Commons, 25 October 1983, Schedule 11, Section 35, 22

11 'Reorganization for Economic Development' (release); Finance, *Economic Development for Canada in the 1980's*, 10

12 See, for example, MSERD, *Canada-Saskatchewan Economic and Regional Development Agreement*, 30 January 1984.

13 'Federal Aid is $100 Million in Arrears, Peckford Claims,' *Globe and Mail* (Toronto), 10 February 1984, 4

14 MSERD, Canada-Manitoba Economic and Regional Development Agreement' (news release), 23 November 1983

15 MSERD, 'Canada and Saskatchewan Sign New Economic and Regional Development Agreement' (news release), 30 January 1984

16 MSERD, Canada–Newfoundland Economic and Regional Development Agreements' (news release), 4 May 1984

17 MSERD, Canada–New Brunswick Economic and Regional Development Agreements' (news release), 13 April 1984

18 'Ottawa Cutting Cost-Shared Programs?, '*Times-Transcript* (Moncton), 6 June 1984, 22

19 MSERD, 'Canada and Nova Scotia Sign Economic and Regional Development Agreement' (news release), 11 June 1984; MSERD, 'Canada and Nova Scotia Sign Strait of Canso Agreement' (news release), 11 June 1984, 3; MSERD, 'Canada and Nova Scotia Sign Planning Agreement' (news release), 11 June 1984

20 MSERD, *Canada–Prince Edward Island Economic and Regional Development Agreement*, 13 June 1984

21 MSERD, 'Canada-Ontario Economic Development Ministers Meet' (news release), 2 November 1984.

22 DRIE, 'Canada and British Columbia Sign New Economic and Regional Development Agreement' (news release), 23 November 1984

23 'Quebec Signs New Economic Development Agreement,' *The Gazette* (Montreal), 15 December 1984, 2

24 DRIE, *Canada-Quebec Economic and Regional Development Agreement* (December 14 1984). See also DRIE, 'Canada-Quebec Economic and Regional Development Agreement' (news release), 14 December 1984.

25 MSERD, 'New Federal Projects Worth $109 Million for Quebec' (news release), 4 June 1984

26 'Reorganization for Economic Development (release)

27 Over a five-year period from the late 1970s to the early 1980s, the GDA spending pattern saw 45 per cent of the funds going to the four Atlantic provinces, 30 per cent to Quebec, 6 per cent to Ontario, and 20 per cent to the western provinces.

28 'Reorganization for Economic Development' (release)

29 Peter Aucoin and Herman Bakvis, 'Organizational Differentiation and Integration: The Case of Regional Economic Development Policy in Canada,' *Canadian Public Administration*, XXVII 3 (fall 1984) 366

30 DRIE, 'Speaking Notes – The Honourable Ed Lumley to the House of Commons on the Industrial and Regional Development Program,' 27 June 1983, 1, 2

31 APEC, *An Analysis of the Reorganization for Economic Development* (Halifax: Atlantic Provinces Economic Council, August 1982); Canada, *Government Policy and Regional Development* (Report of the Standing Senate Committee, September 1982)
32 'Trudeau-Pitfield Bureaucracy First Item on Turner's Overhaul,' *Globe and Mail* (Toronto), 2 July 1984, 5; Ottawa, Office of the Prime Minister, 'Government Organization Measures' (release), 30 June 1984
33 'Government Organization Measures' (release)
34 *Statement by Hon. Brian Mulroney at Halifax, Nova Scotia, 2 August 1984* (Progressive Conservative Party of Canada), Annex A, 1
35 DRIE, 'Adjustments to Industrial and Regional Development Program' (news release), 9 November 1984; 'Provinces May Get More Clout on Grants,' *Toronto Star*, 22 January 1985, 7. See also 'Développement régional: Stevens est prêt à laisser la maîtrise d'oeuvre aux provinces,' *Le Devoir* (Montreal), 22 January 1985, 1.

CHAPTER EIGHT: OTHER REGIONAL DEVELOPMENT EFFORTS

1 Based on information provided by Tom Kent, former DEVCO president
2 See *People in Business Together, A Review* (Cape Breton Development Corporation Industrial Development Division, January 1981), 1–16
3 *Annual Report 1981–1982*, The Cape Breton Development Corporation, 28 May 1982, 8–16 and 1–x(c)
4 Ottawa, Industry, Trade and Commerce and Regional Economic Expansion, 'Background to Community-Based Industrial Adjustment' (news release), undated
5 See, Ottawa, Industry, Trade and Commerce and Department of Regional Economic Expansion, 'Communities Designated for Adjustment Assistance' (news release), 16 March 1981, and Four New Communities Designated for ILAP Assistance, Four Others Get Six-Month Extensions' (news release), 28 January 1982. See also 'Auto Parts Industry Designated for Assistance' (news release) 28 January 1982, and 'Major Appliance and Components Industries Designated for Assistance' (news release) 28 January 1982.
6 Ottawa, Industry, Trade and Commerce and Department of Regional Economic Expansion, 'Five Windsor Firms Receive ILAP Assistance' (news release), 2 July 1982
7 Interview with former DREE officials
8 Ottawa, Office of the Prime Minister, 'Formation of the Canadian Industrial Renewal Board' (news release), 26 October 1981
9 The account that follows is based on Ottawa, Industry, Trade and Commerce, 'Government Policy for the Textile and Clothing Sectors' (release), 19 June 1981. See in particular 'Backgrounder,' attached to the news release.
10 See, among others, Ernest R. Forbes, *Maritime Rights*, 149–72.
11 Atlantic Provinces Transportation Commission, 'Notes for an Address: Skippers Perspective of Atlantic Transportation Subsidies' by Craig S. Dickson, to Trans-

portation Seminar Series, University of New Brunswick, Fredericton, NB, 24 March 1983

12 Ottawa, *Unemployment Insurance in the 1980s*, 52–5, 105–26. For an analysis of the Unemployment Insurance program on a regional basis, see ibid, chapter 3.

13 Canada, *Fiscal Federalism in Canada* (Ottawa: Parliamentary Task Force on Federal-Provincial Fiscal Arrangements, 1981), chapter 6

14 Ottawa, 'Priorities for the 1980's, Text of Remarks by the Honourable Jean Chrétien, president of the Treasury Board, to the Annual Conference of the Institute of Public Administration of Canada,' 3 September 1975, mimeo, 5

15 Ottawa, 'Statement by the Honourable Jean Chrétien, Minister Responsible for the Federal Government Decentralization Program,' 3 October 1977

16 Interview with a federal official and member of the Task Force on Decentralization

17 Ottawa, 'Statement by the Honourable Sinclair Stevens, President of the Treasury Board,' 15 August 1979

18 Ottawa, 'Statement by the Honourable Donald Johnston, President of the Treasury Board on the Federal Government Decentralization Program,' undated

19 Allan Tupper, *Public Money in the Private Sector*, 20. See also 'La bataille du F-18 est perdue,' *Le Devoir* (Montreal), 21 January 1983, 1.

20 Interview with federal officials. See also Savoie, *Federal-Provincial Collaboration*, chapter 7.

21 For an excellent paper on the impact of defence spending on Canada's regions, see J.M. Treddenick, *Regional Impacts of Defence Spending* (Kingston: Centre for Studies in Defence Resources Management, Royal Military College of Canada, 1984). Information on defence spending in this study is by and large drawn from the Treddenick paper. I also interviewed some officials from the Department of National Defence.

22 For helicopter competition, see 'Manitoba wants to be site of helicopter Plant,' *Globe and Mail* (Toronto), 12 January 1983, B 11. For DREE competition, see Savoie, *Federal-Provincial Collaboration*, chapter 7. On visits almost overlapping, see, for example, Canada, *Proceedings of the Standing Senate Committee on National Finance*, 22 February 1979, issue no. 11, p. 10:17; this point was made by John F. Godfrey in his testimony to the Senate committee. Campbell is quoted in 'Maritimes Hope to Co-operate on Regional Development Plan,' *Financial Post* (Toronto), 8 October 1977, 11. Tupper, *Public Money in the Private Sector*, chapter 5, discusses nation-wide competition.

23 Ontario, *Building Ontario in the 1980's* (Government of Ontario, 27 January 1981)

24 Savoie, *Federal-Provincial Collaboration*, chapter 5

25 Interview with former DREE officials

26 'The Public Purse,' *Canadian Business* (Toronto), April 1980, 65

27 Based on a presentation by Hugh Thorburn to the Advisory Council Meeting of the Institute of Intergovernmental Relations, Queen's University, Kingston, Ontario, 9 April 1984

28 Tupper, *Public Money in the Private Sector*, 18
29 See, for example, *Nouvelles*, 'Banque de Montreal au sujet d'un article dans la Revue des affaires,' 14 December 1981. See also 'La conjoncture economique canadienne – une étude régionale,' *Revue mensuelle*, La Banque de Nouvelle-Ecosse, August 1981.
30 Ottawa, *Government of Canada Tax Expenditure Account* (Ottawa: Department of Finance, December 1979)

CHAPTER NINE: AN ASSESSMENT

1 See Economic Council of Canada, *Living Together*, chapter 4. See also Canada, *Proceedings of the Standing Senate Committee on National Finance* (28 May 1981), issue no. 27, 11–29.
2 *Living Together*, 12
3 Economic Council of Canada, *Newfoundland: From Dependency to Self Reliance*, 47–59
4 See C.B. Burke and D.J. Ireland, *An Urban/Economic Development Strategy for the Atlantic Region* (Ottawa: Ministry of State for Urban Affairs, 1976).
5 See Statistics Canada, *Population Estimates for Census Divisions* (Ottawa: Statistics Canada, 1980), catalogue no. 91–206.
6 David P. Ross, *The Working Poor: Wage Earners and the Failure of Income Security Policies* (Ottawa: Canadian Institute for Economic Policy, 1981), 33–60
7 Supply and Services, *Government Policy and Regional Development*, 107–14. See also *Fiscal Federalism in Canada*.
8 This analysis of federal transfer payments is based on data obtained from Statistics Canada.
9 *Living Together*, 188
10 Ibid, 160, 215
11 David Springate, *Regional Incentives and Private Investment*; Carleton L. Dudley, 'Summary of a Theoretical Financial Analysis of the Long-Term Subsidy Value of the Regional Development Incentives Program in Canada: 1969–1972' (Ottawa: University of Ottawa, Department of Geography, April 1974)
12 J.P. LeGoffe and B. Rosenfield, 'Les réactions d'entrepreneurs canadiens à divers programmes d'aide a l'investissement' (Ottawa: Economic Council of Canada, April 1979)
13 D. Usher, 'Some Questions about the Regional Development Incentives Act,' 560
14 Robert S. Woodward, 'The Effectiveness of DREE's New Location Subsidies,' 254. See also Robert S. Woodward, 'Effective Location Subsidies,' 501–10; 'The Capital Bias of DREE Incentives,' 161–73; 'The Effectiveness of DREE's New Location Subsidies,' 219–29.
15 See DREE, *Report on Regional Development Incentives: Cumulative Statistics and Net*

Offers Accepted from July 1, 1969 to December 31, 1981 (undated). See also DREE, *Annual Report*, various dates.

16 See DREE, *Regional Industrial Industries in Selected OECD Countries* (1981), and Douglas Yuill and Kevin Allen, *European Regional Incentives – 1980*. See also *Regional Industrial Development* (London: Her Majesty's Stationery Office, December 1983).

17 *Report on Regional Development Incentives: Cumulative Statistics and Net Offers Accepted from July 1, 1969 to March 31, 1981;* interview with federal officials

18 'Ottawa Paid Generously to Cut 473 Celanese Jobs,' *Gazette* (Montreal), 24 August 1972, 11; 'Treasury Taking Look at Major Spenders,' *Globe and Mail* (Toronto), 10 August 1972, 2; 'DREE: Even Treasury Board Has Doubts,' *Free Press* (Winnipeg), 12 August 1972, 9; 'DREE Has Little Effect in Attracting New Industry,' *Globe and Mail* (Toronto), 6 November 1974, 8; interviews with former DREE officials

19 Ottawa, *Living Together*, 169, 170–1

20 Ottawa, Industry, Trade and Commerce, *Annual Report*, 1973–74 to 1977–78

21 Industry, Trade and Commerce, *New Fighter Aircraft Industrial Benefits Analysis and Evaluation*

22 Ottawa, Industry, Trade and Commerce, *Annual Report 1980–81*. See also *Program Expenditure Plan 1980–81: Illustration of Structure and Content*, June 1981.

23 Interview with a former DREE official

24 Ottawa, 'Priorities for the 1980's, Text of Remarks by the Honourable Jean Chrétien President of the Treasury Board, to the Annual Conference of the Institute of Public Administration of Canada,' 3 September 1975,' mimeo, 6

25 Ottawa, 'Statement by the Honourable Sinclair Stevens, President of the Treasury Board,' 27 July 1979, mimeo

26 Interview with a former member of the task force

27 'Productivité accrue,' *Le Soleil* (Québec), 5 August 1978, 1. The director at Shediac made his observation at a meeting of federal officials to which I was invited. The meeting was chaired by the FEDC for New Brunswick.

28 Information was provided by a former senior DREE official.

29 See André Raynauld ed, *Seminar on Regional Development in Canada* (Montreal: Le Centre de recherche en développement économique, 1980), 12.

30 G. Bruce Doern, 'The Mega-Project Episode and the Formulation of Canadian Economic Developments Policy,' 222

31 Ibid 219

32 'Bickering over Car Plant Led to Cabinet Shake-up,' *Sunday Star* (Toronto), 17 January 1982, 1

33 Canada, *Proceedings of the Standing Senate Committee on National Finance*, issue no. 12, 22 March 1973, 14:24

34 D.D. Husband, 'National versus Regional Growth,' 548

35 See DREE, *Annual Report 1979–80*, and 'Politics Muddles Development Policy,' *Financial Post* (Toronto), 4 February 1984, 9.

36 Jeffrey L. Pressman and Aaron Wildawsky, *Implementation* ..., 186
37 Interviews with officials. See also DRIE, *Annual Report 1983–1984*, 12–60.
38 Michael Jenkin, *The Challenge of Diversity* (Ottawa: Science Council of Canada, Background Study 50, 1983), 167
39 Ottawa, Office of the Prime Minister, 'Reorganization for Economic Development' (release), 12 January 1982
40 Interview on the CBC program *The Journal*, 17 September 1984

CHAPTER TEN: REGIONAL ECONOMIC DEVELOPMENT RECONSIDERED

1 Economic Council of Canada, *Living Together*, 215
2 Paul Streeten, 'Development Ideas in Historical Perspective,' *Regional Development Dialogue*, 1 2 (autumn 1980), 1–38; Benjamin Higgins, 'From Growth Poles to Systems of Interaction in Space,' 5
3 Benjamin Higgins, 'The Task Ahead,' 12
4 Lipsey quoted in André Raynauld ed, *Seminar on Regional Development in Canada: Transcript of the Proceedings* (Montreal: Le Centre de recherche en développement économique de l'Université de Montréal, 24 October 1980), 105; UN official, quoted in Higgins, 'From Growth Poles,' 10
5 Herbert Simon, 'Rational Decision-Making in Business Organizations,' 495–513
6 Higgins, 'From Growth Poles,' 10
7 'Le Québec n'aura que le tiers des retombées des 137 F-18,' *Le Devoir* (Montreal), 23 October 1982, 1
8 T.J. Courchene, 'A Market Perspective on Regional Disparities,' 513
9 Ottawa, *A Commission on Canada's Future – Challenges and Choices* (Supply and Services, 1984), 37; 'Discussion Paper on Major Bilateral Issues: Canada-Newfoundland' (St John's: Government of Newfoundland, May 1980), 4
10 Canada, *The Canadian Constitution 1981 – A Resolution Adopted by the Parliament of Canada, December 1981* (Publications Canada, 1981)
11 *An Analysis of the Reorganization for Economic Development* (Halifax: APEC, August 1982), 34; 'Discussion Paper on Major Bilateral Issues: Canada-Newfoundland,'
12 Information in this and the following paragraph is based on data obtained from Statistics Canada.
13 Ottawa, *Living Together*, 59
14 Ottawa, *Economic Development Prospects in Ontario* (Ottawa: DREE, 1979), 7–11
15 On urbanization, see Michel Boisvert, *La Correspondance entre le système urbain et la base économique des régions canadiennes* (Ottawa: Supply and Services, 1978). Economic Council of Canada, *Living Together*, 123
16 Allan Tupper, *Public Money in the Private Sector*, 53; Kenneth H. Norrie, 'Some Comments on Prairie Economic Alienation,' 211–24
17 Roy E. George, 'Fifteen Years of the Regional Industrial Policy: A Case Study of Nova Scotia,' a paper presented to the Fifth Annual Conference, Atlantic Canada Shipping Project, Memorial University of Newfoundland, 25–27 June 1981, mimeo, 2

18 'Discussion Paper on Major Bilateral Issues: Canada-Newfoundland,' 4
19 See MSERD, *The Canada–Prince Edward Island Economic and Regional Development Agreement*, 13 June 1984, 3.
20 See MSERD, *The Canada–Nova Scotia Economic and Regional Development Agreement*, 11 June 1984, 3.
21 *Living Together*, 229

CHAPTER ELEVEN: PROSPECTS

1 Canada, *Proceedings of the Standing Senate Committee on National Finance*, issue no. 21, 10 February 1981, 11
2 See, among others, Donald J. Savoie, 'Le Canada sans le Québec: Perspectives économiques et politiques pour la région de l'Atlantique,' in J.R. Winter ed, *The Atlantic Provinces in Canada: Where Do We Go from Here?* (Halifax: APEC, 1981), 95–110.
3 There have been numerous difficulties with Ottawa's direct delivery approach. Most important, line departments have not been able to obtain the required person-years from the Treasury Board to open new regional or local offices to deliver the projects.
4 'Province Found Answer to CFB Chatham-Dawson,' *Times-Transcript* (Moncton), 24 May 1984, 26
5 Quoted in Canada, *Proceedings of the Senate Standing Committee on National Finance*, issue no. 3, 21 November 1978, 7
6 Ibid, 11
7 See Douglas Yuill and Kevin Allen, *European Regional Incentives – 1980*.
8 *Regional Development Incentives – Second Report* (London: Her Majesty's Stationery Office, 1974), 49
9 See N.H. Lithwick, 'Regional Policy,' 134.
10 Roy E. George, 'Fifteen Years of the Regional Industrial Policy: A Case Study of Nova Scotia,' a paper presented to the Fifth Annual Conference, Atlantic Canada Shipping Project, Memorial University of Newfoundland, 25–27 June 1981, mimeo, 23
11 Ibid
12 There have been of late thorough studies on Canadian industrial development. See, for example, Michael Jenkin, *The Challenge of Diversity: Industrial Policy in the Canadian Federation* (Ottawa: Science Council of Canada, Background Study 50, 1983). See also Uri Zohar, *Canadian Manufacturing*, I 11. For a more telling version of Canada's industrial difficulties, see, 'Auto Firm Jumps to 90 Cent-an-hour World,' Canadian Press article reprinted in the *Times-Transcript* (Moncton), 13 April 1984, 31.
13 See, for example, John Shepherd and A. Roy Megarry, 'Boosting the Birth of New Business,' *Globe and Mail* (Toronto), 6 December 1984, 7.
14 See, among many others, Brad J. Caftel, *Community Development and Credit Union*.

15 Tom Kent, 'Regional Development,' remarks for the Senate Committee on National Finance, 22 March 1979, mimeo

16 'Local Economic Development Assistance (LEDA) Corporation for Kent County,' (news release, Minister of Employment and Immigration and Minister of Regional Economic Expansion), 16 September 1981

17 Interviews with federal officials and entrepreneurs from Kent County, New Brunswick. See also *A.D.E.L. – Kent – L.E.D.A., Annual Report 1982–1983*, Bouctouche, New Brunswick, undated.

18 Interview with former DREE officials

19 Benjamin Higgins, 'The Task Ahead,' 21

20 Karen S. Christensen and Melvin M. Webber, *On Styles of Noncentralized Planning*, 59–68

21 Canada, *Estimates for the Fiscal Year Ending March 31, 1985* (Minister of Supply and Services, 1984), 22:12

22 See, among many others, G. Bruce Doern and Peter Aucoin eds, *The Structures of Policy-Making in Canada*, chapters 1–3.

Selected bibliography

BOOKS

Aydalot, Philippe, ed, *Crise et espace* (Paris: Economica, 1984)

Balassa, B., ed, *European Economic Integration* (Amsterdam: North Holland, 1975)

Bothwell, Robert, et al, *Canada since 1945: Power, Politics and Provincialism* (Toronto: University of Toronto Press, 1981)

Boudeville, J.R., *Problems of Regional Economic Planning* (Edinburgh: Edinburgh University Press, 1966)

– ed, *L'Espace et les pôles de croissance* (Paris: Presses universitaires de France, 1968)

Brewis, T.N., *Regional Economic Policies in Canada* (Toronto: Macmillan, 1969)

Brown, A.J., *The Framework of Regional Economics in the United Kingdom* (Cambridge: Cambridge University Press, 1972)

Brown, A.J., and E.M. Burrows, *Regional Economic Problems* (London: Allen & Unwin, 1977)

Caftel, Brad J., *Community Development and Credit Unions* (Berkeley: National Economic Development Law Project, 1978)

Cameron, David, ed, *Regionalism and Supranationalism* (Montreal: Institute for Research on Public Policy, 1981)

Cameron, G.C., *Regional Economic Development: The Federal Role* (Baltimore: Johns Hopkins Press, 1970)

Careless, Anthony, *Initiative and Response: The Adaptation of Canadian Federalism to Regional Economic Development* (Montreal: McGill-Queen's University Press, 1977)

Christensen, Karen S., and Melvin M. Webber, *On Styles of Noncentralized Planning* (Berkeley: University of California Institute of International Studies, 1981)

Clout, Hugh, *The Regional Problem in Western Europe* (Cambridge: Cambridge University Press, 1976)

– ed, *Regional Development in Western Europe* (London: John Wiley, 1975)

Dean, Robert D., W.H. Leahy, and David L. McKee, eds, *Spatial Economic Theory* (New York: The Free Press, 1970)

Doern, Bruce G., and Peter Aucoin, eds, *The Structures of Policy-Making in Canada* (Toronto: Macmillan, 1971)

Forbes, Ernest R., *Maritime Rights: The Maritime Rights Movement, 1919–1927* (Montreal: McGill-Queen's University Press, 1979)

Friedmann, John, and William Alonso jr, *Regional Policy: Readings in Theory and Applications* (Cambridge: MIT Press, 1975)

– eds, *Regional Development and Planning: A Reader* (Cambridge: MIT Press, 1964)

Gravier, J.F., *Paris et le désert français en 1972* (Paris: Flammarion, 1972)

Green, Alan G., *Regional Aspects of Canada's Economic Growth* (Toronto: University of Toronto Press, 1971)

Grewal, Bhajan S., et al, *The Economics of Federalism* (Canberra: Centre for Research on Federal Financial Relations, 1981)

Hansen, Niles M., ed, *Public Policy and Regional Economic Development, The Experience of Nine Western Countries* (Cambridge: Ballinger Press, 1974)

Hirshman, A.D., *The Strategy of Economic Development* (New Haven: Yale University Press, 1958)

Holland, Stuart, *Capital versus the Regions* (London: Macmillan, 1976)

– *The Regional Problem* (London: Macmillan, 1976)

Innis, H.A., *The Fur Trade in Canada: An Introduction to Canadian Economic History* (Toronto: University of Toronto Press, 1956)

– *Problems of Staple Production in Canada* (Toronto: University of Toronto Press, 1933)

Izard, Walter, *Introduction to Regional Science* (Englewood Cliffs, NJ: Prentice Hall, 1975)

Kain, John and John R. Meyer, eds, *Essays in Regional Economics* (Cambridge: Harvard University Press, 1971)

Klaassen, L.H., *Location of Industries in Depressed Areas* (Paris: OECD, 1968)

Kuklinski, A.R., ed, *Growth Poles and Growth Centres in Regional Planning* (The Hague: Mouton, 1972)

Lithwick, N.H., ed, *Regional Economic Policy: The Canadian Experience* (Toronto: McGraw-Hill Ryerson, 1978)

McAllister, Ian, *Regional Development and the European Community: A Canadian Perspective* (Montreal: Institute for Research on Public Policy, 1982)

McKee, D.L., R.O. Dean, and W.H. Leahy, *Regional Economics: Theory and Practice* (New York: Free Press, 1970)

Mackintosh, W.A., *The Economic Background of Dominion-Provincial Relations* (Toronto: McClelland and Stewart, 1964)

Mahon, Rianne, *The Politics of Industrial Restructuring: Canadian Textiles* (Toronto: University of Toronto Press, 1984)

Mandel, Ernest, *Late Capitalism* (London: New Left Books, 1975)

Mathews, Ralph, *The Creation of Regional Dependency* (Toronto: University of Toronto Press, 1983)

Matthews, R.L., ed, *Regional Disparities and Economic Development* (Canberra: Centre for Research on Federal Financial Relations, 1981)

Molle, William, with Bas van Holst and Hans Smit, *Regional Disparity and Economic Development in the European Community* (Farnborough: Saxon House, 1980)

Monod, Jérôme, and P. de Castelbajae, *L'Aménagement du territoire* (Paris: Presses universitaires de France, 1973)

Musgrave, Richard A., ed, *Essays in Fiscal Federalism* (Washington: Brookings Institution, 1965)

Myrdal, G.M., *Economic Theory and Underdeveloped Regions* (London: Duckworth, 1957)

Nurkse, R., *Problems of Capital Formation in Underdeveloped Countries* (Oxford: Blackwell, 1953)

Oates, Wallace E, *Fiscal Federalism* (New York: Harcourt, Brace, Jovanovitch, 1972)

– ed, *Financing the New Federalism* (Baltimore: Johns Hopkins Press, 1976)

Perroux, François, *L'Economie du XXᵉ siècle* (Paris: Presses universitaires de France, 1969)

Phidd, Richard W., and G. Bruce Doern, *The Politics and Management of Canadian Economic Policy* (Toronto: Macmillan, 1978)

Pomfret, Richard, *The Economic Development of Canada* (Toronto: Methuen, 1981)

Pred, A.R., *City-Systems in Advanced Economies* (London: Hutchinson and Company, 1971)

Pressman, Jeffery L., and Aaron Wildawsky, *Implementation ...* (Berkeley: University of California Press, 1973)

Reuber, Grant L., *Canada's Political Economy* (Toronto: McGraw-Hill Ryerson, 1980)

Richardson, Harry W., *Regional Economics, Location Theory, Urban Structure, and Regional Change* (New York: Praeger, 1969)

Robinson, E.A.G., *Backward Areas in Advanced Countries* (London: Macmillan, 1969)

Romus, Paul, *L'Europe et les régions* (Paris: Fernand Nathan, 1979)

Savoie, D.J., *Federal-Provincial Collaboration: The Canada–New Brunswick General Development Agreement* (Montreal: McGill-Queen's University Press, 1981)

Savoie, D.J., and André Raynauld, eds, *Essais sur le développement régional* (Montréal: Les presses universitaires de Montréal, 1985)

Shoup, Carl S., ed, *Fiscal Harmonization in Common Markets*, I (New York: Columbia University Press, 1967)

Simeon, Richard, *Federal-Provincial Diplomacy: The Making of Recent Policy in Canada* (Toronto: University of Toronto Press, 1972)

Smiley, D.V., *Canada in Question: Federalism in the Eighties* (Toronto: McGraw-Hill Ryerson, 1980)

Springate, David, *Regional Incentives and Private Investment* (Montreal: C.D. Howe Institute, 1973)

Stevenson, Garth, *Unfulfilled Union* (Toronto: Gage, 1982)

Stilwell, F.J.B., *Regional Economic Policy* (London: Macmillan, 1972)

Tupper, Allan, *Public Money in the Private Sector* (Kingston: Institute of Intergovernmental Relations, 1982)

Yuill, Douglas and Allen Kevin, *European Regional Incentives – 1980* (Glasgow: European Regional Policy Monitoring Unit, 1980)

Zohar, Uri, *Canadian Manufacturing: A Study in Productivity and Technological Change*, I and II (Ottawa: Canadian Institute for Economic Policy, 1982)

ARTICLES

Acheson, Thomas, 'The Maritimes and Empire Canada,' in David Bercuson, *The Burden of Unity* (Toronto: Macmillan, 1977), 87–114

Alexander, David, 'New Notions of Happiness: Nationalism, Regionalism and Atlantic Canada,' *Journal of Canadian Studies*, XV 2 (1980), 29–42

Atlantic Provinces Economic Council, 'Analysis of the Reorganization for Economic Development' (Halifax, August 1982), 1–36

Aucoin, Peter and Herman Bakvis, 'Organizational Differentiation and Integration: The Case of Regional Economic Development Policy in Canada,' *Canadian Public Administration*, XXVII 3 (fall 1984), 348–71

Black, E.R. and Alan Cairns, 'A Different Perspective on Canadian Federalism,' *Canadian Public Administration*, XIV 1 (1966) 27–44

Brewis, T.N., 'Regional Development in Canada in Historical Perspective,' in N.H. Lithwick, ed, *Regional Economic Policy: The Canadian Experience* (Toronto: McGraw-Hill Ryerson, 1978), 215–29

Brewis, T.N., and G. Paquet, 'Regional Development and Planning in Canada: An Exploratory Essay,' *Canadian Public Administration*, XI 2 (1968), 123–62

Cairns, Alan, 'The Governments and Societies of Canadian Federalism,' *Canadian Journal of Political Science*, X 4 (1977), 693–725

Clark, Douglas H., 'Federal-Provincial Fiscal Arrangements for 1972–76 Fiscal Period,' in N.H. Lithwick, *Regional Economic Policy: The Canadian Experience* (Toronto: McGraw-Hill Ryerson, 1978), 206–14

Courchene, Thomas J., 'Avenues of Adjustment: The Transfer System and Regional Disparities,' in *Canadian Confederation at the Crossroads: The Search for a Federal-Provincial Balance* (Vancouver: Fraser Institute, 1978), 145–86

– 'A Market Perspective on Regional Disparities,' *Canadian Public Policy*, VII 4 (1981), 506–8

Crowley, Ronald W., 'A New Power Focus in Ottawa: The Ministry of State for Economic and Regional Development,' *Optimum*, XIII 2 (1977), 19–30

Doern, Bruce G., 'The Mega-Project Episode and the Formulation of Canadian Economic Developments Policy,' *Canadian Public Administration*, XXVI 2 (1983), 219–28

201 Selected bibliography

Francis, J.P. and N.G. Pillai, 'Regional Economic Disparities and Federal Development Policies in Canada,' in *Regional Poverty and Change* (Ottawa: Canadian Council on Rural Development, 1973), 123–60

Higgins, Benjamin, 'From Growth Poles to Systems of Interactions in Space,' *Growth and Change*, XIV 4 (fall 1983), 3–13

– 'The Task Ahead: The Search for a New Local and Regional Development Strategy in the 1980's' (Nagoya: United Nations Centre for Regional Development, undated), 1–42

Husband, D.D., 'National versus Regional Growth: Some Issues,' *Canadian Public Administration*, XIV 1 (1971), 538–55

Lampard, E.R., 'The Evolving Systems of Cities in the United States: Urbanization and Economic Development,' in H.S. Perloff et al, *Issues in Urban Economics* (Baltimore: Johns Hopkins Press, 1968), 81–138

Lithwick, N.H., 'Regional Policy: The Embodiment of Contradictions,' in G. Bruce Doern ed, *How Ottawa Spends Your Tax Dollar – 1982* (Toronto: James Lorimer & Company, 1982), 131–46

McAllister, Ian, 'How to Re-make DREE,' *Policy Options*, I 1 (1980), 39–43

Meyer, John R., 'Regional Economics, A Survey,' *American Economic Review*, LIII (1963), 19–54

Norrie, Kenneth H., 'Some Comments on Prairie Economic Alienation,' *Canadian Public Policy*, II 2 (1976), 211– 24

Savoie, D.J. 'Cash Incentives versus Tax Incentives for Regional Development: Issues and Considerations,' *The Canadian Journal of Regional Science*, VIII 1 (1985), 1–16

– 'Les conférences des premiers ministres,' *Policy Options*, IV 5 (1983), 32–3

– 'Cooperative Federalism with Democracy: The Machinery of Intergovernmental Relations in Regional Development Could Be Made More Open and Accountable,' *Policy Options*, III 6 (1982), 54–8

– 'The GDA Approach and the Bureaucratization of Provincial Governments in the Atlantic Provinces,' *Canadian Public Administration*, XXIV 1 (1981), 116–31

– 'The Toppling of DREE and Prospects for Regional Economic Expansion,' *Canadian Public Policy*, X 3 (1984), 328–37

Scott, A.D., 'Policy for Declining Regions: A Theoretical Approach,' in N.H. Lithwick, ed, *Regional Economic Policy: The Canadian Experience* (Toronto: McGraw-Hill Ryerson, 1978), 46–67

Simon, Herbert, 'Rational Decision-Making in Business Organizations, *American Economic Review*, LXIX 4 (1979), 493–513

Usher, Dan 'Some Questions about the Regional Development Incentives Act,' *Canadian Public Policy* (fall 1975), 557–75

Walton, Frank, 'Canada's Atlantic Region: Recent Policy for Economic Development,' *The Canadian Journal of Regional Science*, I 2 (autumn 1978), 35–52

Woodward, Robert S., 'The Capital Bias of DREE Incentives,' *Canadian Journal of Economics,* VII 2 (1974), 161–73
- 'Effective Location Subsidies: An Evaluation of DREE's Industrial Incentives,' *Canadian Journal of Economics*, VII 3 (1974), 501–10
- 'The Effectiveness of DREE's New Location Subsidies,' in N.H. Lithwick, ed, *Regional Economic Policy: The Canadian Experience* (Toronto: McGraw-Hill Ryerson, 1978), 243–56

GOVERNMENT DOCUMENTS

Boisvert, Michel, 'La correspondance entre le système urbain et la base économique des régions canadiennes' (Ottawa: Supply and Services, 1978)
Burke, C.B. and Ireland, D.J., *An Urban/Economic Development Strategy for the Atlantic Region* (Ottawa: Ministry of State for Urban Affairs, 1976)
Canada, Department of Finance, *Background Paper on Federal-Provincial Fiscal Arrangements* (1980)
- *Economic Development for Canada in the 1980's* (November 1981)
- *Federal-Provincial Fiscal Arrangements in the Eighties* (23 April 1981)
Canada, Economic Council of Canada, *Living Together: A Study of Regional Disparities* (1977)
- *Newfoundland: From Dependency to Self Reliance* (1980)
Canada, Employment and Immigration, *Unemployment Insurance in the 1980s* (July 1981)
Canada, Industry, Trade and Commerce, *New Fighter Aircraft Industrial Benefits Analysis and Evaluation* (1979)
Canada, *Labour Market Developments in the Eighties* (Task Force on Labour Market Development, 1981)
Canada, Royal Commission on Canada's Economic Prospects, *Report of the Royal Commission on Canada's Economic Prospects* (1957)
Canada, Royal Commission on Dominion-Provincial Relations, *Report of the Royal Commission on Dominion-Provincial Relations* (1980)
Canada, Royal Commission on Maritime Claims, *Report of the Royal Commission on Maritime Claims* (1926)
Canada, Supply and Services, *Fiscal Federalism in Canada* (1981)
- *Government Policy and Regional Development* (1982)
DREE, *Annual Reports* (various dates)
- *Atlantic Region Industrial Parks: An Assessment of Economic Impact* (undated)
- *A Better Way to Grow* (undated)
- *Guide d'évaluation des multiplicateurs régionaux* (1982)
- *The New Approach* (1976)
- *Perspectives de développement – la région de l'Atlantique* (1976)

- *The Prince Edward Island Comprehensive Plan* (1969)
- *Province ... Economic Circumstances and Opportunities – Yellow Book 1973* (various provinces)
- *Regional Industrial Industries in Selected OECD Countries* (1981)
- *Regional Policy in the Canadian Context* (1978)

Higgins, B., F. Martin, and A. Raynauld, *Les Orientations du développement économique régional de la province du Québec* (DREE, 1970)

Jenkin, Michael, *Two Challenges of Diversity: Industrial Policy in the Canadian Federation* (Ottawa: Supply and Services), 1983

LeGoffe, J.P. and Rosenfield, B., 'Les réactions d'entrepreneurs canadiens à divers programmes d'aide à l'investissement' (Ottawa: Economic Council of Canada, April 1979)

Swan, Neil M., and Paul J.E. Kovacs, *Empirical Testing of Newfoundland Data of a Theory of Regional Disparities – A Study Prepared for the Economic Council of Canada* (Ottawa: Minister of Supply and Services), 1981

Index

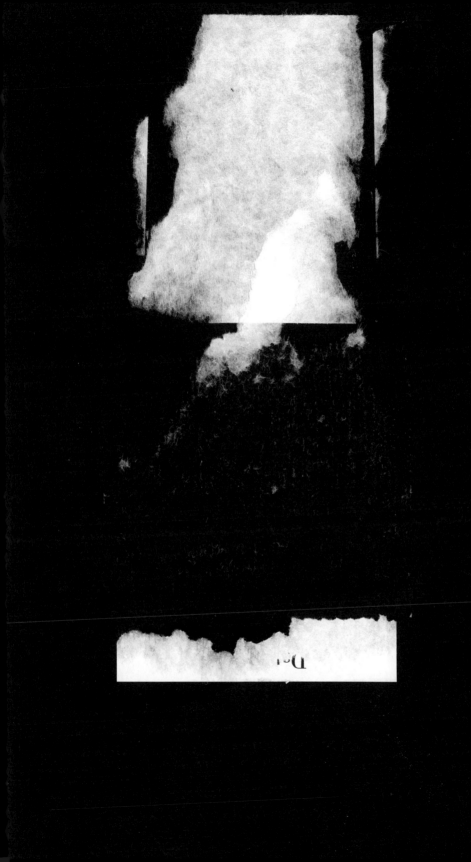